A RAINY NIGHT IN GEORGIA

A LAWMAN'S BRUTAL MURDER, A ROGUE SOUTHERN SHERIFF, AND A PROSECUTOR'S QUEST FOR JUSTICE

J.TOM MORGAN
WITH JOHN CAPOUYA

Prometheus Books
Essex, Connecticut

Prometheus Books

An imprint of The Globe Pequot Publishing Group, Inc.
64 South Main Street
Essex, CT 06426
www.globepequot.com

British Library Cataloguing in Publication Information available

Library of Congress Cataloging-in-Publication Data

Names: Morgan, J. Tom, 1954– author | Capouya, John, 1956– author
Title: A rainy night in Georgia : a lawman's brutal murder, a rogue southern sheriff, and a prosecutor's quest for justice / J. Tom Morgan, with John Capouya.
Description: Essex : Prometheus, 2026. | Summary: "The first book devoted to the political assassination of sheriff-elect Derwin Brown and the ensuing search for justice. Explores the threat of corruption in law enforcement and immerses readers in a gripping true-crime saga, narrated by the man who lived it through every fascinating twist and turn, from beginning to end"— Provided by publisher.
Identifiers: LCCN 2026005353 (print) | LCCN 2026005354 (ebook) | ISBN 9781493094837 paperback | ISBN 9781493094844 epub
Subjects: LCSH: Assassination—Law and legislation—Georgia | Police corruption—Law and legislation—Georgia | Racketeering—Law and legislation—Georgia | Dorsey, Sidney, 1940–2026—Trials, litigation, etc. | Trials (Assassination)—Georgia—Dougherty County | Trials (Homicide)—Georgia—Dougherty County | Brown, Derwin, 1954–2000—Assassination | LCGFT: Trial and arbitral proceedings
Classification: LCC KFG567.H6 M67 2026 (print) | LCC KFG567.H6 (ebook)
LC record available at https://lccn.loc.gov/2026005353
LC ebook record available at https://lccn.loc.gov/2026005354

This book is dedicated to Carol, Caroline, and John

Non sibi sed aliis.

CONTENTS

CONTENTS

CHAPTER 1

By the time Derwin Brown finally made it home that Friday night, it was late and dark. The earlier forecast of hard, pouring rain had been fulfilled, and the temperature in Decatur, Georgia, had dropped into the mid-40s. There were already two cars parked in the driveway, so the lawman parked his sedan on the street. Wearing a full-length leather coat against the chill and damp, Brown reached into the back seat to grab some packages and hurried toward the modest brick ranch.

December 15, 2000, had been both a long and an exceptional day. Months earlier, Brown had been elected sheriff of DeKalb County, Georgia, after a hard-fought political battle, including a runoff election. He was just the second Black sheriff ever chosen there, after the man he'd defeated, and at the time DeKalb was the second-most-populous county in the state. On this Friday morning, he had graduated from the Georgia Sheriff's Academy in Forsyth, about sixty-five miles south of Atlanta, which provides required training for newly elected sheriffs. Derwin's friend and neighbor, Thurbert Baker, the first Black attorney general for the State of Georgia, was the graduation speaker. Sheriff-elect Brown's official swearing in was scheduled for the following Monday, just two days later.

Derwin's wife, Phyllis, and their twenty-year-old daughter, Brandy, were sitting in the front row during graduation. Brandy was her father's only daughter and cherished their special bond; she wished everyone could see her daddy up on that graduation stage. Phyllis was immensely proud, too, wiping away a tear when her husband's name was called and he received his certificate. She had campaigned hard for her husband; like the rest of the family, she was exhausted from that stress but exhilarated by the victory.

Phyllis felt another powerful emotion as well: relief. At five feet ten and 265 pounds, Derwin Brown was an imposing man. But during his twenty-two years as a DeKalb County beat cop and then detective, he had some close calls: stopping dangerous motorists, intervening in volatile domestic violence crises, and doing undercover narcotics work. Luckily, he'd always come out unscathed. Now, as sheriff, "Derwin will be off the streets and out of danger," Phyllis told herself. *He won't even carry a gun except for some formal occasions and while in uniform. I no longer have to worry every time he leaves the house to go to work.*

After graduation Derwin and Phyllis drove north in tandem on Interstate 75 with Phyllis's car in the lead and Brandy riding in the car with her mother. With Christmas just ten days away, they stopped at an outlet mall south of Atlanta to do some shopping. Derwin slipped away from his wife and daughter to purchase gifts without their knowledge, then stowed them in the back seat of his car.

The Browns then headed to Derwin's favorite restaurant, the MVP Sports Bar, for a private dinner and celebration with family, close friends, and campaign workers. The restaurant staff prepared Derwin's favorite dish: rotisserie chicken with Alfredo sauce.

Phyllis left the party early, feigning a headache to prepare a surprise for her husband. She'd had a custom-tailored sheriff's uniform made for Derwin's swearing in on Monday. After dropping Brandy off at her house, Phyllis headed to the family home in east DeKalb County. By this time, the cold December rain was pouring down hard, and she looked forward to the quiet and warmth of their ranch house. Once inside Phyllis hung Derwin's uniform inside the storm door—she wanted the gift to be the first thing her husband saw when he entered the house. Robert Crowder, Derwin's best friend and colleague going back to their days as beat cops, was already there, waiting for Derwin and Phyllis. He was slated to serve as Derwin's chief deputy in the new administration.

Derwin was the last person to leave the party. He thanked the restaurant staff for a great meal and shook hands with patrons who recognized him from the campaign.

Robert, Derwin's eighteen-year-old son, was working on the computer in the family room, a converted garage that was now the main entrance into the home. The glass storm door was closed, but the main door was open, so Robert could see into the front yard. He saw Derwin's broad form coming up the driveway and watched his dad turn his head as if to speak to someone. Suddenly, staccato cracks pierced the night.

Phyllis was in the back of the house when she heard the sounds. "At first I thought they were firecrackers," she said later, but quickly recognized them as gunfire. She called 911 and reported, "There's a shooting next door to my home." Moving to the front of the house, she looked out the window and saw her husband's car. She ran to the family room door with Crowder right behind her. He tried to stop her from going outside, but Phyllis had the door already open.

Still on the cordless phone, she took one step out the door—and screamed. The gunshots weren't next door. Bullets had drilled into the lawman's body front and back, blasting through flesh and smashing bone. "Derwin was lying there near the front steps," his wife of twenty-three years later recounted. She knelt down to hold her husband in her arms and saw the blood streaming from his mouth. "I remember I said on the phone, 'Captain Brown has been shot.' And when I looked in his eyes, I knew he was gone."

Amid the other packages scattered on the wet driveway lay a bouquet of red roses. They were Derwin's surprise gift to Phyllis. The next day, Saturday, was her birthday.

Crowder leaned down and checked Derwin's pulse, but he too knew his friend was dead. He strode farther out into the yard, listening intently, looking in all directions. He heard nothing. He saw only darkness and rain.

CHAPTER 2

Just a short drive away from the Brown house, I was dozing at home on the living-room sofa, the rain steadily pounding the roof. On that same afternoon of December 15, 2000, the DeKalb County district attorney's office I led had lost a difficult and draining case. (DeKalb includes parts of Atlanta and extends to the east where it borders Gwinnett and Rockdale Counties.) My cocounsel and I had prosecuted a grandmother for felony murder after she'd left her eighteen-month-old grandson inside her car the previous summer and he'd perished under the sweltering Georgia sun. As in most cases, we relied on evidence gathered by the police and did not speak directly with the defendant.

After hearing the grandmother tell her story for the first time at the trial, her defense—that she was not used to caring for her grandson and would not intentionally leave her sleeping grandson in a closed vehicle—seemed more believable. The jury agreed and acquitted her. Though I was emotionally and physically exhausted after the trial, I wasn't outraged by the outcome. Unlike the way we are sometimes portrayed, the first duty of prosecutors is to seek justice, not convictions.

When I left the courtroom—my first time outside since six thirty that morning—the sun was nowhere to be seen. The sky was as gray as the granite of Stone Mountain, roughly ten miles away. The drive from the courthouse to my house was just five minutes, but it allowed me some time to decompress after a long, tough week. When I opened the door, the smell of chili, Christmas cookies, a North Carolina Fraser fir tree, and a candle burning somewhere in the back greeted me. After dinner, I went to lie down on the sofa with a glass of wine to unwind and watch the evening news. I dozed off after only a couple of sips.

Then my pager, still on my belt, started vibrating around 10:30 p.m. The message was: "Call Carol Ellis." She was my chief investigator. When I did, she told me, "Derwin Brown's been shot."

"Oh my God!" I said. "Is he okay? Was it an accident?"

"I have no idea," Carol responded. "I just got a call from Director Brown to get you and meet him at the hospital." Tom Brown, not related to Derwin Brown, was the director of public safety for DeKalb County with responsibility for all fire, police, and emergency services.

I called my chief assistant DA, John Petrey, and told him Derwin had been shot and we needed to get to the hospital immediately. I would pick him up at his house in five minutes. Moving swiftly to our bedroom, I reached into the closet and grabbed my blue all-weather jacket with "District Attorney" in yellow letters on the back.

On my way out, when I was on the front porch, my teenage daughter Caroline dashed up the front steps looking a little sheepish. I rushed past her and told her I had to go out and would be back later. I learned afterward she was afraid I was waiting for her on the front porch to chastise her for being a few minutes past her curfew.

Petrey and I picked up Carol at our office within ten minutes of her call. The weather was terrible, but we had no traffic on the way to the hospital, so I did not bother engaging the blue light that came with the Crown Victoria issued to the district attorney.

Parking reserved for law enforcement is near the emergency room door where I planned to park, but I was not prepared for the scene when I arrived. At least twenty marked law enforcement vehicles with their emergency lights flashing were parked along the circular drive and on the sidewalk leading to the emergency room door. The flashing vehicle lights intermingled with the Christmas tree lights that were brightly shining on the large tree standing on the hospital front lawn. Viewed from inside our car, the scene was surreal and blurry with the rain pouring on the windshield, like an Impressionist painting.

After parking, we were ushered past the waiting room and into a private room with Director Tom Brown and Acting Police Chief Eddie Moody. I highly respected both of these men. Like Derwin, Chief Moody was one of the first Black officers in the DeKalb County Police Department, and he had worked his way up to become one of the assistant chiefs. The former police chief had announced his retirement, and everyone expected Moody to be the next chief, making him the first Black person to hold this position in DeKalb County. Director Brown was the first Black person to serve as director of public safety for DeKalb County. On this night both of them, in civilian dress, looked shell-shocked. "Derwin is dead," said Director Brown. "He was shot while walking up the driveway to his front door."

"Good God!" I exclaimed. "What the hell happened?"

Homicide investigators will tell you they draw a small circle around the victim for potential suspects when investigating a murder. Most murder victims are killed by someone they know, including a spouse, intimate partner, or family member. I knew little about Derwin's personal life and had only met Phyllis once while I was campaigning.

"It doesn't appear to be domestic. His wife and kids were inside the home waiting for him," replied Chief Moody. "Nothing was stolen. Also, he was shot multiple times, so it could be more than one shooter."

"It was clearly an ambush by someone who wanted him dead, very dead," said Director Brown.

"Has his body been sent to the medical examiner's office for the autopsy?" I asked.

They said no, that Derwin was still in an examining room. As we walked there, I saw Phyllis standing in an open area. A slight forty-five-year-old woman with short-cropped hair, she was sobbing, her body heaving in anguish. I didn't want to encroach too much on her grief, so I just approached her and said, "I am so very sorry." On that night she struggled to stand without her adult children surrounding her, but Phyllis Brown was a formidable woman. She and I would become crucial allies in the prosecutions that followed.

The five of us walked into the room and saw Derwin's body covered with a sheet. I pulled the sheet back and saw several entrance and exit wounds in his body. His face was swollen; one of the bullets must have struck him there. I pulled the sheet back over his head, and we walked out. I asked for Derwin's address so Carol, Petrey, and I could stop by the crime scene. Brown and Moody showed us an exit door that avoided the main entrance, as press trucks were starting to pull into the hospital with reporters who could not believe the news they were hearing on their police scanners.

We found the house easily. Powerful lights on poles were attached to trucks illuminating the front yard so the crime scene investigators could work through the night. Electric generators were churning loudly to power the bright lights. We stepped out of the car onto the street in front of Derwin's home, which was located near the end of a cul-de-sac. Even though I was wearing my all-weather jacket, I shivered in the cold rain. The first thing I noticed were roses near the front door, and, not yet knowing about Derwin's surprise gift for his wife, I wondered if someone had already placed them there in Derwin's memory.

The investigators had meticulously divided the yard into squares with string. Inside the squares were flags with numbers that represented where they found a piece of evidence such as a spent shell casing, bullet, blood, button from a jacket, or anything else that might be relevant to the investigation. Based on the location of the shell casings, a ballistics expert could often determine where the shooter was standing when the shots were fired and how far the shooter was from the murder victim. I knew that the colored flags in the ground had different meanings and asked one of the investigators why there were so many red flags. "Those represent the shell casings we recovered," he said.

"Damn," I said to myself. "I wonder how many shooters there were." I knew that the Georgia Bureau of Investigation ballistics expert could tell whether the shell casings were fired from the same gun or different guns based on the distinctive marks left on each cartridge. There was nothing more for us to see, so I told Carol and Petrey we needed to go to the morgue for the autopsy.

When we arrived at the morgue, Dr. Gerald Gowitt, the chief medical examiner for the county, was already looking at the numerous X-rays he had taken of Derwin's body before starting the autopsy. X-rays can reveal bullets or bullet fragments that remain in the body before the first incision.

Dr. Gowitt had performed thousands of autopsies in homicide cases and had testified as an expert witness all over the country. We were friends. (I once told him, "Gerry, if I am ever murdered, I want you to promise me you will do the autopsy." He laughed and said, "I couldn't cut you open. I know you too well.")

Dr. Gowitt pointed out on the X-rays what he believed were the entrance wounds and also showed us where some of the bullets were still in the body. It appeared there were five bullets remaining there, he said, and several more had entered and exited. "It looks like there are some defensive wounds in the front," he added; Derwin had probably put his hand up to protect his face. When Derwin turned to run, he was shot three times in the back. One round went through his spleen, another his lung, a third ended in his heart. Any of those three bullets would have ended his life. Derwin's jaw was also shattered by a bullet, explaining why his face was swollen.

Later we would learn Derwin had been shot a total of twelve times with a TEC-9 semiautomatic pistol. He was unarmed; in order to run for the top job in the sheriff's department, he had to resign from the DeKalb PD and turn in his service weapon. (The DeKalb County Police Department and Sheriff's Department are different entities, with no overlapping responsibilities or leadership.) But caught unaware as he was in that furious onslaught, carrying his pistol would likely not have saved his life.

I don't know why, but I left the others and walked down the hall to the room where Derwin's body was lying on the examining table waiting for the autopsy. When I got closer, I could see again the terrible wounds he'd suffered, including his shattered jaw, a horrifically painful wound, but not necessarily lethal. Dr. Gowitt's examination could possibly determine the sequence of shots. If the fatal shot occurred last, the first shots to the body would have caused excruciating pain and suffering. Causing extreme pain and suffering to a victim can be used to support what the law calls an "aggravating factor," which can impact the severity of the punishment for a defendant.

I had witnessed several autopsies of murder victims before, including some of children, but this was the first time I had known the victim in life. As I stood next to this man, I realized that this accumulation of bone, tissue, and water was not Derwin Brown. Derwin was not here. He had left us in his front yard.

"I've seen enough," I told my team. "Let's go." We were all shaken, naturally, but as usual, Carol Ellis was not visibly rattled. I knew Carol when she was an investigator in the DeKalb County Police Department, where she was respected and liked by cops, prosecutors, and fellow investigators. When the chief investigator job in the DA's office became open, I immediately turned to her. Then forty-three, she was a calming force in our sixteen-person investigative division, which also housed a bunch of testosterone-fueled cowboys. The blond, blue-eyed woman of middling height also defied any lingering gender stereotypes by being the best marksman in our unit, consistently getting the highest score at the gun range. She was my integral partner throughout this journey—and Carol's expertise on the gun range would later prove beneficial to me.

When we walked out of the morgue, the rain had finally stopped. Except for my short time on the couch, I had now been awake for close to twenty-four hours. We could see a faint glimpse of daylight in the eastern sky toward Stone Mountain.

CHAPTER 3

It was up to me and my office, I knew, to achieve justice for Derwin Brown. Every DeKalb murder was a tragedy, but this seeming assassination of a public official was a shocking affront to the people we both served. I understood this the moment I arrived back home the morning after the murder. When I left my wife Carol during my rush out the door the previous evening, she was pushing our bed away from a rain leak in the bedroom ceiling. (Coincidentally, she had the same name as my chief investigator, Carol Ellis, but after we married, she went by Carol Ellis Morgan.) She told me, "I got this. Go find out what happened to Sheriff Brown. I hope he is okay."

She greeted me at the front door, wearing the same clothes she had on when I'd left the house—she'd gotten little rest while I was gone. I'd left home at night before when the police needed me, but this was the first time I hadn't come back until the next morning. Carol knew Derwin had been shot when I left; while I was away, she learned he had been murdered. She was shocked and worried waiting for me to come home.

Carol grew up in DeKalb County, attended public schools there, and was proud of her upbringing. I was glad to join her there and make DeKalb our home where we would raise our children. I kissed the top of her light brown hair. She looked at me, and her first words were: "What is happening to our county?"

I would hear that sad and fearful refrain very often in the days, weeks, and months to come. "I have no idea. I really don't know," was all I could tell her.

Sidney Dorsey, the outgoing DeKalb County sheriff whom Derwin Brown had defeated to win that office, released a public statement saying: "Our deepest sympathy is given to the family of Sheriff-elect Brown, all members of law enforcement, and the community for the tragic death of my law enforcement brother. We must stay strong and work through this tragedy, with heavy hearts."

Distress and outrage were palpable, not just in DeKalb County and the rest of Georgia, but well beyond. I got calls from district attorneys in almost every state. Just three days before the murder, the US Supreme Court ruled that the presidential vote recount in Florida had to be discontinued, and that George W. Bush had defeated Al Gore and would be our forty-third president. Yet even as that momentous story continued to play out, the national media focused on Derwin's murder as well. I appeared on the *Today Show* live via satellite from the Atlanta NBC affiliate. Nancy Grace, a host on *Court TV*, whom I knew from her prosecution days in Fulton County, interviewed me. Stories appeared as far away as *The New York Times*, the *Los Angeles Times*, and in at least one paper in Europe. I told one reporter, "We have to solve this case for the public's peace of mind. If the sheriff-elect isn't safe around here, who is?"

But we had no witnesses to the killing, no suspects, and, thanks to the rain, we had no footprints or tire tracks or other forensic evidence at the scene besides the shell casings. No one had heard a car leaving, even though the Browns' home was near the end of a cul-de-sac. In the confusion and, again, the pouring-down rain, a car could possibly have sped off without being heard. After we left the morgue on Friday night, I asked Director Brown and Chief Moody to meet with Carol Ellis, Petrey, and me at a nearby Waffle House. They joined us at a back booth, out of earshot from the other few customers. When I asked them if they had any leads, Chief Moody replied, "Not a one."

Derwin and I weren't personal friends, but I knew and liked the man. I'd had dinner with him just the week before when we shared a table at an event sponsored by a Chinese American organization. He wore a neat moustache and a perfect-fitting suit on his large frame. I marveled at Derwin's deftness with chopsticks. I gave up and asked for a fork. During our meal I was reminded what a good conversationalist he was and how personable he'd been during his campaign. He enjoyed talking to people and connected well one-on-one.

While his affect wasn't intimidating, I also knew Derwin Brown as an activist and a fighter. He participated in a lawsuit against DeKalb County early in his career for failure to promote Black officers; he hosted a TV show, *The Naked Truth*, on a local cable channel; and he wrote a column for a local newspaper called "Tell It Like It Is." Though he'd been defeated by Sidney Dorsey in the 1996 election for sheriff, he was eager for a rematch.

After a brief stint in the sheriff's office, Derwin joined the DeKalb County Police Department in 1978 as one of the first Black officers and came up through the ranks to become one of the county's first Black detectives. He served in the narcotics division until he was promoted to captain, the position he held (and had to give up) when he ran for county sheriff. As a detective he'd been an excellent witness for the state, and in cases we were both involved in, I was especially impressed by his honesty in the courtroom, even when it hurt the government's case. One narcotics case in particular stood out. After the defense had made a motion to suppress evidence, Derwin admitted that the information contained in the affidavit for the search warrant was unreliable, and the case was dismissed.

Our backgrounds were very different—he was Black and I am white, to begin with—but we also shared some strong commonalities. We were born in the same year, making us forty-six years old in 2000. He was elected sheriff, and I won my third term as DeKalb County DA in the same elections. We both started our families and criminal justice careers in DeKalb County because the women we married had established themselves there professionally. Lawmen and public servants, we both wanted to make a difference. I wanted to help make the world safer, especially for children. Derwin often said while campaigning, "My dream is that one day we no longer need a jail in DeKalb County." Derwin's dreams were shattered by an assassin or assassins in his front yard. My dream now—my mission—was to hold accountable those responsible.

***

"Go take a shower and get some sleep," Carol told me that Saturday morning. "I will call Jim and tell him you can't coach this morning." My friend Jim Beaty and I had coached our sons' basketball team in the City of Decatur Recreation league for several years. More accurately, Jim was the coach, and I was the team cheerleader.

I'd completely forgotten it was Saturday. My mind, seared with images of the last many waking hours, had me still functioning on Friday.

"I just need to shower," I told Carol. "But I'll make it to the game. John will be disappointed if I'm not there. Besides, I need some normalcy right now, and a basketball game with eleven-year-olds is the perfect distraction."

When I finished showering and getting dressed, John was already eating cereal and reading a book at the breakfast table, wearing his team T-shirt and basketball shorts. He looked up and asked me, "Who do you think murdered Sheriff Brown?"

John was a voracious reader and retained what he read. His vocabulary was extensive, and sometimes when we were talking, I forgot he was not an adult. I told him, "The only person not a suspect is Sheriff Brown himself."

When we arrived at the gym, the players were already shooting layups. John ran to join his team. Jim looked at me and said, "What the hell happened last night? I heard on the radio that Sheriff Brown was gunned down in his driveway. That can't be right. And by the way, you look like crap."

"The news got it right this time, man," I replied. "And I am not sick, just tired."

"No worries. I got it covered," Jim said. "I have enough kickass for both of us." He, like many others in our community, would give me the cover and support I needed during this arduous time.

During the game, I got a page telling me to call Chief Moody ASAP. I stepped away and called him out of earshot of anyone else, hoping there was news about the investigation. Instead, he told me, "Mr. CEO is hosting a press conference at his office at 1:00 p.m., and he wants you to join us." Mr. CEO was Vernon Jones, the chief executive officer of DeKalb County. He required that all county employees, including the police chief, address him as "Mr. CEO."

"A press conference? To say what?" I asked. "I can't say much of anything during a criminal investigation—ethical rules for prosecutors prohibit it." I told the chief I would be there, but I had nothing to add to Jones's comments. I just wanted to hear what Mr. CEO had to say about the murder. Once again, sleep would have to wait.

I was puzzled why we were meeting in the county administration building instead of police headquarters. It was just a block away from the courthouse, so I parked at my office and walked to Jones's office. Crossing the street, I saw it was lined with media trucks representing all the networks. I passed a guard at the front entrance, unusual for a Saturday. Chief Moody greeted me on the third floor, and we went into Jones's office.

I asked the chief, "Have we caught the bad guys yet?" I noticed both men were impeccably dressed in coat and tie—I was glad I had swapped my basketball jersey for a dress shirt. Just before the press conference, I asked Jones to "please don't give any details regarding the crime scene. And say nothing about any possible leads or suspects because there aren't any." I made a mental note to myself to have a private conversation with Chief Moody about discussing this case with Jones, or any other politician. Nothing can screw up a criminal case more than a politician who has a love affair with television cameras or likes to be quoted in the press. Experience has taught me there is no such thing as sharing criminal investigation information in confidence with a politician. If you do, you can expect that information to be broadcast for all to hear. I also knew that Chief Moody could be in an awkward position, though, because, as in many jurisdictions, the DeKalb chief executive officer appoints the chief of police.

We crossed the hall together and walked into the CEO's media room. The front of the podium was emblazoned with the county seal, showing two barefoot male runners passing a torch with Stone Mountain in the background, and the founding date, 1822. Although the media room was quite spacious, on this day it was filled wall-to-wall with tripods, cameras, microphones, and reporters. When reporters came to see me in the district attorney's office, they just sat in my small office while I sat behind my desk.

Despite my concerns, Jones's comments were subdued. He called it a sad day and said, "I want the citizens of DeKalb County to know that my heart goes out to Sheriff Brown and his family and that the hard work of my police department will bring the perpetrators to justice."

Chief Moody went next, saying his detectives were working around the clock to track down leads, and they were setting up a twenty-four-hour tip line for information about the murder. I felt sorry for the people fielding these tips, as 99.99 percent of the calls would likely come from crackpots claiming that everyone from their weird next-door neighbor to the real killers of John F. Kennedy, Robert Kennedy, and Martin Luther King Jr. were responsible for the sheriff-elect's murder. It's extremely rare that a useful tip comes into a hotline.

When it came time for me to speak, I said that I had no comment other than that my office would be working closely with Chief Moody and his department during this investigation. A reporter I had not seen before asked me if this was a death penalty case. I shot him a look and replied, "It's inappropriate for a prosecutor to comment on whether a case warrants the death penalty before a grand jury returns an indictment. We are a long way from that point." I had no idea how prophetic the words "long way" would be.

Chief Moody and I left together. The weather was cool and dry, unlike the cold rain we shared together the previous evening. Chief Moody, who had a strong, stocky, medium build, exuded a quiet type of leadership. I never heard him raise his voice or sound excited, but I always knew who was in charge when we were in a meeting with his staff. When we walked outside, he asked me where my driver and my security detail were. Surprised, I responded, "I always drive myself and don't think I need a security detail."

The chief replied, "Several elected officials asked me today for security, or extra security, if they already had coverage. I know you have your own staff of investigators in the district attorney's office who work for you. I assumed they were providing you protection."

"Which elected officials are concerned?" I inquired.

I could tell Chief Moody was a little reluctant as he looked down the street toward my office. Nonetheless, he disclosed the names. They were all Black. My tired brain started to register why they would be seeking protection.

I probed a little deeper. "Is there a concern that Derwin was murdered solely because he was a Black elected official?"

"Yes," he said. "It's been discussed."

Until that moment, that thought had not crossed my mind. Considering the history of the South, however, I should have been more in tune with that possibility. In 1979, an antisemitic white supremacist serial killer, Joseph Paul Franklin, shot and killed a Black man in DeKalb County for talking with a white woman. Franklin also shot and severely wounded the famous civil rights leader and Urban League president, Vernon Jordan. Franklin killed or wounded victims in eleven states, including Georgia. He was sentenced to death in Missouri. Before his execution in 1996, Franklin said he wanted to confess to the DeKalb County killing, which had gone unsolved. I sent Carol Ellis to Missouri to interrogate

Franklin and videotape his confession. To this day, it is the most chilling and evil statement from a human being I have ever observed. Franklin showed no remorse at all—he was *proud* of his "accomplishments."

Although I believed, and hoped and prayed, Derwin's killing was not a racially motivated hate crime, I knew we could not eliminate that possibility. However, DeKalb County now had a number of Black elected officials, and it wasn't at all clear to me why the sheriff-elect would be singled out if the murder was motivated by race.

"Why do you think someone would want to murder Derwin?" I asked.

"Likely because he was about to be sheriff," the chief replied.

"I believe you're right," I said. "I suggest we get started looking at who would want the sheriff murdered before he took office on January 1, 2001—and why. Can we meet at your headquarters Monday afternoon? Maybe we will have a preliminary ballistics report and some insight from Dr. Gowitt's autopsy."

"See you Monday at one," he said. "And J.Tom, if you don't want a security detail, at least keep your weapon close by at all times."

Sheepishly, I admitted, "Chief, I don't pack heat. I promised my wife I would never bring a gun into the house. Certainly not as long as we have children at home." As this case unfolded, that promise would reluctantly be broken.

We said goodbye, and I went home and climbed into bed mid-afternoon, having now been awake for over thirty hours. I still woke up barely in time to go to church the next morning.

CHAPTER 4

The sanctuary of Chapel Hill Harvester Church was huge, the largest in the county. It could seat over 1,500 people, but the overflow crowd—perhaps the largest crowd ever for these rites in DeKalb County—had to be diverted to a smaller chapel to watch the service on closed-circuit televisions.

Sheriff-elect Brown's funeral was Thursday morning, December 21, 2000, six days after the shooting. Even though my investigator Carol Ellis and I had arrived more than an hour early, hundreds of cars were already in the massive parking lot at the church. Dozens of police cars, firefighting equipment, and EMS vehicles were in line for the procession to the cemetery after the service. Once again, a cold Georgia rain was pouring.

The leader of Chapel Hill Harvester was Bishop Earl Paulk. He was white, while several members of his clergy and staff were Black. Unlike many churches, this evangelical nondenominational congregation was racially mixed. President George H. W. Bush selected the church as one of his "1,000 points of light," organizations that provide exceptional service to others.

Police officers in formal uniform dress were acting as ushers. One recognized me as we walked in the door and said, "Mr. District Attorney, there is a reserved seat for you up front with the dignitaries."

"No thanks," I told the officer. "We may need to leave early."

The sanctuary's ascending pews were in a semicircle facing a large stage, reminding me of a Roman coliseum. Carol and I climbed many steps before we got to the last pew. Looking down at the stage we saw several tall, cushioned chairs behind an elegantly carved pulpit. Behind the chairs were risers that could accommodate a one-hundred-person choir. During a Martin Luther King Jr. Day celebration, I had the opportunity to speak to a packed congregation from that pulpit. My job was to introduce the famous actor James Earl Jones to give the keynote address. I knew that the view from the pulpit could be both intimidating and inspiring.

My eyes were drawn to the closed solid mahogany casket under a spotlight, draped with an American flag. The casket was on a funeral home gurney immediately in front of the pulpit, which was in the center of the stage. Three images of Derwin came immediately to mind: the warm and talkative Derwin I'd recently eaten dinner with; Derwin's lifeless form under a sheet at the hospital; and Derwin's shattered face and bullet-ridden body on the examining table before the autopsy. Now that body, or what was left of it after the autopsy, was encased in that huge wooden box. Again, I had the sensation that wherever Derwin might be, he was not contained in that box in front of the pulpit. I knew his legacy was in the room, though, and it felt weighty and important.

After several hymns and a prayer from Bishop Paulk, Public Safety Director Brown rose to speak. I had not heard Tom speak in front of a crowd before, and I was impressed with his thoughtfulness and eloquence. He used an unexpected metaphor in describing Derwin, but I thought it worked. The late crimefighter, Tom said, "could be an agitator on a washing machine: He was committed to taking the dirty and making it clean."

Robert Brown spoke next. His youthful face and lanky teenage body reminded us all that Derwin was not only an assassinated elected official, but he was a father with children. The son worshiped his dad, and he was obviously grieving deeply. I reflected on the extreme height and depth of emotions he'd experienced in such a short time—from celebrating his father's remarkable election to seeing his father's face when his father turned to confront his assassins in their front yard.

Ron Brown, Derwin's brother who grew up with him on New York's Long Island, compared Derwin to Martin Luther King Jr. His face bore many emotions all at once—pain, anger, grief, sorrow, confusion. His brother had just been assassinated, and the killer or killers were still at large. I got the sense he felt that no one was to be trusted.

A woman then stood in the pulpit proudly wearing the new blue dress uniform that Derwin had personally selected for his officers. Geraldine Chapman had been an opponent of Derwin in the primary election, but she campaigned for Derwin against incumbent Sidney Dorsey in the runoff. After he was elected, Derwin offered Geraldine a post in his new administration. She concluded her remarks with passion. "I want to say to the person or persons involved in this heinous act: You may have taken the cream, but you left the crop!"

It was a long service, and I was grateful for Carol's company. On the ride back to the courthouse, I discovered a key reason she'd volunteered to go with me. I was driving and couldn't see her face, but I heard what she said in her professional, matter-of-fact way. "J.Tom, I've been talking it over with our investigators," she told me, "and we decided you need protection until this case is solved. We're going to take shifts, from the moment you leave your house each day until you walk back into your home in the evening. And I'm going to ask the police to make rounds by your house when you're home."

"I really don't think that's necessary," I responded. "Accompanying me would just interfere with the work our investigators need to be doing. I'm grateful for your concern, and please tell the others I appreciate it, but this crime is about Derwin, not me."

"You're the boss," she said. "But please leave the thought on the table. Also, I am going to assign you a gun and put it in the safe at the office."

***

Earlier that week, I had met with my executive team: Carol Ellis; Petrey, my chief assistant (no one ever called him by his first name or full name); and Tom Clegg, my office's chief trial assistant, a position I'd created when I first took office. Our three other deputy chiefs joined us. There was just enough room for the seven of us to have a seat in my office.

We went over what we knew about the crime and possible perpetrators: dauntingly little. The vast majority of homicides are solved in the first forty-eight hours because most killings are crimes of passion, or armed robbery of a store (where there's often video), or a drug deal gone bad with a text message trail to the killer. We had no such leads. Derwin was due to be sworn in that very day, and apparently someone or some persons did not want him taking that oath—not your typical motivation for murder.

Beyond our similar goals and values, Derwin and I also shared a commitment to cleaning up corruption in the DeKalb County Sheriff's Department. An important reason for his upset electoral victory the previous August was a series of exposés by a local journalist. His reports essentially accused then-Sheriff Sidney Dorsey of ordering and profiting—financially and politically—from illegal schemes involving his deputies and the inmates in the jail he ran. There were also allegations elsewhere of brutality against those inmates. For his part Dorsey, sixty, touted his "unprecedented accomplishments" as sheriff, adding that the "allegations are unproven assertions."

Derwin made corruption the focus of his campaign, calling the sheriff's department a "cesspool." He sent letters to thirty-eight department employees telling them they would be fired when his term began on January 1, 2001. Chief Moody and I agreed after the initial press conference that we should start looking at those people, but we were nowhere near to identifying any real suspects. Who could be responsible for this brutal murder?

Dorsey could certainly resent, even hate, the man who'd called him out for corruption and booted him from office—but enough to kill him? What purpose would that serve? Dorsey's job was already lost; would killing Derwin for revenge or spite be worth risking life imprisonment or even execution? Dorsey also knew I'd launched an investigation of corruption in his office. Derwin's murder would not stop our work or eliminate that threat.

Besides, Dorsey had a solid alibi, confirmed by Director Brown himself. Brown had seen Sheriff Dorsey and his wife at a celebration that evening for Vernon Jones, who'd been elected the first Black chief executive officer for DeKalb County. Brown had spoken to them as they were all leaving the party around 10:00 p.m., right when Derwin was killed, based on Phyllis's 911 call.

Continuing the meeting with my team, I explained that, due to the magnitude of this case, we would be working alongside Chief Moody and the DeKalb Police Department. Usually, district attorneys' offices have little involvement, if any, in investigations *before* arrests are made; the police fulfill that role. This time was different.

"Carol and I are meeting with Chief Moody this afternoon," I said. "We all need to be in agreement that when an arrest is made in this case—again, because of its significance—we need more than probable cause; we need sufficient evidence to convict the defendant or defendants beyond a reasonable doubt."

Probable cause is the standard of proof needed for an arrest according to the Fourth Amendment of the US Constitution, which also protects all people against "unreasonable searches and seizures." The standard of proof for a conviction is much higher: guilt beyond a reasonable doubt. Law enforcement will sometimes arrest a defendant with only probable cause in hopes that more evidence will develop after the arrest.

"Also, we need to be extremely careful," I continued. "We can't have the kind of fiasco that happened in the Olympic bombing investigation." Everyone knew I was talking about Richard Jewell and the 1996 Olympics in Atlanta. That memory was still vivid because the events were recent—and because our office had been tangentially involved.

One person was killed and over one hundred were injured when a bomb in a backpack went off in Centennial Park at the beginning of the Olympic Games in July. Early the next morning, FBI agents arrived at my house and wanted to see a file in my office. Back in 1990 Richard Jewell was working security at an upscale apartment complex near Emory University. (Emory is in the Druid Hills neighborhood in DeKalb County.) One evening, two students were in a hot tub there, and Jewell arrested the male student for disorderly conduct and had the student taken to jail. The problem was: Jewell had no legal authority to arrest anyone. He was a "wannabe cop," unable to pass the real-world certification. Jewell himself was arrested the next day for impersonating a police officer. We agreed to let him plead to a misdemeanor, receive counseling, and promise never to pretend to be a cop again.

The agents believed that Jewell had planted the backpack bomb and then ushered people away to make himself an Olympic hero. I reviewed the file before giving it to the agents and remarked, "If you told me this guy had planted a fake bomb, I might believe you. But I seriously doubt he could put together a real bomb. Hell, I don't believe this guy is capable of making a pot of coffee."

Someone passed on to the press that Jewell was a suspect, and his life was completely upended. The FBI later looked foolish when the real bomber, Eric Rudolph, a white supremacist and antiabortionist, was eventually arrested and convicted. In our own very public case, we could not have leaks—and we could not falsely accuse an innocent person. The only way I knew to prevent such a screwup would be a coordinated investigative effort with our office involved every step of the way. Also, we would need to control information going to the media. I told the team, "I'm hoping Chief Moody will agree that I will be the spokesperson and the only person allowed to talk to the press about this case."

"Well, who then decides whether there is sufficient evidence to convict a defendant at trial before an arrest is made?" asked Clegg, meaning: Would that be up to us in the DA's office or the police?

"We will make that decision," I said. "There are more than 150 years of prosecution trial experience in this room. Together, we have tried over four hundred felony jury trials. I hope we know what the hell it takes to win a felony jury trial in this county." That being said, this was not a typical murder case but rather the assassination of a political figure. What we would need for a conviction was uncharted waters for me and the team.

When we drove to the DeKalb PD that afternoon, Carol and I were met by Chief Moody, Assistant Police Chief Phil Joyner, and the team of detectives assigned to the case, including Rodney Maddox and Paul Taylor. The latter two were excellent homicide detectives I had worked with on prior cases. Joining us as well, I saw, were two special agents from the Georgia Bureau of Investigation, an agent from the Federal Bureau of Investigation, and an agent from Alcohol, Tobacco, and Firearms. The GBI and federal agents could only be present if requested by Chief Moody.

I asked to see Moody alone for a few minutes. "Chief," I said. "I'm glad you invited all these other folks here today."

"Their agency heads called me and offered their services," he responded. "We can use all the help we can get."

Other police chiefs might have balked and considered others' involvement to be an intrusion on their turf, but not Chief Moody. He was not going to let ego get in the way of solving the murder of his friend and colleague. We agreed we'd form a joint task force—unprecedented, in my experience—of all the agencies present, with Moody's department taking the lead.

"Also," I continued, "I have some favors to ask." I explained that I wanted to assign one of my investigators, Chris Harvey, whom I'd also brought to the meeting, to work as a liaison between our office and Moody's detectives.

Chris had taken an unusual path to law enforcement. After graduating from The Citadel, a military college in Charleston, South Carolina, he enrolled in seminary to become a Catholic priest. While there, he felt a calling to go into law enforcement. Still devout, now married with kids, Chris rose every morning at 4:00 a.m. to go to church for prayers. Then he went to the YMCA as soon as it opened at 5:00 a.m. for his disciplined exercise regimen, which kept him in tiptop physical shape.

Lastly, I said to the chief, "we have never experienced anything of this magnitude with the press. We have to be careful of leaks and what is disseminated, and I would like to be the point person for all press contact. Finally, I want us all to agree that no arrests will be made until the DA's office has determined we have enough evidence to convict this bastard or bastards."

When I walked back in the room, everyone was sitting at a conference table. I made sure Chief Moody sat at the head. GBI Special Agent Fred Mays began by saying, "We have a preliminary report from our crime lab on the ballistics. Sixteen shell casings were found at the scene. All the casings were fired from the same weapon, a 9mm, probably a TEC-9, or an AA Arms, or a Feather Industries 9mm pistol. Also, the five bullets recovered from the body were fired from the same weapon as the one that fired the shell casings," Fred explained.

"Only one gun fired all those rounds? How can that be?" I asked.

"Welcome to America," Fred replied, "where one person can fire a single gun and strike one person many times, or many people one time. This is why law enforcement is scared to death when called to an active shooter. It isn't like the Wild West where a shooter could only shoot six rounds and have to reload. The pistol used to kill Derwin probably had a magazine that held up to twenty rounds of ammunition."

"I guess that now leaves open the possibility of a lone assassin," I said. "I assumed there had to be more than one person firing all those rounds."

"We only know that one gun fired all the rounds," Chief Moody clarified. "We don't have a clue as to how many people could have been at the scene of the crime as backups for the shooter. One shooter could have handed the weapon to another shooter, but that's doubtful since the witnesses said they heard the shots fired in rapid succession."

***

Over the next twenty months I was at the center of—and consumed by—the most tumultuous, harrowing case in DeKalb County's history, and of my decades-long career. The investigation and prosecution included a devastating courtroom defeat, another seemingly unrelated but ultimately crucial murder, and agonizing decisions. Foremost among them: Could we justify giving some wrongdoers immunity or more favorable legal treatment to help solve this abhorrent crime? One newspaper columnist called that possibility "making a deal with the Devil."

Along the way the police and I both made incorrect assumptions that jeopardized our chances of successful prosecutions. During the most difficult times, comments about me in the press and reactions from the public were scathing. The surviving Brown family members lost patience with the DA's office and the halting progress of the investigation. As I'll reveal here for the first time, my family was traumatized, too.

Ultimately, we were able to identify and punish who was responsible for the murder, achieving a measure of justice for Derwin. To accomplish that I used an innovative prosecutorial approach, one that had never before been used by a Georgia district attorney in a case of this kind.

In righting this nearly unthinkable wrong, we uncovered a conspiracy that is to my knowledge unique in the history of American crime. And as the investigation unfolded, I learned that Derwin's murderers had another victim targeted for assassination, another name on their hit list. That second target was me, J.Tom Morgan.

CHAPTER 5

When I arrived at Eddie's Attic after the polls closed on July 18, 2000, my favorite watering hole and music venue was already teeming with enthusiastic supporters and co-workers. People were standing on the outside covered deck or enjoying refreshments at the outside bar and buzzing with excitement and lively conversation. Because it was summer, the sun had not completely set, and natural light filled the space. As was common at Eddie's Attic, music was playing in the background.

This was primary election night in Georgia, and I was running as a Democrat for a third term as DeKalb County DA. Because no Republican was on the primary ballot, the winner of tonight's election would hold the office for the next four years. (At the same time, Derwin Brown forced then-Sheriff Sidney Dorsey into a runoff, which took place the following month.) I held a cold beer in my hand while we waited on the results. It was going to be a long night. Despite the weariness in my eyes and voice, I felt satisfaction that we had done all we could during the campaign to make this night a success. I was surprised at the calm I felt, an innate sense that everything had a purpose, no matter the result.

Eddie's Attic, then owned by Eddie Owen, was located directly across the street from the DeKalb County Courthouse in Decatur, the county seat. It was a popular hangout for the courthouse and local politico crowd, especially on Friday afternoons when Eddie served free hot chicken wings and french fries during happy hour on the upstairs deck. Eight years earlier, after I was elected as DA for the first time, Eddie hosted a party to celebrate. He is best known, however, for helping launch the careers of famous local musicians, including the Indigo Girls, John Mayer, and Sugarland.

In my first two elections for district attorney, I was lucky enough to run unopposed. Earlier that spring, however, just prior to the deadline, an attorney who had never prosecuted a case threw her hat into the ring. For the next three months, my family and I—with the help of many friends, relatives, supporters, co-workers, and perfect strangers—launched and operated a campaign with full intensity and at lightning speed. We quickly had to raise money; write, print and mail campaign literature; design, print, and distribute hundreds of yard signs; produce television commercials; and attend a myriad of campaign events. Our headquarters was the dining room table of our cozy bungalow home, which was constantly humming with the motor of the campaign.

My daughter, Caroline, who had just gotten her learner's permit that spring, became a proficient driver as she practiced on all 271 square miles of DeKalb County while we put up yard signs she designed in her high school graphic arts class. The maroon signs with white lettering were straightforward and simple: Reelect J.TOM MORGAN District Attorney, with my first name centered over the last name. We knew many people would recognize my first name even if they had forgotten my last name. My son, John, who loved to run, raced with his friends from mailbox to mailbox, handing out flyers. Carol, my wife, who was also an attorney, and I squeezed the most out of each twenty-four-hour day as we worked our regular jobs, cared for our children, and ran the campaign in every spare minute. Sleep was a luxury.

Because self-financing a campaign was not an option for me, I depended on the generosity of friends hosting fundraisers. Melita Easters, a well-known political activist and philanthropist in Atlanta, hosted one of the most successful events at her home. The headliner of the event at Melita's home was the famous Southern writer Pat Conroy. Caroline, an avid reader, asked to be his driver for the event. I'm sure Conroy was surprised when a fifteen-year-old with a learner's permit showed up at his Buckhead home, encouraged him to sit in the front seat while I sat in the back, and proceeded to share her thoughts on *The Great Santini*.

I looked over the room full of people at Eddie's Attic, humbled by and grateful for the broad support I'd received. Almost all of my 126 employees were present. Because crime impacts everyone of all races and economic status, I'd strived over the past eight years to develop strong ties with communities and neighborhoods throughout the county. However, because crime disproportionately impacts the Black community—and the DeKalb population of about 660,000 was half Black—as a white district attorney, I worked especially hard developing relationships with Black church leaders and neighborhood and community organizers.

Because I was not a stranger to the church congregations in the southern part of the county, which were predominantly Black, I was often invited during the campaign to attend church services. On many occasions, I was given the opportunity to speak. I was easy to spot, as I was usually the only white face in the audience. Reverend Martin Luther King Jr. once said, "It is one of the tragedies of our nation, one of the shameful tragedies, that 11:00 on Sunday morning is one of the most segregated hours, if not the most segregated hour, in Christian America." Unfortunately, not much had changed since King spoke those words.

During one worship service, a staunch supporter, Reverend Raleigh Rucker, asked me to stand up during the service. Reverend Rucker proclaimed from the pulpit, "My lawyers and accountants have told me I cannot endorse a political candidate from this pulpit. But I will tell you that this morning, I got down on my knees and prayed to God who to vote for. God told me to vote for J.Tom, and I know we listen to the same God!" I prayed that lightning—or the IRS—would not strike me or my friend Reverend Rucker.

I was also overwhelmingly endorsed by the local bar association, and I was surprised and pleased when I was the first district attorney in Georgia to be endorsed by a local gay and lesbian organization. The gay community has had a torturous relationship with law enforcement, particularly in the South. When I started working in the district attorney's office, Georgia law still criminalized sodomy (oral and/or anal sex) among consenting adults as a felony. Although technically the statute could be applied to heterosexual couples, law enforcement sometimes used it to harass and arrest same-sex partners. A conviction carried a maximum sentence of twenty years in prison. I refused to prosecute consenting adults who were charged under the sodomy statute when the acts occurred in private.

As I campaigned, I realized I needed to help voters understand the power of the American district attorney. US Supreme Court Justice Robert H. Jackson, in a speech delivered in 1940, said, "The prosecutor has more control over life, liberty, and reputation than any other person in America." In DeKalb County, we indicted more than five thousand defendants per year during my first eight years in office, with over 90 percent resulting in guilty pleas or convictions. Because of the sheer number of felony cases, I explained at my speeches and events that DeKalb voters needed a DA who had the judgment, temperament, and experience to manage this caseload and make decisions about when and whether to indict, which only a district attorney can do.

Waiting for the first results, I reflected on my unlikely path to this moment: on the verge of a third term as DA of a major Georgia county. I was born in 1954 and raised in a small South Georgia town of fewer than fifty thousand people. Atlanta was two hundred miles north, but it might as well have been on another planet. As a boy, I put Atlanta in the same league as Paris, London, or San Francisco—places I might be able to visit when I became a grown-up.

People call me "J.Tom"—not "Jay," not "Tom," but "J.Tom." The first and middle names on my birth certificate are "John Thomas," names I shared with my father and grandfather. However, my mom wanted me to have my own identity, and she insisted since my birth that I be called "J.Tom." Double first names like "Billy Ray" and "Mandy Sue" are not uncommon in the South, so "J.Tom" seemed not that unusual.

My father was not present for most of my childhood, but my younger sister Claire and I were fortunate to be raised by three strong women. My mother, Virginia Morgan, was a public school teacher; my grandmother, Elizabeth Richardson, worked as a bookkeeper in a sheet metal shop. The third was Sarah Hightower, whom my mother hired to care for us while she and my grandmother worked and when my mother went off to graduate school. Mom was the breadwinner, and she made sure my sister and I never lacked the things we most needed.

Because we could not afford to take vacations, my physical world was limited. However, my mother instilled in me a love for reading, so my imaginary world had no boundaries. After reading *To Kill a Mockingbird* for an seventh-grade school assignment, and later watching the movie, I decided I wanted to be a lawyer. I was inspired to fight for justice like Atticus Finch. It was a gutsy ambition. Not only did I have no lawyers in my family, I did not even know any lawyers. When I told my high school guidance counselor I wanted to become one, she told me I was the first student she had ever counseled with that career goal.

I graduated from the local junior college and then transferred to and graduated from the University of Georgia in Athens. I was accepted into the law school at the university, and the president of the local bank in my hometown helped me secure a loan to pay for law school. I had every intention of returning to my hometown to practice law and maybe get into politics, but then I met Carol, my next-door neighbor in Athens, during my first year of law school. Carol, who was a year ahead of me, and I carpooled to classes, which was how we got to know each other.

By the time Carol graduated, we were dating seriously. Carol knew my desire to return to my hometown after I graduated the following year, so she considered interviewing with local firms. However, she soon discovered that my hometown had few women lawyers. Unimaginable today, some of the firms had a height requirement for lawyers to work there—a thinly veiled discriminatory tactic to keep women out of the firms. Carol, who failed to meet the height requirement by many inches, instead found a job with a reputable law firm in Atlanta. The next year, after I graduated from law school, I followed her to the big city. I was going wherever she planted roots. Thanks in part to gender discrimination, I found myself in DeKalb County.

I owe my career as district attorney to the fact that my predecessor, Bob Wilson, had the foresight and faith to hire me as a neophyte assistant district attorney not long after I graduated from law school. During his twelve years as DA, Bob significantly increased the number of women prosecutors in the office and hired the first Black prosecutor in DeKalb County. I was privileged to be a member of his team for nine years.

Bob also gave me an opportunity that changed the course of my life. After I had been working in the office for two years, Bob decided he wanted to dedicate one prosecutor exclusively to prosecute crimes against children. This decision was bold, because at the time, many prosecutors throughout the country were hesitant about prosecuting crimes against children; these cases were difficult and hard to prove given the ages of the victims. Bob wanted to change that paradigm. He called on me to fill the position, and I heeded the call. I was the first prosecutor in Georgia, and among the first in the nation, to specialize in the prosecution of crimes against children. If a child was sexually abused, physically abused, or murdered in DeKalb County, that prosecution was my responsibility.

Bob had noticed that children who were victims of crime appeared to be comfortable around me, even children who had just met me. Children would sit on the floor in my courthouse office and tell me about horrendous acts done to them by adults. We sat on the floor so I could be at their level, because at six feet two inches, I knew I could be imposing to a six-year-old child. I tried not to speak much or ask many questions; I sat patiently and quietly, and listened to their painful stories. Sometimes I was the first person the child had ever told about their abuse. Tears would strain to leave my eyes, but I never let the children see them. I just listened to what the children had to say. Once they shared their stories with me, I felt deeply compelled to become their advocate and fight on their behalf. And I then encouraged those children to tell their truth to strangers in a courtroom.

Unlike some district attorneys who insist on being referred to by a title such as Mr. or Ms. and their last name, or "Mr. or Ms. District Attorney," I asked that my staff and victims alike call me by my first name. Once people get comfortable calling me "J.Tom," they sometimes forget my last name.

One time, a defense attorney was cross-examining a child, and he asked the witness, "Did Mr. Morgan tell you what to say in court today?"

"Who is Mr. Morgan?" the child asked.

"The man sitting in that chair," the defense attorney said, pointing at me.

"No," the child contradicted him. "That is J.Tom, and he only told me to tell the truth."

I prosecuted more than three hundred defendants for abusing children, including one of the first Catholic priests to be convicted and sentenced to prison for molesting children in the United States. I also successfully prosecuted a prominent child psychiatrist, Dr. Charles Markham Berry, who molested numerous male victims in his office, often while the parents were in the waiting room.

Bob and I wanted to do more to help victims, and in 1987, we co-founded the Georgia Center for Children, which provided free counseling to all victims of child abuse in DeKalb County. This center, now known as the Georgia Center for Child Advocacy, continues to thrive.

Because I was among the first prosecutors in the country with this specialty, I was invited to teach prosecutors and law enforcement officials throughout the United States and other countries how to investigate and prosecute crimes of child abuse. I was featured on a CBS television show, *48 Hours*, and I appeared on *The Oprah Winfrey Show*. The boy who had only been to a few states outside of Georgia growing up had come a long way.

When Bob retired and the DA position opened in 1992, I was ready for a new professional challenge. My work also was taking an emotional toll, especially now that my daughter Caroline was the average age of the child abuse victims I interviewed. A prosecutor needs to be objective to decide whether there's enough evidence in a case file to warrant a conviction beyond a reasonable doubt. And I feared my objectivity could be compromised if I had thoughts of *What would I do if someone harmed my daughter?* Though I wanted to leave it behind, I'm confident my work in prosecuting and preventing child abuse, and the resulting publicity, gave me an advantage and helped me get elected.

Back in Eddie's Attic, my reminiscences ended as I heard "Closer to Fine" by the Indigo Girls playing over Eddie's sound system. As it turned out, that was the perfect song for the moment:

I'm trying to tell you something 'bout my life
Maybe give me insight between black and white . . .
I went to the doctor, I went to the mountains
I looked to the children, I drank from the fountains . . .
There's more than one answer to these questions
Pointing me in a crooked line
And the less I seek my source for some definitive
Closer I am to fine, yeah
Closer I am to fine . . .

John, wearing a "VOTE J.TOM MORGAN DISTRICT ATTORNEY" T-shirt, was heading for the chicken wings when he was suddenly hoisted to the top of a barstool by one of our investigators, who told John to read out loud the first precinct vote counts of the evening. John called out proudly, "J.Tom Morgan, 80 percent, Dad's opponent 20 percent." We were off to a strong start and never lost momentum for the rest of the night.

CHAPTER 6

When the summer 2000 elections came around, I was surprised that Sheriff Dorsey had drawn any opposition. He was popular and charismatic, a good public speaker, and had the backing of much of the Black clergy. Dorsey and I were endorsed by several of the same preachers who wielded considerable influence in the Black community.

Dorsey's wife, Sherry Dorsey, an elected member of the Atlanta City Council, was likewise personable and a great campaigner for her husband. (The Dorseys lived in a section of Atlanta within DeKalb County.) They were a DeKalb power couple, and despite his three challengers, Derwin among them, I thought Dorsey would have little trouble being reelected.

Dorsey was previously a respected City of Atlanta homicide detective, and he had worked extensively on the Atlanta Child Murders, as they were known. Between 1979 and 1981, at least twenty-five young Black males, most in their early teens, disappeared and were later found murdered. Wayne Williams was convicted for two of those murders, and Atlanta PD closed the remaining cases.

However, Dorsey also had a temper and a propensity for violence. He'd been arrested once for domestic abuse, and early in his career was charged with manslaughter when he shot and killed an unarmed teenager. Dorsey maintained that the boy spilled gas on Dorsey's car at a service station and claimed self-defense. The case was never prosecuted by the Fulton County district attorney.

I didn't interact much at all with Dorsey and his staff professionally, as the DeKalb sheriff's office had relinquished almost all law enforcement responsibilities to local police departments. Instead, my encounters with him were mostly political, as we were both elected Democrats. I was expected to attend party breakfast meetings, charity fundraisers, preacher appreciation dinners, and other "must-be-seen" events. Our meetings there were cordial and respectful.

Then sixty years old, Dorsey looked like he still lifted weights. He was of medium height and had a full head of black hair. I also noticed he wore a uniform with epaulets, like some military leaders. The sheriff walked with a swagger, and I always saw him accompanied by a bevy of armed deputies.

As the primary elections approached in the summer of 2000, Derwin began making allegations of corruption in Dorsey's office. They were news to me. No similar suspicions had reached my office, and no one had come to see me behind closed doors to voice any such claims. I thought Derwin's accusations were just campaign noise.

"Corruption" became Derwin's mantra, but he cited few specifics, if any. Instead, he campaigned saying he wanted to "replace suspicion [of the sheriff's department] with respect." He was also quoted saying Dorsey had "demoralized the sheriff's department and offended the police department." He may not have offered specifics because doing so would reveal his source or sources, who were most likely within the sheriff's department. If that happened, those identified could face retribution.

A month before the primary, the *Atlanta Journal* ran an editorial urging voters to strongly consider Dorsey's challengers. Among their reasons: He'd hired his twenty-two-year-old daughter Cherlea as the department's public information officer, starting at $30,000 (about $55,000 in today's dollars), which was more than some deputies' starting salaries. He also appointed a disbarred judge to a $70,000 administrative position. While these hires were legal, they were dubious at best. The *Journal* quoted a former deputy saying Dorsey's performance was "a horrendous example of law enforcement," and the editorial concluded: "The office is in real need of new leadership."

Then Dale Cardwell, an Atlanta investigative reporter for the ABC affiliate WSB-TV, started airing stories about Sheriff Dorsey and some of his deputies with material that could only have come from a department source or sources. A government official being ratted out for unethical conduct by an insider considers the informant a "leak," but the insider is a "whistleblower" under the law, and to the media and the public. As a teenager, I was fascinated with Bernstein and Woodward's reporting on Watergate in 1972 for *The Washington Post* based largely on a whistleblower the reporters only referred to as "Deep Throat." During the primary campaign, the sheriff's department had its own Deep Throat.

Cardwell got a tip that a deputy—in uniform, driving a county car—was working private security at a local bank while getting paid by the DeKalb County Sheriff's Department. There's nothing illegal in Georgia about law enforcement officers working a second job, in uniform. Many officers have to work part-time jobs to make ends meet, and most private companies only want to hire officers in uniform. But those officers have to be off-duty, not on the government clock.

What's more, Cardwell was told, this deputy was not being paid by the bank. Instead, the bank had a security contract with a private firm called SID, Inc., which had a single owner: Sheriff Sidney Dorsey. Again, it's perfectly legal for Dorsey or any sheriff in Georgia to own a security firm and hire his or her own deputies to work for that firm—when and only when they're off-duty.

Cardwell would sometimes call me to clarify legalities and give me a heads-up before he aired a story. In one of our talks, he said he was going to surreptitiously film the deputy at the bank and then ask him questions on camera about whether he was working an off-duty job. I told Cardwell that if the bank was paying SID, Inc. for security services, but the officer was on duty and being paid by DeKalb County, the owner of SID, Inc. would be committing a crime of felony theft from the county.

On June 30, roughly two weeks before the primary, Cardwell and his camera crew filmed the deputy, Sgt. Joe Murray, working at the bank.

When Cardwell approached Murray, he asked Murray for whom he was working, and Murray said, "the sheriff." When asked if he worked for a private security firm, Murray said, "No," and then refused to answer any more questions. Cardwell then got Murray's county timesheet through an open records request, which showed Murray on the county clock at the time of the interview and the four hours preceding Cardwell's confrontation.

Either Deep Throat was feeding both Derwin and Cardwell embarrassing information and details of possible criminal activity separately, or that whistleblower in the sheriff's inner organization told Derwin, and he in turn told Cardwell. (Twenty-five years later, I still don't know who that Deep Throat was.) Either way, when the bank security story aired before the July primary, I knew I needed to start an investigation—and the quicker the better. The sooner I acted, the better our chances of gathering evidence we might need for a future criminal prosecution. Thinking about how best to get that evidence, I had a sudden brainstorm and quickly called Buddy Nix, the director of the Georgia Bureau of Investigation (GBI). I asked him to assign someone on his staff to investigate the case with me, and I wanted one special agent in particular. I told him: "I need Fred Mays."

***

If Dorsey was indeed guilty of breaking the law, he would not be the first rogue sheriff in the South's dishonorable record. In 1984, a year after I became an assistant DA, *The New York Times* reported that twenty-one current or former sheriffs in Georgia and Tennessee had been charged with crimes within the last three years. DeKalb County had its own sordid history: From 1965 until 1996, *every sheriff* in DeKalb County had been arrested:

- Sheriff Lamar Martin, who served from 1965 to 1973, was convicted of taking bribes from bail bonding companies that did business in the county. He extorted 5 percent off the top of every bond paid to them to secure an inmate's release from jail.

- Sheriff Ray Bonner (1973–1976) was charged with misappropriating funds he had helped raise for a local hospital. He was cleared of those charges but lost his reelection. He was later indicted for shooting and killing a sixteen-year-old who he claimed was attempting to break into his car. He was acquitted of those charges as well.
- Sheriff Pat Jarvis (1977–1995) succeeded Bonner and was sheriff when I took over as DA. He'd previously been a pitcher for the Atlanta Braves, and his fans affectionately called him "The Little Bulldog." After retiring from baseball, Jarvis, without any prior law enforcement experience, was elected sheriff.
- Sheriff Bob Morris was appointed interim sheriff in 1995 after Sheriff Jarvis resigned. During his tenure, he was arrested for drunk driving, a misdemeanor. Fortunately, my office only prosecuted felony cases, so that prosecution wasn't my headache. In 1996, when Morris ran for election as sheriff, Sidney Dorsey defeated him.

A sheriff's employee came to see me and confided that he believed his boss, Jarvis, was taking bribes from vendors and bonding companies. I knew that investigating a popular sheriff with seventeen years' tenure during my first term would be a difficult, if not an impossible, prosecution. An incumbent sheriff is hard enough to defeat at the polls, and even more so in a local courtroom. Complicating things even further, Jarvis was married to one of our sitting superior court judges. So I turned to Kent Alexander, the US attorney for the Northern District of Georgia, for assistance. He designated me as a special assistant US attorney so I could stay involved in the Jarvis investigation and prosecution, and then assigned Sally Yates, an assistant US attorney, to be in charge of the case. (Sally would later be the US deputy attorney general under President Obama and the acting US attorney under President Trump.)

Sally and I interviewed witnesses, sheriff's department employees, vendors, and owners of bonding companies. With the power of the federal government, we also issued subpoenas for financial records and bank statements. One vendor, under the promise of immunity, told us how he made his payoffs: He would meet Jarvis at a diner for coffee, and when Jarvis got up to use the restroom, the vendor would stuff money into a Styrofoam cup. Jarvis would then come back to the table, pick up the cup, and walk out of the restaurant. This gave a whole new meaning to the term "to-go cup."

After the investigation was underway, Jarvis resigned in 1995. After we issued a subpoena for Sheriff Jarvis's personal financial documents, his lawyer called Sally and said that his client wanted to enter a plea even though he had not yet been arrested or indicted for any crimes.

That shameful, almost unbelievable litany exposes a little-understood problem in our justice system—not just in DeKalb, not just in Georgia or the South, but in the entire United States. Despite their heroic image in Westerns, local sheriffs across this country have been and often still are granted immense powers with almost no oversight, a combination ripe for exploitation.

Georgia, for example, has 159 counties, the second-highest number of any state (after Texas), and those 159 sheriffs have more unbridled power than any other elected officials. What qualifications must someone have to wield all that authority? Fewer than you might think. To run for sheriff in Georgia requires only a high school diploma, or its equivalent, and no felony convictions. No prior law enforcement experience is needed.

Everybody who works in a sheriff's department in Georgia works at the pleasure of that official. The sheriff can hire, fire, promote, or demote anyone—whether they're a civilian employee who performs non–law enforcement duties, such as a clerk; a jailor detention officer; or a deputy—for any reason or no reason. (Only deputies can be certified police officers who serve warrants, investigate crimes, and make arrests.) The only limitation under state and federal laws is that the sheriff cannot fire employees due to race, age, gender, religion, or other protected category.

The sheriff is also a one-person parole board for inmates in county jails with misdemeanor convictions. He or she has the sole authority to reduce a misdemeanor sentence for "good time served," unless a judge previously ordered the inmate to serve the full sentence. (Only the Georgia State Board of Pardons and Parole can determine sentence reductions for felonies.)

The Georgia sheriff also has exclusive control over the bail bonding businesses in the county. They decide which companies, and how many, are allowed to secure bonds in that county, and what operating criteria they must adhere to.

Bail bonds, which range from a few thousand dollars in misdemeanor cases up to hundreds of thousands of dollars for serious crimes, are designed to ensure that the arrested person shows up for their court appearance. If not, the bond is forfeited. They can put up the money themselves, or a friend or relative can put up the money or collateral, such as real estate. If not, a friend or relative can pay a private bonding company anywhere from 13 percent to 17 percent of the designated amount on the defendant's behalf. That company then secures the bond by using collateral previously authorized by the sheriff.

Requiring bond for court appearances is a holdover from another era. The reality is that an overwhelming majority of people charged with crimes would likely return to court to face the consequences of their actions without a bond. Yet this practice is still pervasive, and due to the enormous numbers of arrests, mostly for misdemeanors, bonding companies remain cash cows. To take one small local example, in Athens, Georgia, where the University of Georgia is located, almost a thousand college students were arrested in one year and had to post bond for nothing more than underage possession of alcohol—a misdemeanor. Clearly, getting the local sheriff to say yes to your bonding company—and no to some of your competitors—can be worth a fortune. The potential for bribery, like what Sheriff Jarvis confessed to, is obvious.

Georgia sheriffs are responsible for housing the defendants who do not make bond, and inmates serving misdemeanor sentences, in the county jails they supervise. All these inmates need and get three meals a day. In most counties, particularly urban counties with large jail populations, food services are provided by private companies. In DeKalb County, the food contract covers up to 3,600 inmates' sustenance: nearly four million meals a year. This contract is a multimillion-dollar award for the supplying vendor. The sheriff chooses that vendor.

Many inmates need medical attention, including prescription drugs, and the sheriff's department is responsible for providing them as well. That's another multimillion-dollar award to the winning contractor, and another unilateral decision by the sheriff. Most often, there's no restriction on the size of these deals. Once the sheriff decides who gets these food-service and medical contracts, the county government must provide the funds to cover the agreed-upon amounts.

All told the amount of money under a sheriff's sole control is staggering. Back in 2000 most citizens of DeKalb were aware that a new jail had been built in 1995. What they probably did not know was that it cost taxpayers $100 million and that it was the largest jail this side of the Mississippi River. The jail could house up to 3,600 inmates, with an average of 2,800 inmates on any given day. In 2000 the annual cost of operating the jail, including salaries, was $51 million; more than $90 million in today's dollars.

You don't need to be the most astute sleuth or have a degree in accounting to see how the office of sheriff can lead to cronyism, conflicts of interest, and corruption.

CHAPTER 7

I was grateful when the GBI director granted my request, assigning Special Agent Fred Mays to work with me on the Dorsey corruption investigation. I'd crossed paths with Fred before and knew his exceptional skills and personality would be very helpful in this case. During the next two years, Fred and I spent countless hours working together and developed a close friendship.

He had been an outstanding high school football player and wrestler. After being injured playing college football, he returned to his parents' farm in Henry County, just south of DeKalb County. During this time, he had a chance meeting with the director of the GBI, who offered Fred a job as long as Fred promised to keep acquiring college credits. Fred began his career with the GBI when he was only twenty years old, the age at which he could legally carry a firearm with the GBI. He was the youngest agent and one of the first Black agents hired by the GBI.

Fred is short in stature but powerful in strength. He was a competitive weightlifter and could squat 650 pounds and bench press 550 pounds. His physical appearance belied his calm and pleasant personality. He had a way of making people feel comfortable during their questioning, which made them speak more candidly. Fred was not confrontational, often humorous, and almost apologetic when questioning a witness or suspect. He was particularly adept at fraud investigations because those guilty parties will usually try to lie their way out of a predicament instead of keeping their mouths shut. Fred made sure they kept talking their way into holes they could not climb out of.

Fred is the straightest law enforcement official I know; he abhors corrupt public officials. I showed him the Cardwell news story I'd recorded and asked him, along with Carol Ellis, to interview Dorsey and see if the sheriff had an explanation for one of his employees double-dipping at the bank. Because Fred and Sheriff Dorsey knew each other professionally, I felt Dorsey would be comfortable talking with him. Fred said he had contacts in the sheriff's department and that, if possible, he wanted to talk to Sergeant Murray—the double-dipper—before he interviewed Dorsey.

On July 18, almost 200,000 votes were cast in the DeKalb primary election, and Sidney Dorsey, the incumbent, beat Derwin Brown, the second-place challenger, by about 20 percentage points. However, in Georgia elections a candidate needs more than 50 percent of the votes to be declared the winner. Dorsey got 49.9 percent; he would have to face Derwin in a runoff election the following month.

Two days later Fred interviewed Sergeant Murray after promising him confidentiality—Murray did not want Dorsey, still his boss, to know he talked with Fred. Murray, who was in his sixties, told Fred that he worked in a unit Sheriff Dorsey called "community relations." Although Murray was not a certified law enforcement officer and couldn't make arrests or conduct searches, Dorsey issued him a sheriff's deputy uniform, a patrol car, and a service weapon. While Dorsey had the authority to do this, giving law enforcement equipment to someone who's not a certified officer is very unusual.

Murray's responsibilities included going to elementary schools to talk about the sheriff's department and manning a booth at job fairs. He often took care of Dorsey's children and drove them to and from school. On several occasions, Murray said, the sheriff or the sheriff's administrative aide, Lt. Roy Baker, ordered him to provide security at a bank. He never questioned the order. Murray was always getting paid his hourly wage by the county while doing that work. He'd never heard of SID, Inc. and was never paid to work for Dorsey's private security firm.

When Cardwell presented himself at the bank, Murray told Fred, Murray did not see the camera—he thought Cardwell was a disgruntled customer. He definitely did not know he was going to be on the news. The day after the report aired, Murray said he was called into the sheriff's office by Lieutenant Baker. Baker told Murray they would have to change his timecard to read "Leave without pay" for the time he was at the bank, but not to worry about it because they'd give him the time back in the next pay cycle. Murray had never been docked before and didn't understand why they were doing that now. He knew he hadn't done anything wrong; he was just following orders. Fred got all this from Murray before he went to interview Dorsey.

I told Fred I wanted him to secretly record the conversation with Dorsey. Georgia, like many states, has a "one-party consent" law, which means that any party to a conversation can record or allow recording of the conversation, even in the most private situation, without the other person's consent or knowledge. I also told Fred and Carol to make Dorsey feel at ease and to tell him that I was only trying to get answers so I could get Cardwell off my back, which was partially true. I honestly hoped for a rational explanation for the double-dipping so we could move on to other matters. A fraud investigation would consume major time and effort from our office, which was already stretched thin with limited resources.

Fred and Carol met with Dorsey in the sheriff's office, along with Lieutenant Baker. Dorsey asked Fred if he was wearing a recording device and Fred said, "Yes, but it is not on." (Citizens are prohibited from lying to the police, but police are not prohibited from lying to suspects to garner information.) To my surprise, Dorsey didn't demand to see the device before answering Fred's questions.

Dorsey explained that Murray was on the county clock while at the bank because of a clerical error by Baker. Dorsey said Murray's time should have been recorded as annual leave and that Baker had made the correction. He told Fred that when Murray worked security at the banks, he was always off the county clock. Dorsey also told Fred that he did not assign deputies to work at the banks. Dorsey said that his daughter ran SID, Inc., and that she called one of the majors in the department if she needed personnel help. Only off-duty officers worked the jobs.

Then, without prompting, Dorsey told Fred and Carol that Derwin Brown, who'd just forced him into a runoff election and was accusing him of corruption, was a "low son of a bitch."

Fred and Carol told me about their conversation with Dorsey, but I didn't need to listen to the recording. I knew Dorsey was lying because of Fred's prior conversation with Murray. I also knew there would probably be no documentation to back up Murray's version of events, and certainly not enough evidence to convict Dorsey of a crime. Fred told me he would have the recording transferred to a playable file and keep it in his evidence locker. I later appreciated that Fred preserved that recording.

After I won my third term in that July 2000 primary, my wife Carol, the kids, and I took a much-needed family vacation in the North Carolina mountains. Unfortunately, our cabin had pager service. I got a message to call Dale Cardwell. He was getting ready to drop another firebomb on the Dorsey campaign. When I called back, he asked, "J.Tom, when can a jail inmate perform labor for private persons or companies?"

"Never," I replied. "The sheriff has trustees [trusted inmates] who can perform community service such as picking up trash. The trustees can also provide services in the jail kitchen and keep the jail clean, but they cannot perform labor for private companies or private persons. That kind of abuse was abolished in Georgia in the 1960s."

"That's what I thought you would say. Can I quote you in my newscast tonight?"

"Dale," I asked, "what the hell are you into now?"

"Stay tuned tonight," he replied.

That night on the news, Cardwell made an astonishing accusation against Dorsey. He reported that sheriff's deputies were taking inmates, many of whom had serious criminal charges pending against them, from the jail and putting them on a bus. Normally, that bus was used to take prisoners to the courthouse. Instead, these inmates were let off and assigned to cut grass, trim hedges, paint houses, and other chores at the residences of private citizens who lived in the political district of Atlanta councilwoman Sherry Dorsey. Apparently, the sheriff's wife was trying to curry political favor with those constituents. Alarmingly, these inmates were doing the work with little, if any, supervision. Some folks who watched the news that night may have wondered how they, too, could get free labor to cut their yards and paint their houses.

Cardwell's cameraman was in place when the inmates got off the bus, and the TV report included a lengthy video of inmates doing that labor to back up his story. He had somehow identified some of the inmates and their pending criminal felony charges, which were to be prosecuted by my office. I was even more convinced that Cardwell was getting inside information from a Deep Throat.

After this story aired, the citizens of DeKalb were once again embarrassed by their sheriff. On the day of the runoff, Tuesday, August 8, 2000, the voters overwhelmingly tossed the incumbent Dorsey out of office. A new sheriff, Derwin Brown, was elected, and I was stuck trying to figure out what on earth to do about the mess created by his predecessor.

* * *

In this story, as in so many Southern stories—indeed, in American stories—race is an important and constant context. In addition to the horrors of slavery and lynchings and the denial of economic opportunity to Black Americans, there's a long, painful history of discrimination within the criminal justice system. After Black people were deprived of voting rights for one hundred years post-slavery, the Voting Rights Act of 1965 finally enshrined their right to enter polling booths (though it was not immediately or universally obeyed).

Long after that became law, however, Blacks were still systematically excluded from the jury box. When I first started as a prosecutor in DeKalb County in 1983, prosecutors throughout the country could, without cause, reject Black citizens during jury selection. I still recall one of my first jury trials, when the white judge called me to the bench after jury selection and told me I had allowed too many Black citizens on the jury to get a guilty verdict with a Black defendant. I proved him wrong.

In the 1986 *Batson v. Kentucky* decision, the US Supreme Court held for the first time that prosecutors could not indiscriminately strike potential Black jurors. If it appears that they are excluding jurors based on race, prosecutors are now required to show a legitimate reason for striking them.

DeKalb County had transformed from 86 percent white in 1970 to majority Black in 2000. In my first two terms as DA and third election campaign, I'd gotten considerable support from the Black community, which I'd worked hard to earn. When considering whether to pursue charges against the first Black person elected sheriff in county history, I could not ignore either my constituency or the long history of injustice against Black Americans.

***

Sheriff Dorsey was apparently guilty of theft for repeatedly using his employees on the county dime for personal services and private gain. Since a theft of any amount from government coffers is a felony, each incident was a felony. My concern was that I, a white prosecutor, could be seen as zealously prosecuting Dorsey for what some might consider "petty" crimes when I should be using my office's limited resources to go after violent criminals such as murderers, rapists, armed robbers, and child molesters. Furthermore, the people had spoken. Sheriff Dorsey had lost the election, so why continue to go after him?

I had almost decided to close the investigation and move on when Fred called me and told me the owner of a DeKalb County bonding company, Shirley McMichael, wanted to see him about her interactions with Sheriff Dorsey. Later that August I met with Fred, along with Carol

Ellis and Petrey, in my office. We sat in a circle in front of my desk, and Fred told us about his conversation with McMichael.

Significantly younger than Dorsey, McMichael told Fred she met him while she was a clerk for an Atlanta bonding company. After Dorsey was elected in 1996, she applied to be a designated bonding company in DeKalb County. He told her that she would have to move her residence to DeKalb County. She agreed to do so if her application for a bonding company was approved. Dorsey also inquired about the collateral required to be posted. She said she could come up with some of it in cash, and a friend would guarantee the remainder with real property. At a second meeting Sheriff Dorsey told her that she was approved to be the first Black owner to operate a bonding company in DeKalb County. And so began Speedy Bonding Company.

Speedy Bonding Company grossed $600,000 during the first year of operation, and McMichael earned over $150,000, a great deal more than she was previously making as a clerk. After about six months of doing business, Sheriff Dorsey called her and said that he wanted to see her. She was worried that she was doing something wrong and told him she would immediately come to his office. Dorsey told her not to come to the jail but rather to meet him at a nearby Church's Fried Chicken parking lot.

When McMichael arrived, she said, Sheriff Dorsey was waiting for her in a county-issued Crown Victoria. Then an unmarked SUV showed up, driven by a man wearing a sheriff's deputy uniform. Sheriff Dorsey told the other man to drive the Crown Victoria back to the jail. He climbed into the driver's seat of the SUV and told McMichael to join him. Dorsey drove to what appeared to McMichael to be an abandoned house. He told McMichael that he had inherited the home from an aunt, and that it didn't have electricity or running water. He then led McMichael inside the home. When they were in the foyer, Dorsey immediately started putting his hands on her breasts and up her skirt and tried to kiss her. He told her, "I didn't just give you the bonding company.

There is a price to pay." Sheriff Dorsey then forced her to have sexual intercourse.

Afterward, he drove McMichael back to the restaurant where she had left her car. McMichael told Fred that when she got home, she wiped off his semen with a washcloth and put the washcloth and her panties in a brown paper bag. She stapled the bag closed and locked the bag in a safe in her home.

McMichael said that while the first sexual encounter in his aunt's home was without her consent, she admitted continuing to have sex with him on subsequent occasions to maintain her bonding business in the county. Sheriff Dorsey would call McMichael and tell her to reserve a room at a designated hotel in the Atlanta area in her name. She always paid for the room and was able to produce four credit card receipts.

Sheriff Dorsey also demanded cash in varying amounts. He explained that she never contributed to his political campaign, so therefore she owed him money. The first time she paid him, McMichael met Dorsey at a Waffle King across the street from the jail and handed him the money in an envelope. Her story reminded me of the prosecution of Sheriff Jarvis for bribery.

McMichael said she made numerous cash payments to Dorsey, approximately $3,000 each. One year around Christmas, Dorsey knew from sheriff's department records that she had secured a $100,000 bond, which meant she had at least $13,000 (13 percent) in cash. Dorsey called and congratulated her for securing such a large bond. He then demanded that she pay him $10,000 that evening in cash.

Once when Dorsey demanded money, she paid him with a check because she didn't have the cash. Dorsey was infuriated with her and tore up the check. She went to the bank and withdrew the money and paid him later that evening.

After hearing about Fred's conversation with McMichael, I asked Fred, "Do you believe she's telling the truth?"

Fred replied, "Yes, I can't imagine why she would make this story up. She also gave me the stapled brown bag. I checked a couple of the hotels she mentioned, and her name does appear on the register. I put the brown bag in my evidence locker at the GBI. I haven't verified the address where she first had sex with Dorsey, but I am pretty sure I will be able to once I find a list of Dorsey's properties, if it's in his name."

If we could find a way to get a sample of Sheriff Dorsey's saliva, a genetic match could possibly be made between his saliva and any semen on the cloth material in the brown bag, even though the sample had been placed on the washcloth several years earlier.

DNA identification still amazes me. When I prosecuted sex crimes against children, DNA testing had yet to be discovered. Petrey was one of the first prosecutors to use DNA evidence in a Georgia criminal case; he was the only prosecutor in our office smart enough to understand the science and convince a judge to allow it before a jury. Juries today expect DNA evidence will be presented in criminal cases.

I asked Fred if he thought McMichael would wear a wire and secretly record a conversation between herself and Sheriff Dorsey. Fred said that with a little coaching, she might be willing and able to pull it off.

Based on what Fred told me, I had a strong suspicion, even before meeting her, that McMichael was telling Fred the truth. We arranged for me to meet her at a GBI office in a neighboring county. We didn't want any of the sheriff's deputies working in the courthouse to see McMichael enter my office.

"Why are you coming forward with these allegations now," I asked her, "since Dorsey lost the election and will soon be history?" McMichael, with short, straight brown hair that barely reached the top of her ears, was wearing a dark skirt and white blouse. She looked very much the professional businesswoman.

"I'm worried that the new sheriff will hear from the other bonding company owners that I'm one of Dorsey's 'favorites,'" she told me, "and that I can't be trusted. I want him to know the truth."

McMichael was at first reluctant out of sheer fright to record a conversation with Dorsey. "It's the only way to verify your story," I told her, and she eventually agreed.

Fred and I coached McMichael to call Dorsey and set up a private meeting. "Tell him I've asked you to come to my office to meet me and my investigators, and that you're worried I might know something about your arrangement. Say you want his advice on what to tell us in that meeting."

When McMichael called Dorsey, a week after my first meeting with her, he insisted that they meet at a crowded restaurant, O'Charley's, for dinner and said he would have his young son with him. Transmitting and recording a conversation over a wire in a crowded restaurant is difficult because of the background noise from the customers, the kitchen, and the servers. We could only hope for the best but realistically expected the worst.

The evening they were to meet, McMichael hid the transmitter in her bra. Fred, Carol, and I were in a GBI surveillance van in the parking lot. I placed one of our newest investigators, Jason Hammer, at the bar in the restaurant. He had just graduated from the University of Georgia and looked younger than his twenty-two years. I was sure Dorsey wouldn't suspect him.

Dorsey arrived with his son and joined McMichael at her table. Inside the surveillance van, we could hear McMichael's and Dorsey's voices. But because of the ambient background noise, we could only distinguish a few words. The recording was not usable.

After they ate dinner and McMichael paid the check, Dorsey gave his son some money to play a video game. McMichael followed the script we had prepared. She asked Dorsey what she should tell the DA when questioned about their relationship. Without saying a word, Dorsey wrote on a paper napkin and handed it to her. He'd written: "Are you wired?"

When McMichael read the napkin, she started shaking. Dorsey grabbed the note from her and tore it up. Jason couldn't hear their conversation, but he saw Dorsey's actions, including passing and tearing up the napkin, from his seat at the bar. Then Dorsey stood up from the table, gathered his son, and left the restaurant.

Now I knew I had to continue the investigation of Dorsey. I could not ignore the ample evidence that he had taken bribes from McMichael, along with other crimes. I'd prosecuted former Sheriff Jarvis for taking bribes.

Once the new administration took over on January 1, 2001, we'd be able to interview members of the sheriff's department when they no longer had to fear retribution or reprisal from Dorsey. However, there was one employee I wanted to speak to before Dorsey's term ended: Deputy Patrick Cuffy.

CHAPTER 8

When Sheriff-elect Brown issued those letters to the thirty-eight sheriff's department employees, telling them they would no longer be working there when he took office, Patrick Cuffy's name was at the top of the list. Dorsey's right-hand man and personal assistant, Cuffy was one of Dorsey's first hires when he was elected sheriff, even though Cuffy had no previous law enforcement experience. Cuffy reported directly to the sheriff instead of through the normal chain of command, and he had replaced Sergeant Murray in "community relations." But no one seemed to know exactly what Cuffy's job responsibilities were, and we suspected he was involved in the departmental corruption.

A computer programmer in the payroll department had alerted me that there were major problems with Cuffy's overtime sheets, which were personally approved by Dorsey. In fact, the number of overtime hours he'd been paid for was so outrageous that the computer payroll program refused to recognize it. For example, in 2000, his base salary was $39,708, and Dorsey had already approved overtime payments of $49,219.

Due to the apparent overtime scam or other corruption, Cuffy could end up facing jail time. I wanted to talk to him and, possibly, offer him a deal to testify against his soon-to-be former boss. In September 2000 I sent word to Cuffy that I wanted to chat, expecting that Dorsey would learn of the meeting.

Carol Ellis and I met with Cuffy in my office. Small in stature, he appeared to be in good shape. In his mid-thirties, he wore his hair in a close-cropped natural with a thin mustache and goatee. I sat behind my desk and offered Cuffy a chair. He refused to take a seat. Instead, Cuffy stood in front of my desk like a soldier during inspection. He was dressed in his uniform, and never took off his uniform hat. Carol sat on the couch behind Cuffy and couldn't see his face as Cuffy stood before me rigid as a board.

"I'm sure you're aware," I told him, "that I'm investigating your boss for possible corruption." I also said I'd reviewed his overtime payments over the past several years and was certain he couldn't justify a large portion of those hours, especially those from 2000. I knew he'd also worked for Dorsey's security firm, SID, Inc., and that he could not have realistically worked all his regular hours, and the overtime hours, plus the extra off-duty hours he claimed. "If I can prove that any of the county payments were for work not performed for the county," I continued, "you'll be facing a felony."

Because Dorsey had approved the overtime payments, he, too, was guilty of theft, along with other crimes I was investigating. "Dorsey's my target," I said, "and if you agree to repay the county for the hours you didn't actually work and testify against Dorsey, I won't press charges against you."

Cuffy bristled and started spewing words like snake venom. "I worked all the hours I was paid for," he insisted, "and Sheriff Dorsey will verify every payment." He told us his community relations work meant representing the sheriff's department anywhere Dorsey needed him to be. He often volunteered for overtime, Cuffy said, usually transporting and guarding prisoners who were in the hospital or needed to go to the hospital.

"Will your overtime sheets tell us which inmates you were guarding so I can verify that those inmates were admitted to the hospital?" I asked.

"No," he replied. "That isn't my job."

He went on to say that "Sheriff Dorsey is like a father figure to me, and I will never testify against him—because there's no need to." He then walked out the door. Carol and I looked at each other in disbelief at this performance.

After interviewing Cuffy, there was little we could do until Sheriff-elect Brown became Sheriff Brown on January 1, 2001. Then, with his approval, we could start interviewing the sheriff's department employees and examine documents kept there.

At the beginning of December, a well-respected criminal defense attorney, Brian Steel, stopped me as I was walking to lunch and told me that I was investigating one of his clients. Brian gets along well with prosecutors, judges, and law enforcement officials.

"Really?" I asked Brian. "Who is your client?"

He replied, "Sheriff Dorsey."

"Oh!" I said. "I didn't know he'd retained counsel. We are just getting started with the investigation. We won't get into full swing until after the first of the new year."

"He has not done anything illegal," Brian said.

"Brian, I'll tell you what," I replied. "I will offer Sheriff Dorsey the same plea deal that Sheriff Jarvis pled to when I first became DA. If he takes the plea before Christmas, it will save both of us a lot of time and headache. If I have to keep digging after the new year, the offer is withdrawn."

"I'll let him know," Brian answered. "But I don't believe he will take it. He says he hasn't done anything against the law, and he should know; he is the sheriff," Brian added with a sly grin.

We wished each other a good holiday season and went our separate ways.

It was around that time that Derwin and I chatted over Chinese food. I told him we needed to meet soon after he took office on January 1, 2001, and share information about our investigation of Dorsey. He agreed. When we left the restaurant, I congratulated him again on his victory and told him I looked forward to working with him at the start of the new year. Sadly, bitterly, that was not to be.

When Derwin was shot, I had an instinctive feeling that Cuffy could also be involved in the killing somehow. After I viewed Derwin's lifeless body at the hospital on the night of the fifteenth, my first words to Chief Moody and Director Brown were: "You need to get a surveillance team on a deputy named Patrick Cuffy. I don't know where he lives, but I am pretty sure it's somewhere in the county, so he can't be hard to find."

Hours later, when Carol Ellis, Petrey, and I met with Director Brown and Chief Moody at the Waffle House, I asked the chief if anything had come out of the surveillance on Cuffy.

"Cuffy and another gentleman, with dreads, got into Cuffy's car around 2:30 a.m.," he told us. "They drove to a Waffle House near Cuffy's home and parked in the lot, but the two never got out of the car. Then they pulled onto the interstate and got off at the exit for the jail and sheriff's department. They drove around the jail and then got back on the interstate. That's when the surveillance team stopped the tail."

"Why did the team quit following him?" I asked.

"Because they figured Cuffy knew he had a tail."

Suspicious, maybe, but hardly evidence of involvement in a homicide.

DeKalb PD later questioned Cuffy directly about his whereabouts and possible involvement in the murder. He told the investigators he was at his house when Derwin was shot, with three friends: his roommate, David Ramsey, and Paul Skyers, both of whom worked for SID, Inc., and Melvin Walker, a sheriff's deputy. They'd been lifting weights, Cuffy said, and "thinking about their futures," since they knew they would lose their jobs soon when Sheriff-elect Brown took over. I had an image of them straining to complete a set, pausing to contemplate their futures, and then picking the weights back up for another set. When questioned separately, the others confirmed Cuffy's story—the four alibied each other.

We had a family tradition at Christmastime of baking cookies, which we would take to the police department for those who had to work the holiday evening shift. Usually, just a skeleton crew was working so the others could be home with their families. On this Christmas Eve, just three days after the packed, emotional funeral, when we took cookies to the DeKalb PD, every desk was occupied by investigators trying to track down leads on Derwin's murder.

***

"Mr. Morgan, without telling us what the evidence is, do you have any evidence of possible corruption in the sheriff's department?"

In early January 2001, I'd sent a letter to Judge Robert Mallis, the chief superior court judge for our circuit. I asked that he and the other eight superior court judges impanel a special grand jury to "investigate the murder of Sheriff-elect Derwin Brown and the alleged corruption within the DeKalb County Sheriff's Department." Judge Mallis responded by inviting me to make my case at their next meeting.

After asking for and receiving assurances of confidentiality for our discussions, I answered Judge Mallis's first question.

"Yes, your Honor. I have personally talked to witnesses and reviewed evidence. I believe there is ample evidence to impanel a grand jury to go forward with an investigation of the sheriff's department," I said.

He continued, "Do you have any leads on any suspect or suspects of the murder of the sheriff-elect?"

This question was trickier: We had no leads, only possible motives.

"No, Your Honor, which is why we need a special grand jury to subpoena witnesses. As you're aware, we would not be able to issue subpoenas in a regular grand jury without a suspect. We know that Sheriff-elect Brown had planned to fire several employees of the department when he took office, but at this time we have no evidence that any of these persons may have been involved in his murder."

"Therefore, it is fair to say that at this time you have no way of linking the alleged corruption to the murder, correct?" asked the judge.

"That's correct."

Now I was worried the judges would only grant us a special grand jury to investigate the corruption, and not the murder, since we could not connect the two cases.

The next day I received an order from Judge Mallis directing the clerk of court to subpoena prospective jurors for *two* special grand juries: one for the sole purpose of investigating Derwin's murder, the other charged with investigating the alleged corruption in the DeKalb County Sheriff's Department.

I was surprised by the judges' decision, since special grand juries are not common. My initial thought was that having two of them would be inefficient and result in duplicating effort and testimony. But after thinking it over more, I realized the division of duties made sense. The judges were right. We had no leads as to who murdered Sheriff-elect Brown, or why. His murder could possibly have nothing to do with Sidney Dorsey and the sheriff's department. If the corruption and murder cases were unrelated, the corruption case, which we already knew would be time-consuming, did not need to get bogged down with the other case.

The judges' order meant that for two days each week for the foreseeable future, I would be presenting evidence to two different special grand juries. The corruption grand jury would meet on Tuesdays, and the murder grand jury would meet on Thursdays. Investigator Chris Harvey and I would be interviewing witnesses, reviewing evidence and documents, and deciding what needed to be presented to each. The daily operations and supervision of the DA's office would be handled by Petrey, Tom Clegg, and the other deputy chiefs. Not for the first time, I was thankful I had a staff that could keep our ship on course without my full attention.

With Chris's help, I would interview all the witnesses prior to their testimony before the special grand juries. I also committed to attending all of their grand jury testimony. If either or both special grand juries recommended an indictment, I would be in charge of those prosecutions, and I believed I should take full responsibility for their success or failure. I wanted to hear any future witnesses testify under oath before possibly questioning them in front of a trial jury.

A few days after I received the judges' order, Shawn LaGrua, a former assistant district attorney in DeKalb County who was now working in Fulton County, called and asked if she could come see me.

"J.Tom," she said, "I want to help you with these two special grand juries. I want to come back to DeKalb, work for you, and help with this case."

"Shawn," I said, "if I hire you, you will also need to manage the cases in an assigned courtroom like other assistant district attorneys do."

"Then assign me to a courtroom that is not as demanding as most," she said. "I promise I can do both. If there is a conflict, my courtroom responsibilities will take precedence."

Shawn had interned with our office; she had a great work ethic and was an effective courtroom lawyer. A strong communicator, she related well with juries, and Shawn was also married to an FBI agent, which seemed to give her credibility when working with law enforcement agents.

Having another lawyer besides me hear the testimony and judge the credibility of the witnesses would be helpful. Also, if I presented a witness to the Tuesday special grand jury, but had to be elsewhere on Thursday, for example, I could leave it to Shawn to present the same witness. I agreed to have her assist. I knew this would be a rare opportunity for Shawn, as most state prosecutors never have the chance to be part of a special grand jury investigation. I was also confident that she was up for the job.

The special grand juries were scheduled to be impaneled beginning April 24, 2001, and to continue until all the witnesses who had information relating to the two investigations had been questioned. I would need to explain to the grand jurors that, unlike most grand juries, which indict individuals, their purpose was to investigate allegations and possibly recommend whether a person or persons should be charged with a crime. However, before the special grand juries could begin their work, a strange—and pivotal—event occurred involving a person of interest in our murder case.

On a Sunday morning in March 2001, I was in the Las Vegas airport waiting to board a plane back to Atlanta. I was there for a meeting of the board of the National District Attorneys Association (NDAA). The NDAA consists of one district attorney from each state, and I was privileged to represent my Georgia colleagues. Saturday's meeting had been an all-day marathon, and I was glad to be on the way home. My pager alerted me to a message from Dale Cardwell: "Call me—important!" I found a pay phone as far away as possible from the other passengers and called Dale's number.

"What's so important that I need to call you on a Sunday morning from Vegas?" I asked.

"Cuffy's dead," he said. "There was a shoot-out in his front yard this morning, and he was killed in the gunfire."

"I must admit, that is the last thing I expected to come out of your mouth this morning. Tell me more."

"That's all I know," Dale replied. "I tried to go to his residence, but there's police tape blocking the entrance to his cul-de-sac. I thought you would know something. So, what does this do to your investigation?"

"I'm not sure if it changes much," I said. "If Cuffy was involved in Derwin's death, he was never going to admit it. And I'm sure he was never going to testify against Dorsey in the corruption investigation. He told me that personally. If Cuffy is dead, I won't be able to indict him for his part in the corruption at the jail."

"Can I quote you on that?" asked Cardwell.

"It's all background," I demurred. "Someday you may have a story to tell, and we can talk about it. I need to call Carol Ellis and find out what the hell happened. Talk to you later, Dale, and thanks for the call."

I immediately called Carol Ellis at home. She was as surprised as I was about the new developments in the case.

"Call Chief Moody and find out everything you can. I will be back in Atlanta this afternoon, and I'll call you when I land. And Carol, why did we hear this news first from a reporter?"

"Good question. The hell if I know," she said in exasperation.

The announcement for boarding first class and business class, which did not involve me, came over the speaker when I got a page from Carol: "Call!"

I quickly walked back to the pay phone I had used a few minutes earlier. "Make it quick," I said. "We are about to board."

"Cuffy's not dead," Carol said. "He is very much alive. Somebody's dead, but the police haven't identified him, and there may be someone else wounded. According to the neighbors, bullets were flying everywhere. Hard to believe only one casualty."

"Find out what you can," I said, "and let's all meet in my office in the morning. Tell Petrey, Chris, and Shawn, and also see if Fred Mays can join us."

After hearing of the shooting on the news, Shawn drove to the crime scene, believing Cuffy had been shot. After discovering that Cuffy was alive and well, she went to police headquarters to learn what investigators knew. At our meeting the next day, Shawn reported on her findings.

"Cuffy was talking to friends when a Ford Excursion drove up at about 10:20 a.m.," Shawn told us. "Gunshots started. We have no idea who fired first. We believe Cuffy was unarmed. Bullets were going everywhere. Children outside playing ran to their houses when the gunfire erupted. One bullet went through a window screen and lodged in a highchair holding a small child, who was, miraculously, unharmed. Police found a bullet-ridden body in a park used for softball games close to Cuffy's home. The police believe the decedent is Jeffery George, a possible drug dealer from Canada. The police have charged a man named Carl Hewitt with George's murder. Cuffy was charged with tampering with the evidence since he took a weapon believed to be used in the shoot-out from his yard and hid it in his house."

"What precipitated this melee?" I asked.

"Early guesswork is that it could be a drug deal gone bad," Shawn said. "Not surprisingly, no one is talking to the police. A man named David Ramsey was in the house when this all went down, but there's nothing to indicate he was involved."

The chaos at Cuffy's home seemed to have little to do with Derwin's assassination or the corruption at the jail. Cuffy was no longer a sheriff's employee. A drug deal gone bad could make sense; Cuffy was newly unemployed and could be looking for sources of income other than the DeKalb County taxpayer.

The local media gave the shoot-out a lot of coverage because it involved Cuffy. Though no one in law enforcement had officially disclosed this, some journalists believed the former deputy was a suspect in the December killing. Cuffy's lawyer, E. Duane Jones, was interviewed by *The New York Times* and said that DeKalb police and prosecutors were trying to frame his client for Derwin's murder. "Let's be clear on this: Patrick Cuffy is being set up as a patsy," Jones said. "Ray Charles could see where this thing is going."

At the end of our meeting, Shawn volunteered to be our office liaison to the police department regarding the murder and shoot-out at Cuffy's residence. Typically, we would let the investigation play out before we got involved. But this was an unusual development in an already unusual case. "Go for it," I told her, "but be careful not to get in the way of the police, and keep me posted."

CHAPTER 9

My investigator, Chris Harvey, and I had the monumental task of determining which key witnesses we'd subpoena to appear before the two special investigative grand juries. Usually, only one witness testifies in each case presented to a regular grand jury. A special investigative grand jury, where no arrests have been made, requires multiple witnesses to determine what, if any, crimes occurred and who committed them. Chris and I often interviewed one witness, who would lead us to more witnesses to be spoken to; all told, we interviewed more than 150 people for the corruption grand jury. And while regular grand juries have a two-month term, special investigative grand juries are in session as long as it takes to get the job done.

Preparing for the corruption grand jury was a more straightforward task than preparing for the one focused on Derwin's murder. We already had a suspect, former Sheriff Dorsey, and possibly his deputy, Patrick Cuffy. What we needed to know was: Were any corruption-related crimes committed by Dorsey, and if so, was there sufficient evidence to prove those crimes beyond a reasonable doubt?

After Derwin's death, Tom Brown, the DeKalb public safety director, was appointed interim sheriff, and in March 2001 he won the position in a special election. Sheriff Brown issued a memo directing all employees in his department to cooperate with our corruption investigation and, if any believed they had information that would be useful to my office, to feel free to contact us. As a result, several employees who were not on our radar reached out to us.

We also interviewed Sheriff Brown early on, and he confirmed what a sheriff can and cannot do with his authority. He explained, "A sheriff can delegate his authority. In the chain of command, an order from Lt. Roy Baker, the ex-sheriff's administrative aide, was the same as if it came directly from Dorsey." We believed Brown would help grand jurors understand the unfettered power of the sheriff in Georgia and the risk of abuse and corruption in the wrong hands.

Under Georgia law, I can't reveal what was said to the grand juries. That testimony is absolutely secret in perpetuity unless a judge orders that the testimony may be revealed, which seldom occurs. However, I *can* report on my personal interviews with witnesses prior to their grand jury testimony. The corruption they revealed was worse and more pervasive than we knew. Sheriff Dorsey ran his department with an arrogance and greed that were both outrageous and, according to what potential witnesses told us, the everyday routine. I remembered what Lord Acton, the English historian, said about power: "All power tends to corrupt and absolute power corrupts absolutely."

Wheel Deals and Happy Meals

Cardwell's report had shown Sgt. Joe Murray guarding a bank for Dorsey's private security company when he was supposedly working in "community relations." But before that time, he told us, "Some of my first duties were taking two of Dorsey's sons to and from school, and on personal errands, including haircuts. After I picked the boys up from school, I would take them to McDonald's." Murray said he did these things almost every day school was in session while driving a marked sheriff's vehicle assigned to him by Dorsey. He also picked up Dorsey's daughter at Georgia Southern University in Statesboro and chauffeured her home, a seven-hour round-trip.

Major Tony Scipio—whose rank placed him above deputies and lieutenants—was also relegated to fast-food duty. Dorsey told him one of his sons did not like the food at his elementary school and wanted

Scipio to get his son a Happy Meal every day for lunch. "When I learned that the school lunch period was over before McDonald's started serving Happy Meals," Scipio told us, "Dorsey told me to go see the manager and tell him to have a Happy Meal ready in time for his son's lunch. The manager refused and said, 'Tell your boss we don't make a special Happy Meal for anyone, including the sheriff.' After I reported on my visit to McDonald's, Dorsey called the manager and yelled at him. The manager still refused." Later, when the son's lunch period changed, sheriff's deputies delivered Happy Meals to the son at school.

Those boys were too young to drive, but it seemed that the Dorsey family members old enough to get behind the wheel were not inclined to do so, or considered it work for others to perform. Deputy Gil Hill told us, "I was ordered by Lieutenant Baker to drive Dorsey's wife, Sherry, and their son to Durham, North Carolina, so she could visit her sister. Sgt. Wayne Fitch followed me in a county car and drove me back to the sheriff's department."

Sergeant Fitch said he once drove his county vehicle to Chattanooga and took Noah Heimlich, a mechanic in fleet maintenance, with him. The purpose of the trip? To extricate the keys that Dorsey's daughter had locked in her Chevy Blazer. However, Heimlich did not have the tools he needed to unlock the Chevy Blazer and told Dorsey's daughter to call a locksmith before he and Fitch headed home.

Once, Fitch said, the sheriff had him drive Dorsey, his wife, Sherry, and their children in a rented RV to Disney World—a nine-hundred-mile round trip. The trip lasted four days. Heimlich beat Fitch's record when he drove Dorsey and Sherry to New York City to visit Dorsey's mother over Thanksgiving. Heimlich was told he could invite his wife, Gail, along for the trip. He and Gail took turns driving the sheriff's department Chevy Suburban through the night to New York with Dorsey and his wife in the back seat. They all stayed in Dorsey's mother's home the entire visit.

"Dorsey took everyone to see a Broadway play and then out to eat," Heimlich told me. "My wife and I never paid for anything on the trip;

Dorsey always paid with a card, though I never saw what type of card or to whom it was issued." A round-trip drive from the DeKalb County jail to New York City is roughly 1,700 miles.

In addition to trips to Chattanooga and New York City, Heimlich told us Lieutenant Baker ordered him to drive Dorsey's son to a Walmart in Moultrie, Georgia, where there was a go-kart waiting for him. Moultrie, located in southwest Georgia, is two hundred miles from the DeKalb County jail. Heimlich said, "I asked Baker why Dorsey's son couldn't just get a go-kart from an Atlanta Walmart, and Baker told me that Dorsey had a relative working at the Walmart in Moultrie."

In all of these instances, the employees in the sheriff's department were on the county clock when performing personal services for Dorsey, and in most instances were using a county vehicle and a county credit card to cover gasoline expenses.

Since Heimlich was a mechanic in the sheriff's department fleet maintenance shop, Dorsey also called on him for upkeep and repairs to Dorsey's personal vehicles: a Mercedes-Benz, a Chevrolet Blazer, a Lexus sedan, a Chevrolet pickup, and a limousine. Heimlich said that Baker ordered him to chauffeur Dorsey to several political and social functions while driving the limousine.

Heimlich added, "I told Lieutenant Baker that all the personal errands and extra work I was doing for Dorsey got in the way of my regular duties in the fleet maintenance shop. But Baker didn't make any changes."

I asked Heimlich, "Why did you perform all of these personal errands for Dorsey?"

"I believed it was part of my job," he responded, "and the sheriff knew what was right."

Legal Aid for the Chosen Few

I was surprised to learn that Dorsey had hired an attorney, Ronald Ramsey, to work in his department, filling a new position he called "Director of Labor Relations." DeKalb County has its own law department, which provides legal representation and advice to all county agencies. I seriously doubted that the county commissioners, or the law department, knew that Dorsey had his own in-house counsel.

Ramsey told us that in addition to his duties at the sheriff's department, Dorsey ordered him to provide representation and give legal advice to Dorsey's friends and family, and to review and revise a contract for Dorsey's security firm. At various times he represented Dorsey's son on a criminal charge in state court, appeared in bankruptcy court for a friend of Dorsey's, and represented Dorsey's nephew in his divorce. Ramsey said he performed all these services on the county clock and without any additional compensation. He ultimately resigned his position because of the private work ordered by Dorsey.

SID's Double-Dipping

When Murray showed up at Atlanta-area banks to work security, he told us, he would often relieve other deputies doing the same work. But Murray did not know and could not give us their names. All of Murray's orders to provide bank security came from Lieutenant Baker. Sometimes his assignments were just for a few hours, but at times Murray was there as long as seven hours. He was always in uniform, with his holstered county-issued firearm, driving his county vehicle, and being paid by the county. Not until he was filmed at the bank by Dale Cardwell was he aware that his services were for Dorsey's private security firm, SID, Inc.

Donna Stone, the computer programmer who'd informed my office about Patrick Cuffy's excessive overtime hours, corroborated Murray's explanation of how his time was computed at the bank that day. Murray's timesheet for June 30, 2000, showed he worked a regular eight-hour shift, and Baker, who approved all of Murray's timesheets, signed off on the time. Then, Stone said, five days after Dale Cardwell's story aired, the timesheet was changed to show Murray took four hours of unpaid leave on June 30. In the three previous years, Murray had never taken unpaid leave, and took none in 2000 until June 30.

I truly believed Murray was unaware he was a pawn in Dorsey's power play. He had worked for the sheriff's department for fourteen years, and his work seemed to be his passion. In fact, after Murray and his wife saw the segment on the evening news, he asked to see me; he said, "I want to explain why I was at the bank."

Although we kept our conversation confidential, soon after our meeting, Dorsey reassigned Murray back to the jail as a detention officer and took away his car and his gun. Murray was never told why he was reassigned. After his reassignment, an errand brought him to the administrative offices, and Dorsey happened to see him. Murray said Dorsey yelled, "Get out of here! I never want to see you near my office again!" Murray was shaken by Dorsey's outrage because he looked up to Dorsey. Dorsey assigned Patrick Cuffy to replace Murray in community relations.

Murray was that rare sympathetic and genuinely credible witness, and I was confident the grand jurors would believe his every word. In preparation for Murray's testimony, we subpoenaed the payment records from one of the banks to SID, Inc. That bank paid SID, Inc. as much as $20,000 a month for security, and that was just one of several banks where Dorsey was apparently defrauding the county.

Subordinate or Accomplice?

Lieutenant Baker would be a critical witness. In addition to assigning deputies to security work, he was the one who ordered the sheriff's department employees to perform personal errands and tasks for Dorsey, all at the sheriff's behest. There were people in the department above him in rank, such as majors and captains, but if he gave them an order, they were to follow it. He corroborated some of the deputies' stories about driving Dorsey family members and other services they provided while on duty. Sheriff Brown retained Baker in his administration, which he justified by saying that Baker had a deep understanding of the workings of the department.

Baker confirmed that when Murray called him one evening to report that he'd been filmed by a television crew while providing security at a bank, he and Dorsey devised the plan to revise Murray's timesheet as Donna Stone had detailed. Baker also told us that Shirley McMichael, the owner of Speedy Bonding Company, was a frequent visitor to the sheriff's office. Personal visits to the sheriff by a representative of a bonding company were unusual. He added that Dorsey told him on several occasions to direct the fugitive squad to find people for whom McMichael's company was holding the bonds, and who had failed to show for court. Dorsey never asked him to help out the other bonding companies in this manner.

I expected grand jurors would want to know whether Lieutenant Baker could be charged, along with Dorsey, with any possible crimes. On a law school exam, Baker could possibly be charged as a coconspirator . In reality, however, we made the judgment call that Baker was just executing his boss's orders without intent to commit a crime. He did not personally benefit from those commands being carried out. And further, his testimony would be essential to prove any possible crimes against Dorsey.

The bribes and sex Shirley McMichael said Dorsey extorted so he'd allow her to operate her bonding company were obviously, egregiously illegal. From a prosecution standpoint, though, these allegations were problematic. We had no corroborating evidence of the cash payments she made to Dorsey. Even if we were to conduct a forensic audit of her bonding company, it would likely only show large sums of cash missing. Dorsey's side could argue that McMichael was siphoning money from her own business. If Dorsey's DNA was on the washcloth McMichael kept after their first sexual encounter, it would only show they'd had sex, which could have been consensual. Without corroborating evidence, we'd be hard-pressed to prove her allegations in court.

On the other hand, we could prove that Dorsey tore up the note "Are you wired?" that he gave to McMichael at the restaurant. We decided to subpoena McMichael to testify before the special grand jury to allow the jurors to determine her credibility.

Coffee and Conflict

The public learned that Sidney Dorsey was being investigated for corruption as soon as the judge signed the order for the special grand jury, which was a public record. One morning before the special grand jury reconvened at 9:00 a.m. to hear more evidence, I walked to get a cup of coffee from the Starbucks near the courthouse. When I came back, several protesters carrying signs were milling around the steps leading to the front entrance of the building.

In hand-painted lettering one sign read, "DA Morgan Is A Racist." Another sign read, "Tell DA Morgan Stop Investigation." Still another proclaimed, "Sidney Dorsey Is Innocent!"

As I got closer, I recognized one of the protesters. He was a regular at a homeless shelter for men in Atlanta. My wife Carol, the kids, and I would sometimes serve dinner at the shelter prepared by volunteers from our church.

I walked toward him, and when he saw me his face lit up with a smile. "Mr. J.Tom," he said. "What are you doing here?"

"I work here, Mr. Jackson. What are you doing here?" I asked.

"Some guy came by the shelter this morning when we were leaving and said he would pay us $25 each to carry these signs for two hours. He and another dude drove us here in vans."

I asked, "Do you know this guy 'Morgan' on your sign, Mr. Jackson?"

"Never heard of him, Mr. J.Tom."

"Have a good day, Mr. Jackson," I said, and then I walked into the courthouse. The fact that at least one of the protesters didn't know what or who he was railing against made me feel better. I never did find out who "sponsored" the protest.

CHAPTER 10

The last time I'd spoken to Phyllis Brown was in the hospital when I saw Derwin's body. The last time I saw her was at her husband's funeral. I barely knew her, but I was aware she had a favorable reputation in the community. She wrote a column for a local DeKalb County newspaper, *The Champion*. She was a driving force in her husband's campaign, and she helped guide him to victory. I grew up, worked with, and lived with strong and powerful women, and Phyllis filled the mold.

Before we started presenting evidence to the special investigative grand juries in April 2001, I asked Phyllis to come and see me to discuss the investigation of her husband's murder. Carol Ellis and I, along with our victim/witness coordinator, Roz Harris, met with her and her daughter, Brandy, in my office. Phyllis still appeared frail, but she was composed and eager to learn what we had to say about her husband's murder.

"Ms. Brown," I began, but before I uttered another word, she interrupted me.

"Call me 'Phyllis,' J.Tom," she said.

"Phyllis, I can't express the total shock and disbelief I felt the night Derwin was murdered. Today, I want to explain the process by which I hope we can find, prosecute, and convict the person or persons who killed him. Carol Ellis is my chief investigator and is responsible for all the investigations conducted by my office. Roz Harris is our victim/witness coordinator. Think of her as our liaison to you and your family. I will give you my pager and cell phone number before you leave—please call me anytime you need me. Roz is also there to answer any questions you may have if, for any reason, you cannot reach me. Also, if there is an arrest and a court case, Roz will be sitting with you and your family during the proceedings."

I continued, "The judges have ordered that two special grand juries be convened—one to investigate the alleged corruption in the sheriff's department, and . . ."

But before I could say another word Phyllis interjected, "There was no 'alleged' corruption, J.Tom. There was actual corruption, and my husband uncovered it. We all know that's why he was elected."

"You're probably right," I said. "But for us to be able to prove there was corruption, and charge those involved, we'll need to subpoena witnesses and have them testify under oath to a grand jury. We've already gathered some interesting evidence regarding the corruption, and I'm sure Derwin was instrumental in bringing it to the surface. The other grand jury will investigate Derwin's murder. Again, we'll subpoena witnesses to testify, and our goal will be to help the police develop some leads to the killer or killers."

"J.Tom, do you and the police have any suspects?" she pointedly asked.

"No, we only have suspicions, and suspicions are not suspects. And, I learned early on as a prosecutor that what I believe is mostly irrelevant. It's what I can prove that's important. Phyllis, all I can say is we don't currently have any clues as to who was responsible for Derwin's murder." I tried to be empathetic and factual at the same time, a difficult task. I couldn't imagine the pain and grief she was experiencing, and I wanted her to know we cared. But I did not want my words to give any false sense of hope.

"J.Tom, my family and I trust that you and your office will find and hold those who murdered my husband responsible," she answered. "Please keep us posted."

The assessment I gave Phyllis was unfortunately accurate: After thousands of hours of hard work by experienced investigators, we still did not have a viable suspect in Derwin's murder. With no eyewitnesses or physical evidence, we were looking for anyone with a motive. As part of the special grand jury murder investigation, Chief Moody told us, all thirty-eight sheriff's department employees whom Derwin intended to fire were being interviewed by his detectives. Cuffy was at the top of that list—could he have been motivated to murder purely by hate and revenge? He was embroiled in the corruption investigation, but killing Derwin would not thwart our efforts.

The other three men who said they were at Cuffy's house on the night of the murder didn't appear to have reasons to assassinate Derwin. Paul Skyers and David Ramsey both worked privately as security guards for SID, Inc. Since they were not on the DeKalb County payroll, they wouldn't be ushered out by the new administration. Melvin Walker was one of Dorsey's deputies, but he was not on Derwin's termination list.

Those four had all given each other alibis. But Maj. Rodney Maddox and Capt. Paul Taylor, both very experienced homicide detectives, felt that the interlocking alibis were contrived. That assessment was based on gut instinct, though, rather than anything concrete.

Cuffy and Ramsey both claimed they never left Cuffy's place that night. We knew that was a lie. The surveillance team had followed Cuffy and Ramsey for a brief period after the shooting, around two thirty in the morning. Why would they lie about something that happened four hours after the murder?

Suspicion was swirling around these four men, but there was nothing of substance we could point to, much less a probable cause for an arrest.

Without any solid suspects, Chris and I focused a good deal on witnesses with knowledge of the crime scene.

Robert Crowder was Derwin's best friend. He and Derwin had worked together as narcotics officers in the DeKalb County Police Department, and Derwin pegged Crowder to be his chief deputy after he was sworn in. Personable and soft-spoken, Crowder had worked tirelessly to get his friend elected sheriff. Crowder no longer worked in law enforcement, though he taught criminal law and ethics as an adjunct college professor. He'd attended the graduation ceremony in Forsyth the afternoon of December 15 and was at the celebration at the restaurant afterward. He left early to teach a class and then went to the Browns' home to wait for Derwin to arrive.

Crowder was in the kitchen talking with Phyllis when they heard popping sounds, which she thought at first were firecrackers coming from the neighbor's yard. After she realized the sounds were gunshots, Phyllis immediately called 911, looked out the window, saw her husband's car, and ran to the front door. Crowder yelled at her to stay back, but she rushed past him to get outside. Crowder was right behind Phyllis when she opened the door and saw her husband's body. In our interview he was distressed that he could do nothing to prevent his friend's death and, as a former law enforcement professional, did not want to speculate about the crime scene due to the darkness and the rain.

The GBI firearms examiner, Bernadette Davy, told us she received sixteen shell casings from the crime scene. As Fred Mays told us at our first task force meeting, after examining the markings on the shell casings made by the gun's firing pin, her expert opinion was that they were all fired from the same weapon. She believed the weapon was either a TEC-9, AA Arms, or Feather Industries 9mm pistol.

Davy also examined the five bullets extracted from Derwin's body by Dr. Gowitt in the medical examiner's office. "When a bullet passes through the barrel of a gun," she told us, "it's spinning at an incredible speed. As the bullet spins, the barrel makes microscopic markings on the bullet that are unique to that gun." Davy concluded that all the bullets were fired from the same gun. Even though she could not match the shell casings to a particular bullet, the fact that the shell casings and the bullets all came from the same gun pointed to one weapon having been used in the shooting.

In a perfect world, this identifying information—the "fingerprint" of the gun from shell casings and bullets—would be placed in a database along with the gun's serial number, similar to the national database we have for serial numbers of automobiles. That resource would be a huge help to law enforcement in solving our country's homicides. However, Congress passed the Firearm Owners' Protection Act in 1986 prohibiting the collection of that information. Probably hundreds of cases each year could be resolved if law enforcement could compare, and possibly match, bullets or shell casings with the weapons used in the crime.

Davy also examined the crime scene diagrams made by DeKalb PD's investigators. They pinpointed where each shell casing was found in Derwin's front yard. She knew how far shell casings from that type of gun are ejected after firing. With those facts she determined exactly where the shooter was standing: The shooter was to the left of Derwin in the front yard and opened fire when Derwin was walking toward his front door and was on the left side of the first of two cars in the driveway.

Dr. Gowitt, whom we'd met with on the night of the murder, gave us his updated findings. "Derwin Brown was struck by twelve bullets," he said, "the five I recovered from the body, and seven more that passed through, leaving entrance and exit wounds." Only one of the twelve entrance wounds had stippling—gunpowder particles surrounding it—which meant that the muzzle of the weapon was three to six inches from the wound when the gun was fired. This wound was to the middle finger of the left hand, which, Dr. Gowitt explained, "was probably a defensive wound when Derwin raised his hand after first seeing the gun. The path of the bullet would put the shooter to the left of Brown."

Another bullet went in and out of Derwin's left arm, entered his jacket, and tore through some papers in his pocket, but did not enter the body. Dr. Gowitt believed these were the first two shots, after which Derwin turned to run.

Gowitt continued, "The next three shots entered his back and traveled upward through his spleen, lung, liver, and heart, most likely after Derwin took a left turn and ran a short distance between the two cars in the driveway, where he dropped the Christmas packages. Amazingly, these shots did not cause him to immediately fall to the ground. The sixth shot hit him in the left side of the face, fractured his lower jaw, passed through the tongue, and exited through the neck. This shot took him down. The remaining six shots were fired from approximately two to three feet away. Derwin was balled up at that point, kicking and moving trying to defend himself, and the shooter was standing over him."

Gowitt added, "I would estimate that Brown lost consciousness within thirty to sixty seconds of the last shot being fired, and died quickly thereafter."

Gowitt's gruesome descriptions, including of the final shots when Derwin was balled up and defenseless on the ground, reminded me of what Tom Brown said at the hospital: "It was clearly an ambush by someone who wanted him dead, very dead." Since the first shots did not immediately kill Derwin, I wondered if he could see his killer's face and, if so, did he recognize his assassin during his last breaths on earth?

Dr. Gowitt told me he would use a manikin for the grand jury presentation with metal rods sticking out of it to show the paths of each of the bullets that entered the body. As the case continued to unfold, he and his manikin would eventually make three more courtroom appearances after his grand jury testimony.

* * *

As time passed after Derwin's murder, the initial spate of national media coverage diminished. Before it dwindled completely, though, I gave one more memorable interview. After I appeared on the *Today Show*, someone from NBC called and asked if they could come to DeKalb for a more extensive interview. That would be disruptive to my office, so I arranged to meet with them on a Sunday morning. The film crew rearranged everything but my desk, and they placed extensive floodlights on temporary fixtures above and around my head.

During a response to a question, a quick look of horror crossed the interviewer's face. What I could not see was a large bulb that had become detached from a fixture heading toward my head. It hit just above my right eye, causing a gash, and then shattered on my desk.

Like any face cut, there was a lot of bleeding, and I guessed I would need a couple of stitches. I was not mad at the crew—mistakes happen—but the crew members were petrified. I told them I was okay, but I needed a ride to the local hospital, the same one Derwin was taken to when he was murdered.

While the emergency room doctor was stitching my face, a nurse came charging into the room and said the waiting room was filling up with reporters wanting to know why the district attorney had been "rushed" to the hospital. I was amazed how fast the news traveled. I told her to tell them I was just getting a couple of stitches and to go enjoy their Sunday afternoon.

Lawyers for the network called the next day; they were worried about a lawsuit. I told them I was fine, and they had nothing to worry about, but that one day I hoped to meet Katie Couric because I was a big fan. They sent me a basket of fruit.

Later, as the murder investigation progressed, I met regularly with the local press. Prosecutors have to adhere to a professional code of ethics when making statements to the press. Failure to follow these rules can lead to sanctions and even disbarment. For example, a prosecutor can't make any statements to the press that could "bring condemnation to the accused." That's to avoid influencing potential jurors before the trial. A prosecutor may truly believe that "this is the most evil son of a bitch I've ever seen charged with a crime," but they can never say that to a reporter. However, most of the rules pertain to comments about cases with a known defendant. Since we had no real suspects, I had more freedom to talk about the case to reporters in general terms.

Dale Cardwell's reporting precipitated Dorsey's defeat and Derwin's election. I kept in touch with him; I knew he still had confidential sources that could be helpful, at least in the corruption investigation. I also trusted that Cardwell would not report anything I shared with him in confidence, and he knew I wouldn't share any information he gave me without his permission.

Other local reporters whom I kept abreast included Don Plummer, Ben Smith, and Bill Torpy, all reporters with the *Atlanta Constitution*; Robin McDonald with the *Fulton County Daily Report*, a legal newspaper for lawyers; and Dale Russell, a reporter for the Fox News affiliate in Atlanta.

Although we never publicly, or privately, told any journalists our investigation was concentrating on any particular person, Cardwell reported that we were concentrating on the four people who by their own admission were together the night of the murder: Cuffy, Walker, Ramsey, and Skyers. Cardwell suspected without my saying it that Cuffy and the three others were on our radar and that we did not believe their alibis. As usual, I was amazed at Dale's ability to acquire confidential information.

When Dale asked me if his sources were correct regarding the four suspects, I replied, "We don't have enough evidence to charge anyone with a crime, much less to get a conviction. However, if and when we do seek warrants for Derwin's murder, you will be the first reporter to know." Dale promised to provide me with information as well.

Don Plummer and Robin McDonald reported the same story. Cuffy even told a reporter that he believed he was a target of our investigation. Also, Cuffy knew we were focusing on him and others as responsible for the shoot-out at his residence and the murder of Jeffery George.

One afternoon, I got a call from Mary Fischer, who told me she was a writer for *GQ* magazine in Los Angeles and wanted to interview me. She said she was staying at an Atlanta Ritz-Carlton, and we could talk during dinner in the hotel's restaurant. I told her I would grant the interview, but that I did not socialize with the media. That was partly true. I did have a beer on occasion at Eddie's Attic with Cardwell and other reporters I knew well, but we always paid our own tabs.

Fischer came to my office and, after a few minutes of pleasantries, started asking me why I was targeting Patrick Cuffy and his friends as suspects. She implied that they—and she named Sidney Dorsey as well—were only suspects because of their race. I told Fischer we didn't have any suspects, and no one would be a suspect because of their race. I then promptly ended the interview. Over six months would pass before Fischer's name resurfaced.

I first met Don Plummer, the *Atlanta Constitution* reporter, not long after Derwin's assassination. At that time, Don introduced himself and said he wanted to gather information about me and my background.

"Why do you need to know anything about me and my background?" I asked.

Don, sort of sheepishly, replied, "For your obituary."

Needless to say, I was somewhat startled by his answer. I replied, "To quote Mark Twain, 'The reports of my death are greatly exaggerated.' Seriously, why the hell does the *Atlanta Constitution* want information on my background?"

"Newspapers have obituaries 'in the can' of local politicians and celebrities," Don replied. "When Derwin Brown was murdered, we realized we had not done a good job of collecting information on our local sheriffs and district attorneys."

"That's a relief, I guess," I responded. "As long as it is not because you know something about my future that I don't."

In August 2001 Don dropped by my office to chat one afternoon and asked how both of the investigations were going. I said, "Don, to be honest, the murder investigation is dead in the water. We have not developed any new leads in months."

Of course, the next day the headline screamed, "Slaying Probe Hits a Wall." I regretted that I hadn't asked that my comments be off the record. I later acknowledged to the press that "dead in the water" was too strong. I added that "we're not going to Ray Lewis this case," referring to the bungled prosecution in Fulton County of NFL linebacker Ray Lewis and two companions who were indicted hastily for the murder of two men before all the facts were known.

When Derwin's brother, Ron, read the headline, he told reporters, "I know if my brother was leading this investigation, he'd be shaking the world upside down." He added that the US Justice Department should take over the investigation.

I understood the family's frustration and their concern that the murder might not be solved. My response was: "The task force has relied heavily on other agencies in the investigation. The FBI has provided us with tremendous assistance. The Justice Department has been able to provide us with intelligence that we could only get because of their cooperation. They have been involved in every possible way that we could have used them in a homicide investigation."

My unfortunate comments also created tension with the police department. I had already asked them to apply a standard higher than probable cause to an arrest, I had assumed the role of spokesperson in the case, and now I'd used language that could be construed by the public as critical of them. I hastily told the press I knew the police were doing all they could. Chief Moody explained to a reporter that even though the original task force had been scaled down to work on other homicides, "we're still working our butts off. We continue to work this case."

In fact, over two thousand people had been interviewed, and rewards totaling over $100,000 had been offered. Chief Moody acknowledged to the press that if the one-year anniversary of the Derwin Brown murder arrived without an arrest, "they will write about this as a JonBenet case." He was referring to the famous unsolved 1996 death of a six-year-old child named JonBonet Ramsey in Denver, Colorado.

The next day, Tom Clegg, the chief trial prosecutor in my office, and I were working out at the YMCA at lunch when a YMCA employee came to the weight room and told me two men needed to see me in the lobby immediately. I grabbed a towel to wipe off the sweat and went to the lobby.

Chief Moody and Vernon Jones, the DeKalb CEO, were waiting. Jones was visibly upset that I told the press the murder investigation was not succeeding. Jones said, "You have insulted my entire police department!"

"I admit I should have chosen better words," I replied. "I didn't mean to imply the police were twiddling their thumbs. But it's clear no one is to blame for the lack of arrests in the case. The criminal justice system depends on facts and not fantasies."

I didn't mention to Vernon Jones something that both Chief Moody and I knew. The chief's homicide detectives were diligently pursuing evidence against Cuffy and others related to the homicide of Jeffery George in Cuffy's front yard in March 2001. Major Maddox and Captain Taylor, who were overseeing the Derwin Brown case, redirected a number of detectives to pursue all leads regarding the shoot-out at Cuffy's house, with the hope that they could shed light on Derwin's murder.

CHAPTER 11

The day of the March shooting in his front yard, Patrick Cuffy was charged with tampering with evidence; he'd removed one of the weapons believed to be used in the gun battle and hid it inside his home. That was a misdemeanor offense. The DeKalb PD homicide detectives worked hard in the weeks that followed and uncovered the following scenario:

- The dispute was over ten pounds of marijuana once possessed by Cuffy and Cuffy's friend, Carl Hewitt. Jeffery George, a Canadian, had apparently stolen the marijuana from those two men. On the day before the shoot-out, Hewitt, along with German Montes and his brother, Antonio Montes, retaliated by stealing George's SUV in an armed robbery.
- On Sunday morning, March 18, 2001, George and an associate, Theophilus Williams, arrived at Cuffy's home and dragged him out of bed. Cuffy, George, Williams, and Dania Hewitt, Carl's older brother, then gathered on the front lawn in an attempt to resolve the disputes over the stolen drugs and the theft of George's SUV.
- As they were talking, Carl Hewitt and his friend, German Montes, drove onto Cuffy's lawn in the stolen SUV. They got out of the vehicle, and Hewitt started hitting George with his fists. Montes hit George with the butt of an AK-47.
- George's associate Theophilus Williams opened fire with a pistol at Carl Hewitt and Montes to try to protect George. Williams then yelled to Cuffy to make the others break it up. Cuffy instead raised

his hands and backed away from the melee. Two women in the house shouted to Cuffy and asked if they should call 911. Cuffy told them no.

- German Montes and Carl Hewitt returned fire at Williams, who was wounded but managed to escape by hopping in the bed of a pickup truck driven by an acquaintance who happened to be in the neighborhood.
- German Montes, Carl Hewitt, and Dania Hewitt forced the injured George into his own SUV, where Carl Hewitt shot George twice as they drove off with Montes behind the wheel. Hewitt fired four more shots into George, then dropped his body in a nearby park.

The DeKalb detectives, with the help of the FBI, eventually tracked down all of the players, including German Montes, who was arrested in Los Angeles, and Williams, who was arrested in New York City. On June 11, 2001, German Montes, Dania Hewitt, and Carl Hewitt were indicted for the kidnapping and murder of Jeffery George. They also indicted Carl Hewitt, German Montes, and Antonio Montes for the armed robbery of George's vehicle. Williams was indicted for being a convicted felon in possession of a firearm.

Shawn LaGrua, our liaison to the police, continued to work with them during July and August as they gathered more information. In early September, she and Chris met with Petrey and me to make a case as to why Cuffy should be charged with felony murder.

A person is guilty of felony murder if a homicide occurs during the commission of a felony. The death could be unplanned, even accidental, and a person can still be guilty of felony murder. For example, an armed robber goes into a convenience store with the sole intent to rob the cashier. Once inside the store, he slips on a mat and drops the gun. The gun accidentally fires and kills a patron who just happened to be in the wrong place at the wrong time. The robber is now guilty of felony murder.

Most countries other than the United States don't recognize felony murder, and not every US state does. States that do recognize felony murder usually limit the crimes that can be used as a basis for felony murder to "inherently dangerous felonies," including armed robbery, kidnapping, rape, burglary, and aggravated assault. Many courts, including the Georgia Supreme Court, have also interpreted sales of illegal drugs as an inherently dangerous crime. If an illegal drug transaction becomes violent and someone gets killed, everyone involved can be charged with felony murder. In Georgia, the punishment is the same as the punishment for first-degree murder: the death penalty, life without parole, or life with the possibility of parole.

The rationale for having felony murder in the criminal code is that people won't commit dangerous felonies if they know they could get charged with murder if someone dies during that felony. However, many criminals are ignorant about felony murder or don't know that the punishment is the same as that for murder.

Because Cuffy had been in possession of ten pounds of marijuana, he was presumed to be a drug dealer under Georgia law, which was a felony offense. In the course of a dispute over the marijuana, in which he was involved, there was a murder. Although Cuffy likely did not plan for massive gunfire and a murder in his front yard that Sunday morning, if he was in any way involved in the drug activity, he could be charged with George's death under the felony murder rule.

We definitely had probable cause to indict Cuffy. But proving him guilty of murder beyond a reasonable doubt at trial was a different task. If he were acquitted, the public, the press, and Cuffy himself might conclude that he had a Teflon shield when it came to committing murder.

Shawn told us the police were able to get statements from several of the suspects linking Cuffy to the drug deal. Williams, who was arrested in New York City with ten pounds of marijuana and a .44-caliber handgun in his possession, had already told police that he would testify against Cuffy and Carl Hewitt. Dania Hewitt and Carl Hewitt, along with

German Montes and Antonio Montes, were also willing to testify against Cuffy. I wondered if there was actually any honor among thieves. Why did five codefendants want to throw Cuffy under the bus?

Shawn convinced me that the facts and the legal argument warranted prosecuting Cuffy for felony murder, even though he was not the shooter. I told her that she could take Cuffy's case to the regular grand jury (not the special grand jury) for their consideration. She and Petrey would be responsible for the prosecution of Cuffy and everyone else related to the shoot-out. On September 13, 2001, Patrick Cuffy was indicted by the regular grand jury for felony murder and kidnapping of George, and he was arrested the next day, the fourteenth. He was facing possible life imprisonment. However, his fate and legal woes were overshadowed by the world-changing events just three days prior.

On Tuesday morning, September 11, 2001, as we were presenting evidence to the corruption investigation grand jury, I heard a knock on the door, which was unusual. Presentation of evidence to a grand jury was rarely disturbed.

I opened the door and Roger Lindsay, our top homicide investigator, said, "J.Tom, you need to step outside and see this. It's important."

Several people were standing around a small TV on the desk where the grand jury bailiff sat. They were saying nothing. All I could see was what appeared to be a tiny plane flying into a building. "I wonder if the pilot passed out while he was flying," I said. "Where is this, Roger?"

"That's not a single-engine plane, J.Tom," he replied. "It's an airliner. Two airliners apparently flew into the World Trade Center in New York City." As he was speaking, we saw the buildings start to crumble to the ground.

I had no idea of the magnitude of what we were witnessing, but I recessed the grand jury and told them they might want to go home to their families. I also got word to all our employees to go home as well. Caroline's high school and John's middle school were just a short walk from the courthouse. I said a prayer for my children and hoped the schools would be the safest place for them today. We all were glued to the news broadcasts for the next several days.

***

By November we were wrapping up the special grand jury investigating corruption in the sheriff's department during Dorsey's tenure. Over 150 witnesses had given testimony, and the evidence supported multiple charges of several crimes, including bribery, theft, and violation of oath. We needed to decide whether to include a few of each of the various crimes or charge all of the violations. For instance, do we charge each time Noah Heimlich performed personal tasks for Dorsey, or just a sample of many?

We had no such decisions to make regarding the grand jury investigating Derwin's assassination. After nine months, it was to conclude soon because there was no evidence to support recommendations of indictments for anyone.

In the meantime, the judge assigned to the Jeffery George murder case had scheduled trial for November 26, 2001, for Cuffy and his codefendants. The grand jury investigating corruption in the sheriff's department was also considering recommending indictment of Cuffy. However, Cuffy's trial for George's murder was set to occur before any corruption indictments.

Shawn and Petrey were preparing for the George murder case when I got a call from one of my former assistant district attorneys, Keith Adams, now a criminal defense attorney. He said he wanted to speak in private at my home. I was puzzled by his request, but I said he could come by that evening after seven o'clock.

Keith had been a star prosecutor among great prosecutors in my office. I was preparing to promote Keith to a deputy chief position when he told me he was entering private practice. I was extremely disappointed, but not terribly surprised. Skilled attorneys like Keith can make far more money representing clients in private practice than prosecuting defendants. I was hoping Keith's call meant he wanted to come back to the district attorney's office.

I welcomed Keith into the front room of our home that evening. The only piece of furniture in that room was a Mason & Hamlin grand piano that consumed all the floor space. I told Keith we could go to the back of the house and sit down. He told me that he would only be there for a minute, and we could keep standing.

"I'm representing Patrick Cuffy in the George murder case," he told me, "and my client has important information to reveal regarding the murder of Derwin Brown." Keith said Cuffy would share this information under two conditions: (1) Cuffy wanted immunity from prosecution for Derwin Brown's murder and any possible corruption charges related to his time working for Dorsey; and (2) he wanted a reduced charge for the murder of George.

On the outside I maintained a professional demeanor, but I was stunned. My mind started spinning about the implications. One thought immediately flashed across my mind: My suspicions from the moment I saw Derwin's lifeless body in the hospital were proving true—Patrick Cuffy was somehow involved in Derwin's murder.

I collected my thoughts and told Keith, "I'll give your proposal serious consideration, but only if you can assure me that Cuffy was not the triggerman in the Brown assassination and that he was not the instigator of the killing." Keith assured me on both fronts.

"I'll need to interview Cuffy personally," I added. Usually, a defense attorney will offer what is known as a proffer, either oral or written, of what he expects his client to say. This practice protects the client in the event plea negotiations fall apart. The downside of a proffer for prosecutors is that they can't evaluate the witness's credibility firsthand. The answers to some questions are only known to law enforcement and the suspect. I wanted to hear Cuffy answer those questions so I could determine if he was telling the truth. "As long as Cuffy is truthful during our interview," I told Keith, "I won't use anything he says against him."

Finally, I told Keith I needed to consult with Phyllis Brown before I gave him an answer. I wanted Phyllis to be included in the decision to grant Cuffy immunity for his involvement in the murder of her husband.

Before Keith left, he paused and said in a serious tone, "J.Tom, one more thing. I can't disclose my source, but I have reason to believe that Derwin Brown was not the only target. Your name is on the list. You need protection. You should not go anywhere outside your home without a bodyguard. I know you don't carry a weapon, but you should reconsider. That's all I can say."

I couldn't demand that Keith divulge where this information came from, though I desperately wanted to know.

"Thanks, Keith," was all I could say. "I understand."

When Keith left, I stood dumbfounded and speechless. Keith had just dropped two bombshells in a matter of minutes: First, after almost a year, we might finally have a break in Derwin's murder case. And second, my life was at risk.

I immediately called Derwin Brown's widow.

"Phyllis, this is J.Tom. Are you alone? I have something urgent I need to discuss with you in private."

"I'm in my bedroom," she said. "The boys are watching television in the family room. What's up?"

"We may have a break in the case," I told her. "But acting on this break will mean giving immunity from prosecution to someone involved in Derwin's murder. Patrick Cuffy's lawyer says his client has important information to offer and wants to make a deal," I said. "Phyllis, I told him I could not agree to immunity if Cuffy was the instigator or the shooter. I also told him I needed your blessing before I went forward."

"How do you know Cuffy will tell the truth?" Phyllis asked. I was asking myself the same question.

"Honestly, we won't know until we interview him, which I will do. It depends on his answers and the story he tells us."

Phyllis didn't hesitate. "As long as Cuffy is not the instigator or the shooter, I can live with the immunity deal," she said. "Promise you will call me right after the interview and tell me what you decide to do next. J.Tom, I want answers."

***

I called Keith back the next morning and told him we could proceed with Cuffy's interview, to be scheduled in the near future.

I brought Chris and Petrey into my office and closed the door. Petrey, as second-in-command, always needed to know what I knew. Chris knew the case inside and out and could propose questions to Cuffy without referring to his case file. I explained that I was prepared to offer transactional immunity to Cuffy for Derwin's murder in exchange for his cooperation and truthful testimony against the others involved. Transactional immunity means that a person can't be prosecuted for their involvement in a crime if they cooperate and testify truthfully for the government. "I've consulted with Phyllis Brown," I said, "and she supports this approach."

I'd also agreed to allow Cuffy to plead to lesser charges for the felony murder of George he'd been indicted for. As I'd told Keith, I wanted to hear from Cuffy directly and make my own assessment of his credibility. "If at any time evidence shows that he's lying regarding his role," I said, "I'll use his statements against him, and we'll prosecute him to the fullest extent of the law."

We were about to walk into a minefield. Offering immunity to a participant in a murder can not only be viewed with disdain by the public, it can also backfire on a prosecutor. What if the jury chooses to believe that the snitch was actually the triggerman or the instigator, and everyone charged with the crime walks free after a trial? Would I be able to convince a jury to believe Cuffy beyond a reasonable doubt?

After Petrey and Chris left my office, I paged Carol Ellis to come see me. "Carol," I began, "I learned last night from a trusted source that my life could be in jeopardy. This is somehow related to Derwin's murder." I expected her to give me a "I told you so" look, but she kept her usual calm demeanor.

"Who is the source, and is the source credible?" she asked.

"I can't reveal the source at this time. But yes, the source is credible," I said.

"Well," she said. "I'm going to start a signup sheet with the investigators. You will always have one of us with you at all times when you're not at home. Do you want someone to stay with you and your family in the evenings?"

"That won't be necessary," I said. "I don't want to complicate the kids' lives even more."

"You need to cancel any appointments you have this afternoon," Carol said. "I'm taking the Glock I assigned to you after Derwin was murdered out of the vault. We're going to the range this afternoon, and I will teach you how to shoot. Promise me you will keep it on you at all times when you're outside your home. You can keep it in a shoulder holster inside your suit jacket, and it won't be noticeable to most people. When you're at home, make sure it's always close at hand. I'm also getting you a bulletproof vest from the police department. Same rule applies."

I didn't like what Carol was telling me to do, but I also knew there was no sense arguing with her.

I now have a greater appreciation of people who need armed guards for protection. Another person close to you at all times can be irritating and nerve-racking. I almost always drove by myself to places I needed to be. Now I would have an armed driver everywhere. I had to modify my daily routine.

Chris, who also regularly worked out at the YMCA in the mornings, came to my house at 6:00 a.m. I was dressed to work out, but I also wore the body vest, and the Glock was under my sweatshirt. The YMCA is only a few hundred yards from my house, but Chris insisted we drive. Once inside the YMCA, we put the guns and vests in a locker and secured them. I refused to wear a bulky vest on a treadmill. We worked out, showered, got dressed, put on our protective equipment, and went to the courthouse.

If I left the office during the day, one of our investigators was always with me. During the week Carol Ellis would usually drive me home in the evenings. Fortunately, we agreed that once I was home or in the courthouse, I could be left alone. Carol also asked that the Decatur Police Department routinely canvass my yard during the evenings when I was home. I remember waking up at night to flashlights shining outside our windows. Fred Mays also volunteered on his time off to take me places in the evenings and on weekends.

This time was fraught with fear and anxiety for our family, especially for the children. My wife Carol and I had always been open and honest with them about my work, even when I was a child abuse prosecutor. Carol and I sat the children down at the kitchen table. I told them, "There is reason to believe that my life might be in danger—whoever killed Derwin Brown also had it in for me. The investigators in my office and the police will be providing protection to keep everyone safe. I want to assure you that I don't believe the threat extends to the rest of my family or that you are in any danger."

Appearing visibly shaken, the children's questions poured out, "What kind of protection? How will you be safe? What does this mean for us?"

I tried to comfort them. "Investigators in my office will accompany me everywhere, and the police will patrol our house regularly. I think we will be well protected." I did not tell them that I would be carrying a weapon, since that would only worry them more.

I cautioned them to avoid being at home alone and told Caroline, then sixteen and a newly licensed driver, not to drive alone.

I added, "Keep this information private. Don't share with your friends or other family members what we know or the measures we are taking to protect ourselves."

High school and middle school years can be filled with isolation, anxiety, and loneliness in the best of times; my children feared for my life, for our family's survival, and at times, for their own safety. In addition to focusing on their schoolwork, sports, and other activities, they were dealing with existential fears—all because of me and my job. I grew up without the presence of a father, and I was determined to avoid the same fate for my own children.

As John, then twelve, wrote in an essay for school, he was afraid for our family's safety from the moment of Derwin's murder, and now his premonitions were coming true. He had nightmares and crawled around the house to avoid walking in front of windows. He did his homework behind furniture. Caroline took on the role as her brother's protector and confidant. They became more than siblings: They were partners and best friends, facing fear together. John and Caroline would talk and cry while she drove to their piano lessons or sports practices. The car was the one place they were together, alone, and could share their feelings without worrying their parents or their friends.

Driving near the house one day, Caroline lost control of her emotions. She began banging on the steering wheel, sobbing and screaming. "What is happening to us? To our dad? To this world?"

Overwhelmed, she pulled over and held hands with her brother. He was quiet, stunned, and scared: His protector was breaking down. As he crouched below the window of the stopped car, she felt that she needed to get herself together for her brother. Then, looking in the rearview mirror, she saw a police car trailing them, and began driving home.

Our family, thankfully, still had a sense of humor. One moment of dark comedy came when one of my bodyguards joined us for our Thanksgiving dinner. Other than Carol and our children, no other family members at the table—including my mother-in-law, her brother, and several cousins—knew the real reason for the investigator's presence. Since the bodyguard's parents were deceased, having him at the table seemed perfectly reasonable. They embraced him as a member of the family and peppered him with questions about his life and hobbies. Little did they know he was on the job, enjoying turkey and dressing armed with two pistols. I winked at Caroline and John from across the table, and we conspired in our secret.

During one of my workday outings, Roger Lindsay was assigned to drive and guard me. Roger had been an excellent homicide detective with the DeKalb County Police Department. I was fortunate to convince him to move over to our office to work homicides in preparation for trial. One of the reasons Roger liked working for the DA's office was because I didn't require our investigators to carry weapons if they chose not to. Roger locked his weapon in a drawer. But Carol told him he had to holster that weapon when he was on my detail.

As Roger drove, he said, "J.Tom, I'm glad to be doing this, but you know we really can't protect you from getting shot."

"What do you mean?" I asked.

"If the Secret Service can't protect President Kennedy or President Reagan from being shot, how do you think one of us can protect you? But don't worry, whoever shoots you will get some serious return fire from me."

"Thanks for the reassurance," I said.

***

The judge postponed Cuffy's trial in the George murder case, pending plea negotiations between our office and Cuffy. On November 28, 2001, he pled guilty to the charges of assault, tampering with evidence, and making false statements to the police in the George murder case, and we postponed disposition on the felony murder charge, pending our interview with Cuffy. Phyllis Brown was present in the courtroom for this plea deal.

Petrey, Chris, and I met again to discuss the Cuffy interview. We were doing something that was extraordinary for a prosecutor, much less an elected district attorney, and something I had never done before: conducting the first interview with a suspect. Usually, prosecutors rely on interviews of suspects conducted by the police or other law enforcement agencies in making decisions. But this case was not an ordinary case, and the stakes were extraordinarily high. At the end of the interview, I told Petrey and Chris, "we'll need to make the most difficult decision of our careers: to use Cuffy's cooperation and go forward with a prosecution, or remain silent for the rest of our lives about what he tells us in confidence."

That call would be mine, but I very much valued our collective wisdom in determining what next steps we would take, if any. The three of us were different in the way we analyzed cases: Petrey was more cautious and skeptical; Chris was methodical and logical; and I depended on my instinct and could be impetuous and risk-taking. I needed all three sets of skills to help me make the ultimate decision.

Interviewing Cuffy in secrecy was paramount. Doing that in the jail or my office in the courthouse, or probably anywhere in the county, would be difficult without word leaking that the two of us were meeting. Chris said that some task force members had heard rumors of a possible deal with Cuffy. Dale Cardwell had also paged me and wanted to know if anything was "brewing."

We could not have any leaks. No one else involved had been arrested, and they could flee the state or the country if they knew Cuffy was snitching. I called Richard Read, a friend and the district attorney in neighboring Rockdale County. I didn't tell Richard why I needed a secure and private location to conduct an interview, but I'm sure he could easily surmise that it had something to do with Derwin's murder. Richard offered a building owned by Rockdale County in a secluded area with only one way in and out. He also said his office would provide additional security.

So the three of us would not be seen leaving the courthouse together and driving away in my car—something we didn't ordinarily do—we arranged that Chris would pick Petrey and me up in his county-issued Ford Taurus in front of the Starbucks on the opposite side of the Decatur Square from the courthouse.

When Chris and Petrey left, I felt an overwhelming sense of aloneness and trepidation. By coming forward, Cuffy had presented the big break we'd been seeking during the past year. But it also created a predicament for me personally. We had almost accepted the fact that this case would not be solved, or certainly not in the near future. I could not be blamed for failing to find a suspect to arrest and prosecute. However, because of the high-profile nature of this case, I would be held accountable and my career could be at risk if a suspect or suspects were arrested and I failed to get a conviction. At this point, our only hope was Cuffy—a person with a less-than-stellar past. But I realized I needed to suppress my own personal fears and focus on what was in the best interest of the Brown family and the people of the county who had elected me.

CHAPTER 12

The square, one-story gray metal building sat in an unpaved area without any grass or trees. Richard Read and his chief assistant were standing outside, and they assured me no one knew they had arranged this meeting place. They would stand outside and make sure no one entered the building during our interview.

Entering the building, we saw it contained just one large, austere room, with a gray concrete floor and bare walls. Overhead fluorescent lights lit the place from a high ceiling, and an industrial floor fan operated on a slow speed. The weather outside was mild for November; a good thing, it turned out, since there was seemingly no heating source. The furnishings consisted of just one rectangular folding table in the middle and several folding chairs.

Cuffy and his attorney, Keith Adams, were already sitting together at the table. Chris, Petrey, and I sat down opposite them. Cuffy, who was being held in the Rockdale County jail after his arrest in September 2001 for felony murder due to the shoot-out at his house, was wearing an orange jumpsuit and was in handcuffs locked behind his back. He still looked fit, and still wore his mustache and goatee. Cuffy appeared unemotional, impassive, and calm.

Rockdale sheriff's deputies were standing inside the door. "Please take his handcuffs off," I asked them, explaining that Chris and I were both armed. They could watch the discussion, but out of hearing distance.

Interrogating a suspect or a witness is a learned art. I'd watched, or listened to, hundreds of recordings of detectives' interviews, including those of people who'd done horrific things. Good interrogators maintain a sense of composure, almost nonchalance. Nothing the suspect says will rattle them. Sometimes, a detective will even say at the beginning of an interview, "Hey man, it's cool, nothing you can tell me I haven't heard before."

I didn't have the same experience, but I had interviewed hundreds of children who were victims and a handful of adult defendants. When I interviewed a child, I tried to project the same calm demeanor. However, when I interviewed a child, I had empathy for them. I had no empathy for Cuffy.

"Mr. Cuffy," I began. "I will first read to you your Miranda warnings. I have also included a statement that nothing you say during the course of our conversation this afternoon can ever be used against you as long as you are truthful in your statements to us. Do you understand and agree? If so, please sign at the bottom of the page next to my name and signature."

"I understand," Cuffy said, and he signed the form. Keith also signed, then told Cuffy, "I'll be right outside the door, and available to answer any questions." The attorney would not be present for the interview so that, if we determined Cuffy lied to us and we prosecuted him, Keith could not be called as a witness against his client.

"Mr. Cuffy," I began, "your attorney has told me that you have some information that could be helpful in our investigation into the murder of Sheriff-elect Derwin Brown. Mr. Adams told me that you will only provide us this information if we agree not to prosecute you for your possible involvement in that homicide or any other potential charges against you related to your service as a DeKalb County sheriff's officer. Further, you requested a dismissal of a felony murder charge and a plea to lesser charges relating to an incident that occurred at your residence on March 18, 2001.

"I told Mr. Adams that I would only consider your offer if, one, you were not the instigator of Sheriff-elect Brown's death and, two, you were not the triggerman that caused his death. In addition, every statement you give us must be truthful. Finally, you must agree to testify against everyone involved in the death of Sheriff-elect Brown and the corruption within the DeKalb County Sheriff's Department.

"If at any time I find out you have lied to me, all bets are off, and you may be subject to prosecution for those crimes. If, after this interview, I decide not to go forward with a prosecution, your statements to us cannot be used against you. They will be kept confidential forever. Do you understand our agreement?"

"Yes, I do," Cuffy responded without hesitating. His voice was utterly flat.

"Okay. During our first meeting in my office, you mentioned briefly your relationship with Sheriff Dorsey and how you came to know him. Please elaborate on that if you will."

Open-ended, nonthreatening questions are the best way to begin an interview.

"I moved here from St. Croix when I was a teenager," Cuffy began. As he spoke, I could hear a Caribbean lilt in his voice. "I attended high school with one of Dorsey's sons. His dad, Sidney Dorsey, took me under his wing. After a brief time in the Marines, I went to work for Dorsey's security company, SID, Inc. He was like a father figure to me; sometimes he would introduce me as his son."

Cuffy added that he'd volunteered for both of Dorsey's campaigns for sheriff, and accepted the deputy position Dorsey had promised him after his victory in 1997. He confirmed one aspect of Dorsey's corruption schemes, telling us, "I would also cover security for SID when they needed a private security guard at a bank," he said. "Usually, I was on the county clock when I worked security for SID, and I was never paid by SID."

In 1998, Cuffy told us, Dorsey had him secretly record conversations with "enemies" whom the sheriff thought were plotting against him. One of them was Derwin Brown. Cuffy maintained he didn't know what Dorsey did with those recordings.

After Dorsey lost the runoff to Derwin in the summer of 2000, he moved Cuffy to community relations, the position previously held by Joe Murray. Cuffy had his own office on the same floor as Dorsey's, and was issued a uniform, a gun, and a sheriff's department Crown Victoria, an unmarked vehicle used by the department. "Basically, my job was to do whatever Dorsey told me to do," he said. "Sometimes I ran personal errands for him, his wife, and his kids, and I still covered security at the banks. I pretty much came and went as I pleased."

Then, one day in August, Cuffy continued, "Dorsey called me to come to his home. I got there sometime after work, around 8:00 p.m. Dorsey was wearing a robe and pajama bottoms. He looked tired and angry, and his hair was messed up. He handed me a folded piece of paper. I opened it. The note said, 'Kill Derwin Brown.' I asked him why he wanted Derwin killed. He said, 'Because Derwin is going to kill me.'"

I remained composed—"Nothing you can tell me I haven't heard before"—but Dorsey's response was astonishing, nonsensical. I was also struck again by Cuffy's matter-of-fact, expressionless recitation of this bizarre story. Nothing was making much sense in this case.

"Do you by any chance still have the note?" I asked. I knew that would be too good to be true, but I was hoping.

"No," Cuffy answered. "Dorsey took the note back from me, tore it up, and ate it."

Melodramatic as that sounds, Shirley McMichael had told us Dorsey had destroyed written evidence—twice. If nothing else, Dorsey was consistent in destroying evidence. After all, he was a former homicide detective.

***

"How did you respond that night when Dorsey told you to kill Derwin Brown?" I asked Cuffy.

"I told him I could not do it alone," he said, "and Dorsey brought up the names of Paul Skyers, David Ramsey, and Melvin Walker." All four had worked together at SID; Ramsey, Cuffy's roommate, was also a friend of Cuffy's from the islands. By the next day, the other men had all agreed to participate.

"What was in it for those three to kill Derwin Brown?" I asked.

"Skyers wanted a job in the sheriff's department," Cuffy said. "Ramsey wanted a job in the sheriff's department as well, but he wanted to work in narcotics because he did not want to cut his braids. He has very long braids. Walker wanted to be sent to the police academy to be trained to work on the SWAT team. Eventually, he wanted Dorsey to promote him to SWAT commander."

Amazing. These men readily agreed to kill another human being based on the mere hope of future employment.

"What did Dorsey say to all these demands?"

"He was cool with it. He said he could make it happen. No problem."

"I don't get it." I was thinking out loud. "Even with Brown dead, Dorsey wasn't the sheriff. How could he possibly meet all those demands?" This had baffled us all along: While we had suspicions about Cuffy, and we knew he and Dorsey were joined at the hip, we could not imagine what Dorsey's motive would be to have the man who defeated him killed.

"Dorsey told us there would be a special election to fill the vacancy once Brown was dead," Cuffy explained. "He was certain he would win the special election. He also told me the judges would have to appoint him as interim sheriff even before the special election, since he already had the experience."

That absurd fantasy had never occurred to me, or to anyone else working on the case—how could Dorsey be so delusional? "Continue," I asked, as nonchalantly as possible.

"We went into the planning stage. Dorsey wanted us to strangle Brown because there would be little evidence, as long as we did not leave the garrote at the scene. We did not think that was convenient."

Not *convenient*? Cuffy used that term several times; I suppose he meant practical.

"Brown was too big for even the four of us to try to strangle. So we told Dorsey we were going to shoot him with a gun that could not be traced, and he agreed. None of us knew where Brown lived, and neither did Dorsey. So we went to the public library in Decatur, and the librarian showed us how to find his address using the public records. That is how we also found your address."

My nervous system began to sound its internal alarms, but outwardly, I think I maintained the interrogator's demeanor. "Why did you need my address?" I asked, as coolly as possible.

"Because Dorsey ordered us to kill you after we killed Derwin."

"Interesting." I channeled poise I didn't know I had, responding as if he had just told me he had bacon and eggs with wheat toast for breakfast. "Why kill me?"

"Because Dorsey knew you were looking into the corruption at the jail. He was worried that if you found anything, he might lose the special election or even go to jail," Cuffy replied. "He believed you were in a conspiracy with Derwin Brown to keep him from being sheriff."

"So you found my address at the library," I said.

"Uh-huh."

"Did you ever think about just looking in the phone book for my address?"

"Are you in the phone book?"

"Yes, and I am the only J.Tom Morgan listed in the directory. Not hard to find," I said.

"I guess we wasted our time," Cuffy continued, adding: "You shouldn't list your name in the phone book."

This afternoon was shifting from strange to surreal. Here I was, calmly conversing with someone who, along with others, had planned to kill me at my home. And he was chiding me for being listed in the phone book!

"What did you do after you learned Sheriff Brown's address?" I asked.

The four began surveilling Derwin's home several nights a week, Cuffy said, meeting in an elementary school parking lot and walking through a wooded area to observe the Brown house. "We would wear all black," he added, "black shirts, black pants, black shoes." One night in September, school resource officers approached and questioned the group in the parking lot, but a phone call to Dorsey satisfied the officers and defused the situation.

"Where did you find a gun, and what type of gun was it?" asked Chris. This was the first question we asked to which we already knew the answer. It would be a test of Cuffy's knowledge of the facts.

First, Cuffy said, he'd tried to borrow a weapon with a silencer from a former Fulton County sheriff's deputy he'd met while guarding prisoners. After that man refused, he and Ramsey turned to a different, extremely risky tactic. "Ramsey and I would drive in known drug areas in Atlanta in my Crown Vic," Cuffy said. "We both were armed, and acted as if we were narcotics agents or SWAT team members. We'd confront people we thought looked like drug dealers, arrest them, and search them looking for a gun. But we never found a gun, and we let the people we apprehended leave."

"Eventually," Cuffy continued, "Ramsey was able to acquire a semiautomatic TEC-9. We made our own silencer from items we bought from Home Depot. We tried using a potato for a silencer, but it was not convenient." Again, his pet term, "convenient." Ultimately, he said, "It took us two weeks to make the silencer."

The TEC-9 was consistent with our knowledge of the possible weapons used in the murder. I also mused to myself that their amateur efforts to make a silencer were an abysmal failure, since everyone in Derwin's house heard the gunshots.

"Who had the TEC-9 on the night of the shooting, and how was that determined?" asked Chris.

"Dorsey wanted Ramsey to be the shooter because he did not work for the sheriff's department and had not lived in Atlanta for long," replied Cuffy. "But we disagreed. We did not think Ramsey was up to it, and besides, he did not have the training with firearms. Skyers wanted to be the getaway driver. Walker and I drew straws. Walker got the short straw, so his job was to carry the TEC-9 and be the shooter. Ramsey and I would also carry weapons for backup in case we needed them at the scene. Skyers would be waiting for us with the car running."

After all we'd learned today about the planning, the logistics, and the irrational motivation behind this heinous crime, we'd finally come to the agonizing heart of it: an honorable lawman who'd just reached the pinnacle of his career executed at his home, essentially in front of his family.

"Why did you pick that night?" Chris asked.

"We made several attempts before then, but we never fired any shots. We needed to get up our courage," Cuffy admitted, still without any visible emotion. "The weekend before the shooting, we watched him clean out his car for forty-five minutes. But we kept coming up with excuses—say, a dog was barking—not to kill him.

"But Dorsey told us we would have to kill Brown before December 31, 2000, so that the judges could appoint him sheriff before Brown took office on January 1. He told us Brown would be coming back from sheriffs' training in Forsyth the night of the fifteenth."

Throughout the interview, Cuffy's dispassionate delivery did not change at all as he betrayed his "father figure."

"I worked that day and then went home," Cuffy continued. "Ramsey was living with me. Walker came over around 7:30 p.m. Skyers went to work at his security job, to show his face so he would have an alibi. Later that night, Skyers came to my house to join me and the others. We were all dressed in black pants and black tops, except Ramsey, who was wearing a camouflage top. We left in Skyers's car since he was the getaway driver. We went back to the woods near Brown's home and parked at a dead end near a church.

"Skyers stayed in the car. Skyers and Ramsey had walkie-talkies Skyers had borrowed from his security firm. Ramsey, Walker, and I walked into the woods. I had a 9mm I got from Skyers, Ramsey carried a .38 pistol that I borrowed from a friend in the sheriff's department, and

Walker had the TEC-9. Walker's job was to shoot and kill Brown. Ramsey was to take out any passenger that happened to be in Brown's car, and I was backing up Ramsey."

Another shocking—and repugnant—admission. We hadn't known they were fully prepared to take another innocent life that night. If it had been Derwin's wife, or one of his children or grandchildren, would they have followed through? I didn't ask; I wanted Cuffy to keep talking.

"We walked through the woods and initially took positions near what appeared to be an abandoned house next to Brown's home. It was dark and drizzling rain. After about fifteen minutes, Brown arrived in his car and parked on the street because there were cars in his driveway. Walker ran and put himself between the two cars in the driveway, and I positioned myself behind a car across the street. Brown was alone. He reached in and retrieved some packages from his car and started walking down the driveway toward the house.

"I heard gunshots, but I could not see Walker. The only shots fired that night came from the TEC-9. I ran toward Brown's house and collided with Walker, who was running in the opposite direction, back toward the woods. He yelled, 'Let's go!' and pushed me toward the woods. Ramsey had frozen. I told Ramsey to tell Skyers on the walkie-talkie that we were on the way and to get the car running.

"We ran through the woods, and Ramsey fell to the ground. Walker and I had to pick him up to keep him moving. We hopped in Skyers's car and drove back to my house."

At this point, Petrey, Chris, and I were speechless. We had just heard a chilling, meticulously detailed firsthand account of the assassination of Derwin Brown. And the entire time, Cuffy spoke in a monotone—I've heard people read the US Constitution out loud with more feeling. Chris brought us back to the subject at hand.

"What did you do when you got back to your house?" Chris asked.

"The plan was to change clothes at my house and go to our respective alibis. Skyers was going back to his security job, Walker was going home to give his wife a shot of medication that she needed at 11:00 p.m., and I was going back to the sheriff's department to work overtime. Ramsey stayed at home.

"I heard Skyers say, 'How can you be so stupid and drop your gun?' I asked Ramsey if he had dropped his gun and he said, 'Yeah, I think so.' This was the .38-caliber pistol I had borrowed from a friend in the sheriff's department. I knew it could be traced back to my friend."

"What did you do after you learned Ramsey had lost the pistol?" I asked. I thought I already knew the answer. We had intentionally kept our knowledge of Cuffy and Ramsey leaving his home in those early morning hours a secret from the press and most everyone else—including Cuffy.

"Skyers left to dispose of the TEC-9 on the way to his job, and Walker went home to be with his wife," Cuffy said. "I decided not to go to the sheriff's department to work. Instead, about three in the morning, Ramsey and I went to go find the pistol. We left in my Crown Vic, pulled into the parking lot of a Waffle House, and sat there for several minutes to make sure no one was tailing us. We never went in. We then got on I-285 and exited on Memorial Drive near the jail and drove around the jail without stopping."

A voice inside my head screamed, "Son of a bitch!" We'd been told about their maneuvers after the police surveillance I'd suggested to Chief Moody at the hospital. However, the officers following Cuffy believed he knew he was being tailed and therefore would not do anything suspicious. In fact, Cuffy was unaware—and if the officers had kept on his tail throughout the night, we might have solved the case in twenty-four hours.

"Did you find the .38?" I asked. Again, I tried to remain calm.

"I dropped Ramsey off where we had parked near Derwin's house and told him to crawl back to where he had fallen and find the gun. I waited at a girlfriend's house for him to call me to go back and get him.

"About an hour and a half later, Ramsey called, and I drove back to pick him up. He could not find the gun. We were real worried you guys would find it and trace it back to me. Later, we even bought a metal detector from Radio Shack to go back and find the gun." They never used the machine, Cuffy told us, "but we kept the receipt, so we took the metal detector back for a refund."

They may have been murderous coconspirators desperately trying to avoid arrest, but they weren't about to waste those few dollars.

"Do you remember the Radio Shack where you bought the metal detector?" asked Chris.

"Yeah, the one in South DeKalb Mall," said Cuffy.

Petrey asked what the four did the next day, the sixteenth.

"I went to Dorsey's house that morning. A whole bunch of cars were parked in front of the house. I walked in and greeted Sherry Dorsey. Dorsey was being interviewed by several members from the media. I gave him a nod, and he nodded back."

Cuffy left, picked up Walker, and the two of them later brought supplies to a holiday party the Dorseys were giving for their children and their friends. "The party was on Moreland Avenue," Cuffy said. "Dorsey and Sherry were there with a bunch of kids." The image I got listening to this—of Cuffy and Walker enjoying a party with joyful, boisterous children—was a stark contrast to the brutal assassination they'd carried out the night before.

That night, Cuffy said, he went back to Dorsey's house to speak with him privately. "I told him about Ramsey dropping the gun, and he exclaimed, 'Oh my God!' and his knees kind of buckled. I thought he was going to faint. He wanted to know if the gun could be traced. I said it could be traced back to my friend who worked at the jail.

"Dorsey said, 'We have to get rid of your friend.'"

Yet another murder he was ready and willing to order. Cuffy reassured Dorsey that killing his friend "would not be necessary because we would find the gun."

He and Dorsey only met "a couple times" after that, Cuffy said. "We knew we were suspects, and Dorsey did not want us to be seen together."

One of those meetings occurred when he, Walker, Skyers, and Ramsey were invited, along with their dates, to have dinner with a reporter at the Ritz-Carlton in Atlanta. "She said she wanted to interview us about how you were unfairly targeting us for Derwin's murder because we were Black."

Cuffy confirmed that this reporter was Mary Fischer, who'd approached me saying she was working for *GQ* magazine. "What does that have to do with meeting up with Dorsey?" I asked Cuffy.

"Before we sat down to eat," Cuffy said, "Fischer whispered in my ear that someone wanted to see me, and she handed me a room key. I went upstairs, and Dorsey was sitting on a bed in the room."

"Hold on," I said. "A reporter from California invites you and your friends to have dinner at the Ritz-Carlton. She whispers a message to you and gives you a room key. When you get to the room, Dorsey is there waiting for you. What the hell did you and Dorsey talk about?"

I was starting to lose my ability to appear nonchalant.

"This was after the shoot-out at my house and the possibility of you guys arresting me for that dude's death," Cuffy replied. "Dorsey wanted to make sure we were holding up okay and keeping our mouths shut. I assured him we were.

"I asked him if we should go forward with killing you. He gave me a tongue-lashing and told me, 'No. Call that off!' He said we were in the mess we were in because I did not take orders and listen to him. We talked about thirty minutes, and then I rejoined the group and gave Ms. Fischer back her key. That was the last time I saw Dorsey in person."

"Follow-up questions?" I asked Chris and Petrey.

"Where did Skyers dispose of the TEC-9?" asked Chris.

"I have no idea. Only Skyers knows where he got rid of it," said Cuffy.

We had interviewed Cuffy for about three hours. Petrey, Chris, and I left him at the table and walked to a corner of the room where no one could hear us. "You believe him?" I asked.

"His story fits with the facts as we know them," Chris replied, "and we can verify a few things, like the meeting with the officers at the school and the Radio Shack purchase."

"I believe Cuffy," I said. "But we have a problem. We have nothing to corroborate that he was not the shooter or the instigator, or that Dorsey was involved. I hate to do this, but I think we need to offer immunity to another player, probably Skyers, since he seems to be the least culpable, but that isn't saying much. Also, Skyers appears to be the only person who can provide the location where he disposed of the murder weapon."

"I think we could be giving away too much," Petrey said, with his usual dose of caution. "A jury and the court of public opinion will not like it."

"I agree, but we lose if we don't have Skyers's testimony, and we might lose anyway," I said.

After a little more discussion, we agreed that we needed Skyers on our side.

We went back to the table and approached Cuffy. "We want to interview Skyers," I said. "We will offer him immunity under the same conditions that we offered you. Can you call him and tell him to come in?"

"When do you want to talk to him?" asked Cuffy.

"Now," I said. "We will give him an address. Call him now so we can listen to you talking to him."

We gave Cuffy a phone, and he dialed. Cuffy spoke: "Hey man, it's me. Yeah, I'm not in jail. I am somewhere in Rockdale County with Mr. Morgan and others. I told them everything. I need you to come in and talk to them. It's cool. Everything will be okay." There was a brief pause. "No man, you don't need a lawyer, just get here right away," said Cuffy.

Paul Skyers arrived about an hour later. When he walked in, Cuffy hugged him and told him to tell us everything, reassuring him again that it would be okay. Cuffy was then taken back to the county jail, and his attorney also left.

Even though Skyers had arrived voluntarily and was not under arrest, we read him his Miranda warnings as a precaution and explained that based on what Cuffy had told us during our interview, we were offering him the same immunity as we had offered Cuffy. He said he understood, and he waived his right to silence and to have a lawyer present during questioning.

Skyers's story dovetailed with Cuffy's version. Skyers knew one detail that Cuffy did not know, however: where he disposed of the murder weapon. He told us he had disassembled the silencer and tossed it and the TEC-9 down a storm sewer drain. When asked if he could find the drain again, he said he could and would show us the location. We told Skyers he could go and that we'd be in touch about retrieving the weapon. We also warned him not to discuss our conversation with anyone, especially Walker and Ramsey.

At this point, the sun had set; we could see from the windows in all four walls that it was dark outside. I asked Chris to contact Carol Ellis and Tom Clegg and have them meet him, along with Petrey and me, at the police station. In an office of almost fifty lawyers, Tom was the undisputed best trial lawyer. I wanted him in this meeting for his judgment and his courtroom skills. Chris also reached out to Chief Moody as well as Maddox and Taylor, the lead DeKalb PD detectives, on the case. We would meet with them later in the evening.

My four staff members and I first met privately in a stark conference room at the police department, which had bare walls and no windows. Chris, Petrey, and I brought Tom and Carol up to speed. We discussed the statements and agreed that certain elements—the encounter the four assassins had with the resource officers at the elementary school, the purchase of the metal detector at Radio Shack, the location of the murder weapon, and the friend who provided the .38 pistol—could all be corroborated. We also agreed, though, that the only real piece of evidence linking Dorsey to the four mentioned in Cuffy's and Skyers's interviews was the meeting at the Ritz-Carlton. That would have to be corroborated by the *GQ* reporter.

Cuffy coming forward was the big break we'd been seeking for the past year. But with the addition of Skyers, we were contemplating letting *two* killers walk free, essentially, to punish two others and the man behind the murder, Sidney Dorsey. And convicting those three in court was far from a certainty.

Finally, Tom looked at me and asked, "You're the boss. You have to make the final decision. Your career as a prosecutor is at stake. What's your call?"

I took a deep breath. "Based on the evidence before us, let's bring in the team and prepare arrest warrants for Walker, Ramsey, and Dorsey for the murder of Derwin Brown."

***

Once everyone else arrived, I went over the events of the last twenty-four hours and explained that the prosecution team believed we had enough evidence to prove guilt beyond a reasonable doubt.

Chief Moody was quiet. Then he reached over to a whiteboard that had a list of unsolved homicides in the county. Picking up a marker he wrote, "Solved—Dorsey" next to Derwin Brown's name.

Petrey helped write the warrants. It was about 10:30 p.m. when he and Chris took them to the magistrate court judge for review and issuance. I called my wife Carol and told her briefly about the day and that I would be home very late. She said she would wait up, for which I was grateful.

Three sets of SWAT teams went to the homes of Dorsey, Walker, and Ramsey. We waited tensely in the police department conference room to hear news of the arrests, passing the time with idle conversation. We also watched TV reports of the death of the former Beatle George Harrison from cancer.

When the SWAT team assigned to Dorsey arrived at his home, he wasn't there, and they tried frantically to locate him. The SWAT teams assigned to Walker and Ramsey took them into custody at their homes without incident. After a stressful hour, the police received a call from Dorsey's attorney, Brian Steel, that Dorsey would turn himself in.

Chief Moody finally received the call we were waiting for: All three defendants were now in custody. He must have been relieved that the pieces had fallen into place and the arrests made two weeks before the one-year anniversary of Derwin's murder. Once the defendants were booked into the jail, after midnight, we breathed a sigh of relief and dispersed to our homes for much-needed rest. I paged Dale Cardwell and told him to call me. He needed to be the first to know. In many ways, his reporting had led us to this moment.

For the first time in almost a year, Carol, my children, and I could fall asleep soundly. Only I had a sense that some of the most challenging moments were yet to come.

CHAPTER 13

Brian Steel immediately filed a motion for bond for Dorsey's release from custody pending trial. The bond hearing would be the first opportunity for the defense and the press to have a glimpse of the nature and quality of evidence against the defendants. Walker and Ramsey had not hired private attorneys, so they were appointed public defenders for the hearing.

Under Georgia law, the court must consider the following criteria before granting the defendant a bond to be released from custody: (1) Is the defendant a flight risk from the jurisdiction of the court? (2) Is there a likelihood the defendant will commit other crimes while out on bond? (3) Is there a likelihood the defendant will intimidate witnesses or obstruct justice if granted a bond? Judges are allowed to consider the nature and quality of the evidence against the defendant when deciding bond; however, guilt or innocence is not a factor for the court's consideration. That is for a jury to decide.

I seriously doubted that a judge would grant a defendant who was charged with the assassination of a public official a bond. On the other hand, Dorsey was a former public official himself, one who, for much of his long career in law enforcement, had enjoyed a positive reputation. We decided to let the court know that I had been a target for assassination because of my office's investigation of corruption by Dorsey. I knew this would set off a firestorm in the press and would result in a motion to recuse my office, and me, from the case. Both of my intuitions proved to be true. We would eventually have to let the defense attorneys know of this threat, so we decided to go ahead and introduce it during the bond hearing. However, I did not want to be a distraction, so I told Tom and Petrey to handle the bond hearing.

I was surprised to learn that the superior court judge who should have handled the bond motions had appointed a retired juvenile court judge, Judge Ed Wheeler, to hear the motion for bond. Since his retirement, Judge Wheeler often sat in for judges who were attending a conference or on vacation, so his appearance was not that unusual, except for the circumstances of this case. I thought a full-time superior court judge would want to hear the case.

The courtroom was packed with reporters, security, and people just wanting to see a glimpse of Dorsey in handcuffs. Because hearsay is admissible in a bond hearing, only one witness, Chris Harvey, was called by the prosecution to summarize the facts of the case. Chris's knowledge of this case, both the big picture and the tiniest detail, was encyclopedic. He could recall facts, dates, and participants without referring to his notes. That day, he proved once again how important he was to the case.

Because we had determined that the corruption in the sheriff's department under Dorsey's tenure was a large part of the motivation for murdering Derwin, we needed to lay a framework so that the judge could see that the case went far beyond the arrest warrant for murder. Chris was able to give a broad overview of what led to Derwin's murder. Because he was present for Cuffy's and Skyers's statements, he also gave the court a detailed description of the murder and the role each person played.

Steel used the bond hearing to cross-examine Chris to find out as much about the case against his client as possible. Although not relevant for the issue of Dorsey acquiring a bond, Steel did establish that all of the evidence related to the murder charge came from Cuffy and Skyers, and that Cuffy was the only person to have direct contact with Dorsey. We knew Steel's strategy would be to try to destroy Cuffy's credibility.

Judge Wheeler denied granting bonds to all three defendants. They would have to remain in jail pending their trials. For his own safety

Dorsey was held in the Hall County jail north of Atlanta, and Walker and Ramsey were held in the DeKalb County jail.

With these three defendants off the streets, the security detail that had been assigned to me was suspended. After months of dedicated work, the special investigative grand juries were also dismissed without the need for reports.

Shortly after Judge Wheeler rendered his decision, I learned that eight of the nine superior court judges had recused themselves from presiding over Dorsey's trial without a request from either side that they do so. The judges' rationale was that because of their long-standing relationships with the sheriff's department, including the use of sheriff's deputies to guard their courtrooms, they could not preside over the trial of a former sheriff. This case did not present a legal conflict, and I doubted that attorneys from either side would try to have any of the judges removed from the case. However, I couldn't blame the judges for not wanting to be involved in such a high-profile case. Most judges shun media attention. Judge Lance Ito took a beating from the press, public, and media pundits for his handling of the O. J. Simpson trial.

The only judge who did not recuse herself was the one I knew the least about. I had never appeared before this judge, and knew nothing about her qualifications or judicial demeanor. Judge Cynthia J. Becker was elected to the bench at the same time Derwin won the runoff. I was surprised that she, too, would not try to find a way to recuse herself since she had only served as a judge for a short time.

I had a brief encounter with Judge Becker when we were both campaigning the summer before Derwin was murdered. It was during the Fourth of July celebration in 2000 on the Decatur Square. Every Fourth of July, Decatur hosts a hometown parade led by a city fire truck, followed by kids on bicycles and smaller children in wagons and strollers decorated with streamers and flags. After the parade, families spread their blankets on the Square to enjoy picnics, listen to music, and watch fireworks launched from the courthouse parking deck.

In 2000, my children and their friends decorated a borrowed convertible with campaign signs and rode in the parade while handing out candy. When I was passing out campaign literature on the Square during the picnic, a woman with her own campaign brochures stopped to chat. She introduced herself as Cynthia Becker, but she said everyone called her "CJ." CJ looked athletic and self-confident. I learned later she played in an adult soccer league. Because our paths had not crossed, I assumed her private practice was probably limited to civil cases.

"I know you have your own race to run so you cannot endorse a candidate in another race publicly," CJ said to me. "But I hope you tell anyone who asks you to support me."

"I don't know you at all," I said. "But if I were a betting person, I would bet you will be the next judge on the superior court bench."

CJ gave me a puzzled look and asked why I was so sure she would win, since this was her first foray into politics and few people knew her.

I explained, "Three people including you are running for judge of superior court for an open seat without an incumbent: two women and one man. Sadly, 99 percent of people who vote are unfamiliar with candidates in judicial races—or in district attorney races, for that matter. Female voters exceed male voters in DeKalb County. You and the other female candidate will likely get the most votes. However, because there is a third candidate, you will probably be forced into a runoff. In races without an incumbent, the person with the first name on the ballot often wins. With your last name being before your opponent's name on the ballot, you should get the most votes."

"That sounds pretty cynical," she said.

"It may sound cynical, but it's a reality of our current system, for good or for bad," I said. "Personally, I believe the justice system would be better served if we followed the European model. In that system, lawyers go back to school and must pass an exam before being considered for appointment to a judgeship. Here, the candidate with the most votes wears the robe."

"Well, I believe I'm qualified to be a judge, and I hope you're right about how the votes will be cast," she said.

"I look forward to trying a case in your court," I said.

As it turned out, the first case I would try in her courtroom would be a career-defining one for both of us.

***

For his entire career, Emmet Bondurant has been a premier attorney in Georgia. The *National Law Journal* recognized Emmet as one of the top ten trial lawyers in the country. He was only twenty-six when he won his first US Supreme Court case. The firm that includes his name, Bondurant Mixson & Elmore, is known for both its stellar legal work and its commitment to community service and pro bono work.

I only knew Emmet personally, not professionally. Emmet's wife, Jane, and my wife Carol had attended college together, and we went to a couple of functions at their house. Jane, a former Supreme Court clerk for Justice Sandra Day O'Connor, made the transition from being a lawyer to becoming a Presbyterian minister and served as a seminary intern at our church during summer 2000. After my grueling reelection campaign that summer, Jane had offered a respite in the mountains for my family and me at the home she and Emmet had built in North Carolina.

Because Emmet and his firm were civil attorneys, we had no occasion for our paths to cross in a courtroom. So I was surprised when I had a message to call Emmet a few days after the bond hearings for Dorsey, Walker, and Ramsey in early December 2001.

Emmet does not mince words.

"J.Tom," he said, "I see you and your office have a big case on your hands. I think it might behoove you to meet with one of my partners, John Floyd."

"Emmet," I said, "I didn't know your firm did any criminal trial work."

"We don't," he replied. "But John has some ideas that might assist you with your prosecution. I hope you can find time to meet with him."

"I have some time in the morning," I told him. "I look forward to hearing what Mr. Floyd has to say."

That last sentence was a bald-faced lie. The absolute last thing I wanted to do was to meet with a civil attorney who had ideas on how to prosecute a criminal case. I have nothing against civil lawyers; some of the best and brightest lawyers I know are civil attorneys, and many supported my campaign. But not many of them have practiced criminal law. In fact, many civil lawyers who call themselves litigators have never argued a case before a jury. Only out of respect for and deference to Emmet did I agree to meet with Mr. Floyd.

I walked across the hall to Petrey's office and told him I needed him to join me for a meeting the next morning.

"Who is the meeting with?" Petrey asked.

"An attorney from the Bondurant firm who may have some suggestions regarding how to prosecute Dorsey," I replied.

"What time?" Petrey asked.

"Ten," I responded.

"I'm scheduled to get a pedicure at that time," Petrey said.

"You don't get pedicures," I responded.

"Tomorrow looks like a good time to start. Certainly a better use of my time than meeting with a civil attorney telling us how to try a criminal case," he said.

"Look, you already have some things in common with this guy," I argued. "You both have Ivy League educations: You went to Harvard, and he went to Brown. You both graduated from Emory Law School. That should give you something to talk about. See you at ten."

***

The next morning, John Floyd met Petrey and me in my office. Bespectacled, with a slightly receding hairline and a round face, John looked like a nerdy lawyer, except for his stocky build. I later learned John is a competitive weightlifter, not a common hobby among lawyers.

"Thank you for taking the time to meet with us," I told him. "I look forward to your thoughts on the Dorsey prosecution." Petrey gave me a look.

"I only know what I know about this case from what I have read in the papers," John began. "But it looks to me that the Georgia RICO law was tailor-made for this kind of prosecution."

RICO stands for the Racketeer Influenced and Corrupt Organizations Act, which was passed by Congress during the Nixon administration as a prosecutorial tool to take down Mafia organizations. After its passage, the fifty states passed their own versions of the law, but RICO was seldom used by state prosecutors. We had our problems in DeKalb County, but to my knowledge the Mafia had not made its way down to Georgia. As a result, I was only vaguely familiar with the RICO statute. Not only had I never prosecuted a case under the statute, no one in my office during my administration had prosecuted a RICO case.

"I guess my first question, John, is why a civil lawyer is so knowledgeable about RICO," I said.

"Most of my practice is filing RICO complaints, primarily against corporations," John replied.

"I'm a little confused," I admitted. "What does RICO have to do with the civil practice of law?"

John acknowledged most prosecutors were unaware that civil actions can be brought pursuant to the RICO law. Politely and patiently, he explained: "When I draft a civil RICO complaint, I'm seeking monetary damages on behalf of my client. When a prosecutor drafts a RICO indictment, the prosecutor is seeking a criminal conviction, which may result in jail time. However, the civil complaint and the criminal indictment basically look the same except for these differences. I believe RICO can be used to fight local political corruption. However, state prosecutors haven't used the RICO law for this purpose."

I noticed John had brought a book with him.

"This is a book I wrote called *RICO State by State: A Guide to Litigation Under the State Racketeering Statutes*," he said. "It's a favorite doorstop in law firms all over the country."

Self-deprecation and humility are rare traits among lawyers, especially trial lawyers, and I smiled at John's humor at his own expense. I also thought to myself: *This guy needs to get a life if he has time to read the RICO laws in every state in the country.*

"Seriously," John continued, "I have examined every RICO law on the books, and the Georgia law is the best there is for going after a corrupt public official, even better than the federal law."

"How so?" I asked.

"I understand that Sheriff Dorsey is alleged to have committed many different crimes, in many ways, involving many persons, and maybe in different counties," John said. "Instead of piecemealing the offenses in separate charges, you bring them together under one umbrella of RICO. Furthermore, a RICO complaint, or indictment, is like a short novel. It tells a story of crime and corruption and how the persons interacted before there is even an opening statement to the jury."

"I have a question," Petrey piped up. He was apparently paying attention and not thinking about his pedicure. "Dorsey committed many crimes, either alone or with the help of others. All those crimes, but one, I can see putting under this umbrella you describe. What about the murder charge? It carries a life sentence upon conviction, and RICO only has a twenty-year maximum penalty. If we put the murder charge in with RICO, it arguably cannot be used again to support a life sentence."

"I'm not an expert on criminal law," John confessed. "If I were drafting a civil complaint for monetary damages, it would not be an issue. I can do more research, but to be safe, I would keep the murder charge out of the RICO count."

I said, "John, my first impression—and I will have to discuss it more with Petrey—is that what you're saying might be useful, but I have a couple of concerns. First, no one in this office has ever drafted or prosecuted a RICO indictment. Even if you had a sample that we could use for a template, we would need your expertise to write this so-called umbrella RICO count."

"I'll be glad to help in any way I can be of use to you and your office," he replied.

"The second problem is an even bigger obstacle," I countered. "I don't know if you have ever participated in a criminal trial, but at the end of the prosecution's case, the defense will stand up and ask the court to throw out the indictment. Dorsey has two of the best criminal attorneys in Georgia, and they will come after us like sharks on a swimmer when they make their motion to have this indictment dismissed. Petrey is a smart guy, but I don't want him defending his first RICO dismissal in this of all cases."

"Another possibility is to swear me in as a special assistant district attorney, and I can make the argument for the prosecution," John volunteered.

"John, I don't think you understand. This is going to be a very long trial, and your sole purpose in the trial would be to make this argument outside of the presence of the jury. You would have to sit through the entire state's case, which could take a few weeks, before you get the chance to argue before the judge. I know your office is famous for its pro bono work, and we damn sure can't pay you. Are your partners really going to let you spend weeks with us without pay?"

John smiled and replied, "Yes. Our firm encourages, maybe even demands, all our attorneys to do pro bono work to help charitable organizations and worthwhile causes. I want to spend my pro bono hours helping prosecutors."

"Well," I said, "a district attorney's office is certainly a charitable organization. Let me discuss this with Petrey at lunch and get back with you. Thanks again for taking your time to meet with us, and thank Emmet for me."

After John left my office, I looked at Petrey and said, "Thoughts?"

"He may be onto something. I need to think about it," Petrey replied.

Given Petrey's initial resistance to the meeting, I could tell John Floyd had made an impression on Petrey. "I defer to your judgment on how to handle the corruption allegations. That prosecution is complicated," I said.

Without explicitly stating it, Petrey and I had just divided the case from that point forward. Petrey would be responsible for managing the corruption charges, and I would be responsible for the murder charge. Though we were uncomfortable prosecuting a charge—RICO—that we had never tried before a jury, what Floyd told us made sense. We could bundle all the allegations of corruption into one count, which would make the case easier for a jury to understand and for us to prosecute. With Floyd's promise of unlimited assistance, we decided to move forward with indicting Dorsey for corruption under RICO. We called John and added him to our prosecution team on a pro bono basis.

Petrey needed a place where he could concentrate and work undisturbed on writing the indictment that included RICO charges. Nothing is quiet about a district attorney's office. Lawyers accost other lawyers walking down the hall for advice or help. During breaks in trials, lawyers are yelling at investigators to make certain the next witness is ready to testify. And there's always cursing by a prosecutor about what they believe is an idiotic decision by a judge. Petrey needed to get away from the chaos and mayhem of the everyday district attorney's office. We were able to secure a month-to-month lease on a small office in a nearby bank building. Petrey holed himself up in the office for eight weeks writing the first RICO indictment of a public official in Georgia. John Floyd made himself available throughout this period to assist. Only a few of us knew why Petrey had disappeared and what he was doing for the case.

Georgia law gives two special privileges to former and current sheriffs and other certified law enforcement officers who are facing criminal charges relating to the performance of their duties. First, before a sheriff can be indicted for a crime in Georgia, the sheriff and the sheriff's attorneys must be provided with a copy of the proposed indictment fifteen days before the presentation to the grand jury. Everyone else facing criminal charges sees the charges for the first time after the grand jury has returned an indictment in open court.

Second, the sheriff and the sheriff's attorneys have the right to be physically present in the grand jury room when the evidence is presented against the sheriff. In all other cases, only the grand jurors, the witnesses, and the prosecutor are allowed in the grand jury room at that time. No other person on the planet—not the governor, a member of Congress, or the president—is provided the opportunity to get advance notice of a pending indictment or to appear before a Georgia grand jury. These special privileges just underscore the political power Georgia grants to sheriffs and other certified law enforcement officers.

We were under time pressure to get Dorsey, Walker, and Ramsey indicted. If they were not indicted within ninety days after their arrest on November 30, 2001, they would automatically be entitled to a bond. I did not want that to happen. On Super Bowl Sunday, February 3, 2002, as twenty-four-year-old Tom Brady took the Patriots to their first Super Bowl victory against the St Louis Rams, I watched two of the finest legal writers, John Petrey and John Floyd, put the finishing touches on a fifty-two-page proposed indictment with counts against Sidney Dorsey for murder and RICO violations. Most indictments are just a few pages.

We decided the death penalty was not feasible in this case, in part because we had given immunity to two of the coconspirators. If we had made a different decision about the death penalty, we would have been required to give notice at the time of the indictment. Because we believed the RICO charges explained Dorsey's motive for the murder, we wanted to indict Dorsey and try him individually for both corruption and murder. We also prepared a separate murder indictment for Walker and Ramsey.

The indictment was hand-delivered the next day to Dorsey's attorneys, fifteen days before the date scheduled for the grand jury. I'm certain it was not the indictment that Steel and Don Samuel, Dorsey's other attorney, were expecting from the DeKalb County district attorney's office. For the first time in Georgia, a former elected state official would face a RICO charge for acts that occurred while in office.

On February 19, 2002, I read the entire indictment against Dorsey aloud before testimony was introduced to the grand jury. It took over thirty minutes to read every paragraph on every page of that epistle. As he was in the earlier bond hearing, I wanted Chris Harvey to be the sole witness. I told him to keep his testimony as brief and simple as possible.

After they heard the evidence, we left the grand jurors alone to consider the indictment. The grand jurors were faced with two choices: to enter a true bill of indictment, which means the case would move forward to trial, or a no-bill, which means the case would be dismissed. The standard of proof for a true bill of indictment is probable cause. The grand jury returned a true bill about thirty minutes after we left the room, indicting Dorsey for the murder of Derwin Brown, and for corruption under RICO.

We then presented the separate murder indictment against Walker and Ramsey. The same grand jury returned an indictment against them as well. The arraignment, pretrial hearings, and trials were now set into motion.

After a grand jury returns a true bill, a defendant receives a copy of the indictment and a notice for arraignment in court before a judge. At the arraignment, the defendant must enter a plea of guilty or not guilty. If the defendant pleads not guilty, the judge sets a date for trial. A defendant may waive an arraignment by entering a plea of not guilty prior to the date of the arraignment.

As expected, Judge CJ Becker was assigned the case of *State v. Dorsey*. *State v. Walker and Ramsey* was randomly assigned to Judge Robert Mallis.

Dorsey's lawyers waived the arraignment and entered a plea of not guilty on Dorsey's behalf. In addition to filing detailed discovery motions requiring us to reveal evidence, his attorneys also immediately filed motions to recuse me and my office from prosecuting the case, and a motion for a change of venue to move the trial away from the Atlanta media market.

At the motions' hearing before Judge Becker, Petrey argued that if all it took to get a district attorney removed from a case was a threat on the DA's life, defendants would be making threats in every case when they didn't want a particular prosecutor handling their case. Judge Becker agreed and added that, because I was not a named victim in the indictment, we could stay on the case. Judge Becker also issued a gag order prohibiting anyone on the prosecution and defense teams from publicly saying anything about the case outside the courtroom.

We did not oppose the defense motion for a change of venue, believing it was warranted due to the enormous pretrial publicity over the past fifteen months. Normally, criminal cases must be tried in the county where the crime occurred. However, where there has been such overwhelming publicity that a defendant's right to a fair trial has been compromised, the court must move the trial away from the media market where the crime occurred.

Judge Becker instructed both sides to pick three locations, in order of preference. She would decide where to move the trial from that list. Under Georgia law, we had to propose locations that were racially and demographically similar to DeKalb County. She scheduled the Dorsey trial for June 2002.

We suggested Columbus, Augusta, and Savannah, in that order. Columbus and Augusta have large military and military-connected populations. Military personnel are usually pro law enforcement jurors. Savannah was our third choice because Savannah is a great town, with excellent restaurants and a close beach if we had time to get away. If you have to be stuck somewhere away from home in Georgia for at least five weeks, that's a good spot, even in the summer. The defense proposed the same cities, but in reverse order: Savannah, Augusta, and Columbus. I predicted we would try Dorsey in Savannah.

While waiting on Judge Becker to rule on the location for the Dorsey case, we turned our attention to the first trial on the calendar: *State v. Walker and Ramsey* in DeKalb County. That trial would begin March 11, 2002, less than one month after the grand jury indicted Melvin Walker and David Ramsey for the murder of Derwin Brown.

DeKalb County, Georgia, sheriff-elect Derwin Brown.
COURTESY OF THE *ASSOCIATED PRESS*

Funeral possession for sheriff-elect Derwin Brown. COURTESY OF THE *ASSOCIATED PRESS*

Dr. Gerald Gowitt, medical examiner, using a manikin to show the jury the twelve bullet entry wounds to Brown's body. COURTESY OF THE *ASSOCIATED PRESS*

Defense attorney Brian Steel (right) cross-examining killer turned state's witness Patrick Cuffy (left).
DIEGO RADZINSCH / © 2025 ALM GLOBAL PROPERTIES, LLC

Shirley McMichael testifying about her conversation with Dorsey before the murder.
COURTESY OF THE *ASSOCIATED PRESS*

Special GBI agent Fred Mays testifying about the secret recording he made with Sidney Dorsey.
COURTESY OF THE *ALBANY HERALD*

Derwin Brown's widow, Phyllis Brown, testifying during the Dorsey trial about finding her husband's body.
COURTESY OF THE *ASSOCIATED PRESS*

Judge C. J. Becker presiding over the trial of former Sheriff Sidney Dorsey. DIEGO RADZINSCH / © 2025 ALM GLOBAL PROPERTIES, LLC

Lead prosecutor J.Tom Morgan giving the final closing argument for the state.
COURTESY OF THE *ASSOCIATED PRESS*

Sidney Dorsey waiting for the verdict.
COURTESY OF THE *ASSOCIATED PRESS*

J.Tom Morgan and Phyllis Brown minutes after the verdict is read.
COURTESY OF THE *ALBANY HERALD*

Ron Brown, Derwin Brown's brother, and the jury foreman, Willie Hayes, after the verdict. Carol Ellis, DA chief investigator, in the background. COURTESY OF THE *ALBANY HERALD*

DeKalb County District Attorney's Sidney Dorsey prosecution team at the Snuffy Smith Cabin: Carol Ellis, chief investigator; Roz Harris, victim/witness coordinator; Shawn LaGrua, senior assistant district attorney; J.Tom Morgan, district attorney; John Floyd, RICO expert; Tom Clegg, chief trial attorney; Chris Harvey, homicide investigator; John Petrey, chief assistant district attorney.
COURTESY OF J.TOM MORGAN

CHAPTER 14

The first trial, *State v. Walker and Ramsey*, began in Judge Robert Mallis's courtroom on Monday, March 11, 2002. Tom Clegg and I were responsible for trying this case, and we split the responsibilities. I would make the opening statement, and Tom would argue the closing. We evenly divided the witnesses, but Tom was responsible for preparing Cuffy, our key witness, to testify. I prepared Skyers for his trial testimony, which would corroborate Cuffy's testimony. This first test, in the DeKalb County Courthouse, would be a trial run for the bigger show that summer: *State v. Dorsey*.

Walker and Ramsey both found the funds to hire private lawyers. Max Richardson represented Walker, the alleged triggerman, and Xavier Dicks represented Ramsey, the backup who Cuffy claimed lost his gun in the woods near Derwin's home. Richardson was a pleasure to deal with in and out of the courtroom. He had starred as a wide receiver for the University of Michigan football team and received his law degree from Indiana University–Indianapolis. Handsome and charming, Richardson had a great presence with juries. I knew who would be the lead defense attorney in this trial.

Before the trial date, Judge Mallis had directed both sides to submit questions to be answered by the prospective jurors before they arrived for jury duty. Juror questionnaires are standard in high-profile cases that have garnered significant press attention.

I'm a fan of juror questionnaires for two reasons. First, they speed up the process of jury selection and quickly identify those who may be disqualified for a legal reason, such as a substantial hardship regarding their health. Second, jurors seem to be more forthcoming when writing an answer to a question than when answering out loud in a crowded courtroom with other prospective jurors present. For example, I included the question: "Do you have a family member or close friend who has been prosecuted and convicted of a felony crime in DeKalb County?" Many people with an affirmative answer to this question would rather write the answer than publicly share their reply with strangers.

The juror questionnaire revealed that they were all aware of the murder of Derwin Brown and that the former sheriff, Sidney Dorsey, had been charged, along with others, with his murder. Only a few of the prospective jurors recognized the names Melvin Walker and David Ramsey, and all the jurors said they had read or heard nothing that could influence their decision in this case.

Some attorneys abhor jury selection and want to get it over with as quickly as possible. I enjoy jury selection because I like talking to strangers. The trick to jury selection is to get the prospective juror to start talking, so you can discern if they could be harmful to your case.

"Jury selection" is a misnomer. In reality, it is jury de-selection. Lawyers try to determine if a potential juror will harm their case despite overwhelming evidence and strike that person. It only takes one juror to hold out and cause a mistrial in a criminal case; in the 2020 case *Ramos v. Louisiana*, the US Supreme Court ruled that all verdicts in criminal cases must be unanimous.

I was uncertain whether race would be a factor in this case. The victim and his family were Black, the defendants were Black, key witnesses for the prosecution were Black, and the attorneys on the legal defense team were Black. Tom and I, who are both white, had tried many cases where the defendant and victim were Black and were represented by Black attorneys, and the color of our skin didn't seem to matter in the outcome of those cases.

In Georgia, at the time of this trial, the defense was granted twenty juror strikes, but the prosecution was only allowed to strike ten jurors.

(Georgia law changed in 2005 and now grants equal strikes to the prosecution and defense.) We surmised that the defense team would use the majority of their strikes to strike white jurors, and we were correct. The seated jury consisted of eight Black women, three Black men, and one white man. Walker and Ramsey could not argue they were discriminated against during jury selection.

Prior to jury selection, Dicks had approached me in the hall and wanted to talk in private. We walked into the stairwell where no one could see or hear us talking. Dicks said, "J.Tom, my client will testify against Walker and Dorsey, but he wants the same deal you gave Cuffy and Skyers—immunity and dismissal of all charges." Dicks was acting extremely nervous as he spoke.

I was highly irritated that Dicks waited until the last minute, before jury selection began, to hit me with this proposal. Still, I decided not to chastise him as he was already nervous. I said, "I'm done with immunity deals for murderers. Your client can plead to five years on a conspiracy charge. If he is convicted of murder, he must serve thirty years before even being considered for parole."

"Please give me five minutes to talk with my client," he said.

I waited patiently in the stairwell until Dicks reappeared. "Ramsey will plead to conspiracy and three to serve," he said.

"No deal," I replied. "Let's get this trial moving."

I believed we had a rock-solid case with two coconspirators testifying, and we did not need Ramsey's testimony to convict Walker and Dorsey. When I walked back into the courtroom, Ramsey was sitting next to Walker at the defense table. Five minutes earlier Ramsey had been willing to testify against Walker.

In many ways, this was a typical murder case, like others Tom and I had tried. There was direct evidence of the defendants' participation. Cuffy and Skyers were eyewitnesses, albeit coconspirators. We also had corroborating circumstantial evidence:

- Walker and Ramsey admitted during their interviews with police that they were with Cuffy and Skyers at Cuffy's home before Derwin was murdered.
- Although the school resource officer we tracked down, Officer Cary Harris, could not identify anyone except Cuffy, he could testify that four men, all dressed in black, were together late one evening in the elementary school parking lot near Derwin's residence prior to the murder. He also could testify that Dorsey told the school resource officer by phone that the men worked for him and that they were on a "special assignment."
- Skyers had led police investigators to the storm sewer where he disposed of the weapon, a TEC-9, used in the murder, which the police investigators found there.
- The GBI firearms examiner could testify that a TEC-9 was used to fire the bullets that killed Derwin. However, the TEC-9 that the police retrieved was too corroded to make a ballistic comparison since it had been in the storm sewer for almost a year.
- The medical examiner's testimony could corroborate Cuffy's description of the shooting.
- A friend of Cuffy's at the sheriff's department could confirm loaning Cuffy a county-issued firearm (the one that Ramsey dropped), which was never returned.
- Documentation could be produced showing the date, time, and place of the purchase and later return of a metal detector at Radio Shack. Cuffy had said they'd planned to use it to find the gun that Ramsey dropped, but then changed their minds.
- Officers from the surveillance team the night of the shooting could testify that two men got in the car at Cuffy's home during the early morning after the shooting. Although they could not identify Ramsey because it was dark and raining, they could see the man with Cuffy had dreads, as did Ramsey.

We could verify everything that Cuffy and Skyers told us about their involvement in the murder except for one thing: We did not have independent direct evidence that Walker and Ramsey were with them at the scene of the murder. We had to rely on the presumption that, since Cuffy and Skyers were telling the truth about everything else, they were being truthful about Walker's and Ramsey's participation in the murder. Tom and I both had successfully prosecuted murder cases with far less evidence.

I gave the opening statement, which was straightforward and laid out the facts. Concluding the opening, I addressed what I already knew was on the minds of the jurors. What was in it for these two men to kill Derwin Brown?

"Ladies and gentlemen, as preposterous and crazy as this may sound to you at this moment," I said, "the evidence will show that these two defendants conspired with others to kill Sheriff-elect Derwin Brown for one purpose—the promise of future employment in the DeKalb County Sheriff's Department. Former Sheriff Dorsey believed that if Brown were out of the picture, he, Dorsey, would be appointed interim sheriff and then reelected. Dorsey promised Ramsey a job and Walker a promotion when he resumed his reign, and they believed him."

Tom and I started with testimony from the crime scene technicians at the murder scene. We then moved to Dr. Gowitt and his autopsy. He was followed by the GBI firearms examiner and her explanation of the type of murder weapon and the fact that all the bullets were fired from the same gun. We strategically placed Cuffy and Skyers in the middle because we did not want Richardson's cross-examination of them to be the last thing the jury heard from the prosecution. Cuffy went first, and Tom worked him through all the details with little prodding.

Then Richardson stood up, and his cross-examination went straight for the jugular vein. First, he brought up the immunity deal in exchange for his testimony. "Mr. Cuffy," Richardson began with a voice that was both authoritative and incredulous at the same time, "you were facing life in prison for a murder that took place in your front yard while you looked on when you decided that you wanted to cut a deal with the district attorney's office."

"I didn't have anything to do with that murder," Cuffy replied as if he were being insulted.

"You were about to go to trial for murder when you told your lawyer to see if he could cut a sweetheart deal for you with the prosecutors, correct? And you knew the investigators were at a dead end as to who killed Derwin Brown," Richardson hammered. "And what a sweetheart deal you were given: reduced charge on the murder of Jeffery George, and no charges for your involvement in a murder that could get you the death penalty. All you had to do was concoct a wild and unbelievable story accusing my client and Mr. Ramsey of murdering Derwin Brown."

Cuffy became very angry, agitated, and snarly as Richardson continued pressing him. The angrier Cuffy got, the harder Richardson drilled him. Richardson questioned Cuffy for almost two hours without a break. He was a fierce advocate for his client but, to his credit, acted professionally and did not attack the prosecutors or our decisions about immunity. When Richardson's grueling cross-examination was over, I was very glad I had also made a deal with Skyers to testify. Because of his demeanor, Cuffy would have difficulty persuading the jury alone. Dicks didn't have any questions for Cuffy.

Skyers appeared anxious and scared on the witness stand: He fidgeted with his hands, moved around in the chair, and spoke haltingly. He corroborated everything Cuffy said regarding Walker's and Ramsey's involvement.

I wanted the jury to understand something important. "Mr. Skyers, were you under arrest or facing any criminal charges in any matters when you came to see me in Rockdale County?" I asked.

"No, sir," he answered.

"When Mr. Cuffy called you and told you to come to Rockdale, did you know that he had confessed to his involvement in the Derwin Brown matter?"

"No, sir."

"What did Mr. Cuffy tell you when he called you?" I asked. I knew the truthful answer to that question because I was standing next to Cuffy when he made the call.

"He told me to come see you and to tell the truth, and everything would be okay," Skyers answered.

"When you came to meet with us, was Cuffy present while you were being questioned?" I asked.

"No, sir."

"Prior to your coming in and giving us a statement, had you and Mr. Cuffy rehearsed what you would say if questioned by the authorities?" I asked.

"The only thing we talked about was what the four of us would say if we were questioned about where we were on the night of the murder. We agreed we were at Cuffy's house working out and talking about possible job openings," he said.

Like any trial lawyer, I knew the answers to my questions before I asked them, and I thought Skyers did a good job answering my questions and corroborating Cuffy.

Richardson could not make Skyers out to be a dealmaker for his immunity—because he wasn't. As I'd had him tell the jury, he wasn't under arrest when he came to see us. Technically, we weren't even required to read him his Miranda warnings because he was not in custody. The immunity agreement was simple: Tell us the truth about your involvement in the murder of Derwin Brown and your words cannot be used against you. I wanted the jury to understand this.

Richardson, like any good trial lawyer, knew that the best way to deal with a witness who is hurting your case is to ask few questions, not allow the witness to repeat his story, and get the witness off the stand and away from the jury. So he kept his cross-examination brief. "Mr. Skyers, you just testified you collaborated with Mr. Cuffy to commit the most horrible murder in the history of DeKalb County, correct?"

"Yes, sir," Skyers replied meekly.

"And you conspired with Mr. Cuffy as to what to say if you were ever questioned about the killing, right?" Richardson asked while standing next to the jury. Before Skyers had a chance to answer, the attorney had already returned to his seat.

Again, Dicks asked no questions on behalf of his client, David Ramsey.

We rested our case after presenting all of the direct and corroborating circumstantial evidence pointing to the fact that four men were involved in this murder, and that Walker and Ramsey were with Cuffy and Skyers when Derwin was killed. The defense did not present any evidence.

Richardson gave the closing argument we expected: Cuffy was unworthy of belief because of the deal he was able to extract from the prosecution. He basically ignored the corroborating evidence and Skyers and focused on Cuffy personally. He was clear, thoughtful, and persuasive in his delivery.

Tom presented the closing argument for the prosecution. In his cogent and methodical way, without any notes, he meticulously went through all of the evidence that substantiated Cuffy's and Skyers's statements. He explained to the jury, "This case is not about Patrick Cuffy's immunity deal, but whether the evidence proves that he is telling the truth."

Tom continued, "When you go into that jury room, you are not being asked to determine who pulled the trigger that fired the bullets that killed Derwin Brown. The undisputed testimony is that Melvin Walker was the triggerman. But even if he did not pull the trigger, he is guilty of murder. Judge Mallis will instruct you that anyone who aids, instructs, or participates in the commission of a crime is guilty of the crime. If you believe Mr. Walker and Mr. Ramsey participated in any way in the murder, they are guilty of murder as parties to the crime."

The jury sat stone-faced throughout all the arguments. I never saw a juror write a note on their notepad.

After the jury was excused to deliberate, I walked over to shake hands with Richardson and Dicks, congratulated them both on a job well done, and went upstairs to wait for the call telling us the jury had reached a verdict.

The jury deliberated until late Friday afternoon and was sent home to return on Monday morning. After lunch on Monday, March 18, 2002, we received a call that the jury had reached a verdict. Tom and I, along with most of the office, went to Judge Mallis's courtroom to receive the verdict. Phyllis and her family members were sitting two rows behind the counsel table. Roz Harris was seated with Phyllis.

The jurors were led back into the jury box by the bailiff. Judge Mallis asked the foreperson if they had reached a verdict, and she said, "Yes we have, Your Honor."

Judge Mallis asked the defendants to stand. Walker and Ramsey rose with their attorneys. Clegg and I remained seated at the prosecutors' table. The tension, the anticipation, the angst, and the magnitude and responsibility of the moment were palpable. I was committed to bringing justice to Derwin. I *wanted* this moment of justice. For Phyllis, for his mother, for his children, for the entire Brown family. For the people I was sworn to serve as their district attorney. For Carol, Caroline, and John. I thought this was the moment.

"What is your verdict, Madam Foreperson?" Judge Mallis asked.

"As to the defendant, Melvin Walker, Not Guilty.

As to the defendant, David Ramsey, Not Guilty."

***

Phyllis collapsed and wept inconsolably. Derwin's mother, Burvena Brown, suffered complications from asthma and was taken to the hospital in an ambulance. I could sense there were angry people, supporters of Derwin, in the courtroom. I was in a state of shock. How could the jury render a not guilty verdict in the face of such strong evidence?

I felt terribly for Derwin's family. I felt terribly for the people of DeKalb County. I felt like I had personally let everyone down. I could sense chaos all around me, yet at the same time, I felt very alone.

Walker and Ramsey were now free to leave, and they walked out of the courtroom with their lawyers. Carol Ellis grabbed me by the arm and she, Tom, and I quickly left the courtroom and walked up the four flights of stairs to the seventh-floor DA's office.

I thought we could evade the reporters, but a crowd had gathered outside my office when we got to our floor. I was relieved we were still under a gag order—the last thing I wanted to do was talk to a reporter. But I also felt compelled to be answerable for the verdicts. As soon as I opened my mouth, I knew I would be held in contempt of court for speaking in violation of the gag order. *The New York Times* quoted me saying, "I take full responsibility for the prosecution of this case, including the grant of immunity for those conspirators who came forward with information. Without their cooperation, there never would have been any attempt to hold those responsible for this horrible crime. Unfortunately, no one now can be held accountable, and I must bear that burden."

One reporter, whom I did not recognize, pushed my button.

"Mr. Morgan," he said. "Do you still believe Mr. Dorsey is guilty of the murder after today's verdict?" he asked.

I looked straight at him and the camera, and said, "It would be unethical, illegal, and immoral to prosecute Mr. Dorsey if I believed he were innocent." I said under my breath, "What a dumbass!"

My emotions had gotten the best of me. Judge Becker fined me $250 for commenting on the case to the press, which I paid with a personal check. I wanted to write, "It was worth every word" in the memo section of the check. But I liked Judge Becker, and I did not want to get on her bad side. She had good reason to hold me in contempt.

What I had to remind myself, and what the public often confuses, is that a not guilty verdict is not the same as a determination of innocence. Rather, a not guilty verdict in a criminal trial means that the prosecution did not meet its burden of proving the defendant's guilt beyond a reasonable doubt. Now I needed to reflect on how we failed in meeting that burden despite compelling evidence. And I had to determine what we needed to do differently in the Dorsey case—and quickly.

Tom and I went to our respective offices and closed our doors. I had not read my mail or emails, or listened to phone messages on my office landline since the trial started, so catching up gave me something to do besides obsess about the verdict. My personal phone rang. It was Dale Cardwell. I almost didn't answer, but I did anyway, saying, "You know I'm not supposed to be talking to you."

"Pretend I am not a reporter, just a friend," Dale said, "and we are so far off the record we are in another country. First, I wanted to tell you that everyone in the media pool room was shocked. We were certain the first trial was a slam dunk, and it would be Dorsey's trial, not this one, that would be difficult for you." The media pool room was where the camera video from the courtroom was fed into a large room where reporters could watch the proceedings.

"There is no such thing as a slam dunk in criminal cases," I said. "I've been trying cases for more than twenty years, and the only certainty is that there is no certainty when it comes to jury verdicts."

"The other thing I wanted to say is that I am truly sorry," Dale lamented. "My reporting probably caused Derwin to win an election that cost him his life. Now it may have cost you your career as a prosecutor."

"Dale, you did the right thing. You are not responsible for Derwin's death or for any impact on my career. Your reporting exposed insidious corruption in the DeKalb County Sheriff's Department. Because of your reporting, Dorsey is no longer in office, and the county is better for it," I responded. "Are you going to cover the Dorsey trial?"

"Hell, yes," Dale said. "I will be there every day. You won't see me because I will be in the media pool room. Can I ask you a big favor?"

I was curious what that favor would be. "You can ask," I said.

"Whatever the verdict is in the Dorsey case, will you talk with me one-on-one on camera after the verdict?" asked Dale.

I was in no mood to think about an interview now or in the future. "Let's wait. But don't worry. If I talk with anyone, it will be you."

I walked over to Tom's office and opened the door. "Let's play golf at nine in the morning at Southerness," I said. "I need to decompress and get away from the phone and the office. Besides, misery loves company, and we can take out our frustrations on some golf balls."

He looked up from the file he was reading and replied, "Sounds good. See you in the morning."

It was after six before I left. I considered walking the mile home between the courthouse and my house, but Carol Ellis insisted that she drive me. We rode the short distance together, mostly in silence.

CHAPTER 15

My home was a refuge for me, and my wife Carol was the pillar of strength who kept everything from tumbling down. Before and during the trial, I had to be laser-focused on the case. But time does not stand still.

As the Walker and Ramsey trial preparations were in full swing in late February 2002, I got a call from Caroline that she was leaving school early. A midday call was unusual. She told me that Sarah, one of her best friends, was dying.

Caroline met Sarah during elementary school, and they shared many of the same interests: They both played the flute; they loved to listen to music; they were high-achieving students; and they enjoyed life fully. After Caroline and Sarah got their driver's licenses, they drove around Decatur blasting Indigo Girls songs through the car speakers and singing along at the top of their lungs.

When Sarah was sixteen, she was diagnosed with Ewing sarcoma, an aggressive form of bone cancer. Caroline and other friends supported Sarah during her rigorous chemotherapy treatments and spent time with her at the hospital. When Sarah's cancer went into remission soon after the arrests of Dorsey, Walker, and Ramsey, they made the most of their time together.

But just a few months later, Sarah's cancer had returned, and she was at home in hospice care. At Sarah's request, Caroline and other close friends visited her, one by one, to say goodbye.

Emily Saliers and Amy Ray of the Indigo Girls came to her bedside and played, sang, and cried with Sarah and her family just hours before her death.

On Saturday, March 9, 2002, Caroline competed with her high school team in the state Mock Trial competition. She was the lead prosecutor on the Mock Trial team, which was coached by Petrey and another Decatur dad who was a federal prosecutor. Caroline was headed home when she got a call that Sarah was near the end. That evening, Sarah died; she was seventeen years old.

The Walker and Ramsey trial began the Monday after Sarah died. Her memorial service was the following weekend. The sanctuary was packed, as it often is when the light goes out on a young person who was so promising and full of life before death. After the minister gave a comforting sermon, yet still not able to explain the inexplicable, Emily Saliers of the Indigo Girls performed "Southland in the Springtime," a song she and Amy Ray had written and released twelve years before. When Emily sang the chorus, there was not a dry eye in the congregation.

And there's something 'bout the Southland in the springtime
Where the waters flow with confidence and reason
Though I miss her when I'm gone
It won't ever be too long
'Til I'm home again to spend my favorite season.

As a parent, I could only imagine the tremendous pain Sarah's mother and father, Donna and Bill, were experiencing. My trial stress could not begin to compare to the anguish of losing a child.

Because of the trial, I could not be as present for Caroline during her intense grieving immediately after Sarah's death as I would have liked, but I was glad I could be with her during the service. I was grateful that Carol could provide much-needed support for our daughter during the week following Sarah's death, and now Carol would help me deal with a devastating trial loss.

When I walked inside our home after the verdict, Carol asked, "Are you going to be okay? Do you feel like talking? I heard you on the news, and I was proud of the way you accepted responsibility for the verdict."

Carol was exactly the person I needed to talk to about the acquittal. She was not only my wife, but also my best friend, and a fellow lawyer who could understand and help me digest what had happened and what needed to happen next. Carol could be methodical and caring at the same time. I can't say I felt better after our conversation, but I can say I felt a sense of renewed purpose.

After we finished talking, Carol said, "You may want to talk to the kids. They are both worried about you. Caroline is still at tennis, but John is home."

I went to the family room and found him on the couch watching CNN *Headline News*, where he absorbed the problems of the world to distract himself from his fears closer to home. As a voracious reader of news and nonfiction, John consumed facts and figures like a supercharged vacuum cleaner. I thought he might be a great *Jeopardy!* contestant someday. When he wasn't reading or watching the news, he was an active member of lacrosse, tennis, basketball, and track teams. In fact, he learned about the not guilty verdict on his carpool ride home from track practice.

"How's it going?" I asked.

"Okay," he said. "I have a question: Are the men who killed Mr. Brown out of jail?"

"Yes. The jury returned a 'not guilty' verdict this afternoon, so they are free to go home," I said. At twelve years of age, he was between a child and a teenager, but I needed to talk to him like an adult.

"Will they come here and try to kill you?" he asked.

Good grief, I thought to myself. The thought of Walker and Ramsey hurting me, or anyone else, after the trial had not even crossed my mind, yet I could now see it was troubling my son.

"Those men killed Mr. Brown because they thought killing him would help get them jobs in the sheriff's department," I told John. The sound of that didn't even make sense to me. No wonder it didn't make sense to a jury. "People usually kill people for a reason, and there is no longer any reason to kill me."

"Will the jury decide that Mr. Dorsey is not guilty?" he asked. His inquisitive mind wanted answers.

"A different jury with different evidence in a different place will have to decide whether Mr. Dorsey is guilty or not guilty. I've learned I can never guess what a jury will decide," I said.

I left John to find Carol, who was working on our Gateway computer. "I'm going to grab a beer and sit outside on the deck," I told her. "John seems okay for now. Thanks for our talk. I was better prepared to answer his questions."

I needed to ponder the impact of the verdict. I understood how prosecutors Marcia Clark and Christopher Darden must have felt after the O. J. Simpson not guilty verdict. Both resigned from the DA's office after that gut punch. I had no plans to resign. However, I needed to be realistic. Today's verdict could damage my chances for reelection, but a not guilty verdict by the Dorsey jury would ensure I would not seek reelection for district attorney.

More important than the impact on my career, I considered the impact of the verdict on the well-being of the county. Although Walker and Ramsey just beat a murder charge, I seriously doubted they would kill anyone else. To our knowledge, this was their first criminal act. They did not fit the profile of career criminals or serial murderers. My hope was that the world was no less safe because they were walking the streets.

I believe in our system of trial by jury, but it is not infallible. Like most career prosecutors, I won the vast majority of my jury trials, but there were a couple I lost that had serious repercussions after the not guilty verdicts, and those cases will trouble me forever.

One was back in the 1980s. "Jenny," as I'll call her, told her best friend that her father was sexually abusing her. The friend told her mother, who told Jenny's mother, and Jenny's mother called social services, who contacted the police. Jenny was only eight years old when she made her disclosure, but she was able to describe in graphic detail sexual acts with her father. Her father, however, was careful. None of the acts could be corroborated with a forensic physical examination.

Unfortunately for Jenny, her parents were going through a divorce in another county. The judge presiding over the divorce case believed that Jenny's mother coached Jenny to fabricate the abuse so that she could gain sole custody of the child. This same judge had said in another case that child sexual abuse was just a fantasy of children who were oversexualized by television. The judge ordered that, if the jury in the criminal case I prosecuted against the father in DeKalb County returned a not guilty verdict, Jenny would have to leave the courthouse with the man she testified had sexually abused her.

Although Jenny made a credible witness, the defense attorney argued that Jenny had been brainwashed by her mother. The jury returned a verdict of not guilty. Jenny was waiting in my office when the verdict was returned, and Roz had to lead Jenny to her father's car. Several years later, Jenny committed suicide. My faith does not allow me to wish another man dead, but when the judge from that other county died, I did not shed a tear.

Out on the deck, another case came to mind—another that will always haunt me. A young woman, Gwendolyn, fell in love with a graduate student majoring in English when she was an undergraduate student in Mississippi. The feeling was mutual, and the couple married and had a child, Natasha, in 1966. A biracial marriage—Gwendolyn was Black and her husband was white—was not tolerated by many residents of Mississippi at the time. The marriage did not last.

Gwendolyn moved to Atlanta to start a new life with her young daughter and went on to get her master's degree. She landed a good job in state government, met Joel Grimmette, remarried, and had a son, Joel Jr.

Grimmette physically and emotionally abused Gwendolyn. Grimmette also tormented Natasha, but she was too scared to tell her mom about his conduct. Finally, with the help of domestic violence advocates, Gwendolyn found the strength to move to her own apartment. She took her children—Natasha and Joel Jr.—with her.

Grimmette was a car mechanic. One afternoon, he put battery acid from an old battery into a hypodermic needle, went to Gwendolyn's apartment, wrestled her to the floor, and tried to inject the acid into her arm. Neighbors heard Gwendolyn screaming, the police were called, and Grimmette was arrested with the needle still in his hand.

The case was assigned to Judge Curtis Tillman's courtroom where I was the prosecutor. This was in 1984, just a few months before Bob Wilson assigned me to the new crimes against children unit. Grimmette was indicted for aggravated assault with intent to kill and simple battery.

I met with Gwendolyn, and she recounted the story as outlined in the police report. It seemed a straightforward case: a credible and likable victim of domestic violence, a history of abuse, neighbors who heard her screams, and police officers who caught the suspect at the scene of the crime with the hypodermic needle. Instead of a guilty verdict on the felony aggravated assault, however, the jury only returned a guilty verdict on simple battery, a misdemeanor. Judge Tillman was furious at the jury and told them they had rendered a verdict contrary to overwhelming evidence in the case. He ordered that Grimmette serve 365 days in jail, the maximum sentence, and told the sheriff that Grimmette could not be given any time off for good behavior. When interviewed after the trial, the jurors said they thought this case was just a "domestic spat."

Judge Tillman ordered Gwendolyn and me to come to his office. Tillman told Gwendolyn she needed to pack her bags and her children and leave Georgia. He said Grimmette was dangerous and crazy, and he was concerned Grimmette would try to kill her again when he got out of jail.

Gwendolyn told the judge she had a good job in Atlanta and that she would be careful, but that she could not leave. She also told us that her daughter was a high school cheerleader and had been offered a scholarship at the University of Georgia. Gwendolyn was clearly proud of Natasha's accomplishments. She thought Grimmette would calm down while in jail and forget about her.

When Grimmette got out of jail in 1985, he immediately began calling Gwendolyn. She called my office and said he was threatening to kill her and then himself. Bob Wilson sent our chief investigator to Gwendolyn's apartment to await the next call. The next morning, Grimmette called again with the same message, and our investigator listened in on the call. He left to get a warrant for Grimmette's arrest for terroristic threats against Gwendolyn. While he was getting the warrant from the magistrate, Grimmette showed up at the apartment with a gun, pointed it at Gwendolyn's head, and pulled the trigger.

I was immediately notified of Gwendolyn's murder, and I learned that Grimmette had told the jailer upon his release that he also planned to kill me. Fearing for the life of my wife and our one-month-old daughter, Caroline, I arranged for them to move quickly to the nearby house of my wife's parents.

After a couple of days, Grimmette was arrested in a neighboring county. To my surprise, he did not kill himself. He eventually pled guilty to murder and served his full prison sentence of thirty years.

Natasha was a freshman at the University of Georgia and on the cheerleading squad when her mother was murdered. She learned of her mother's murder from the university campus police department. As the only adult relative in the state, Natasha was responsible for emptying her mother's apartment and getting it cleaned of her mother's blood. After Grimmette's sentencing, I lost contact with Natasha. I could not blame her for holding the criminal justice system, including me, responsible for her mother's death.

Years later I was driving to the office listening to Atlanta's National Public Radio station when the reporter announced that an Emory University English professor, Natasha Trethewey, had just been named Poet Laureate of the United States by President Obama. I had to pull the car over into a Chick-fil-A parking lot. A flood of visuals came to my brain, including the picture of Gwendolyn with the bullet hole in her head, and also of Natasha at her stepfather's sentencing for her mother's murder. I thought about resiliency, and I wondered why some abused children commit suicide and others become poets. Natasha would eventually write a book, *Memorial Drive*, about life with her mother in Mississippi and Georgia, and about living with an abusive stepfather, her mother's murderer.

The egregious cases involving Jenny and Gwendolyn are painful reminders that the criminal justice system sometimes fails. Because there's more public awareness now about the realities of child sexual abuse and domestic violence, the verdicts in the cases of Jenny and Gwendolyn might be different today than they were in the 1980s.

These cases helped me put the Walker and Ramsey verdicts in perspective. I did not believe that today's acquittals would lead to more deaths, as did the not guilty verdicts in Jenny's and Gwendolyn's cases. Although I was convinced that justice had not been served, something Bob Wilson told me after the Grimmette verdict came to mind. "You learn the most from the cases you lose," he said. "But you cannot dwell on them. We protect hundreds of people every year, including the most vulnerable, the children, by holding those responsible who commit violent crimes. Do your job and look back, but not too far back, because there will always be a case to replace the case you just finished trying."

I looked at the beer in my hand and realized I had been so deep in thought I had not finished it. I went back in the house to get ready for bed. I had at least one more case to try while I was still the district attorney.

CHAPTER 16

Most people who have never played golf think of golf courses as beautiful, manicured lawns with ostentatious clubhouses where the pros compete on Sunday afternoons. Those are private courses. I rarely played on one of those. My skills (or lack thereof) and my temperament are better suited for public courses for the common folk, such as Southerness.

A public course in the southeast part of DeKalb County away from civilization, Southerness was located where there were fewer homes for me to hit with a golf ball. There was no clubhouse—just a double-wide trailer where you checked in and paid for a cart. A plumber pulling a set of clubs from his company van in the gravel parking lot, or a schoolteacher, or a retired veteran, was not an uncommon sight at Southerness.

Tom and I paid for our cart, and I drove to the first tee. Because it was a Tuesday, there were few players on the course, and no one was ahead or behind us.

"Fire away," he said.

I drew back and swung with all the might my 180 pounds and six-foot-two-inch frame could pass through the grip and drive shaft into the club head. I powered a lot of anger and frustration into that swing. I surprisingly made direct contact. The ball took off like a bullet high and to the right, over towering pines and out of sight.

"I think it landed in Alabama," Tom quipped. "Drop your ball next to mine," he added, and he hit one straight down the fairway.

After we made the turn, we addressed the subject weighing heavily on both of our minds.

"What happened?" Tom asked.

"That's a good question. I have been thinking a lot about this, replaying everything in my mind. The jury despised Cuffy, which is perfectly understandable," I replied. "They despised him almost as much as we do. We relied a lot on Cuffy's testimony, and we overestimated his ability to come across as a credible witness. Max did an excellent job decimating him on cross-examination. And I'm sure the jurors didn't like that I gave Cuffy and Skyers immunity in exchange for their testimonies. They may have thought those two would say anything for those deals."

"Yes, I get that. But we had evidence that corroborated everything they said; we weren't just relying on their oral testimony. The jury seemed to disregard all of the corroborating evidence," Tom said as we drove our cart down the fairway. The grass was already a lush green in March, but it would be a few weeks before the azaleas behind the greens would start to bloom.

"True, but the one piece of independent evidence we didn't have was that Walker and Ramsey were at the scene of the murder. We were counting on the jury believing Cuffy and Skyers about that because everything else they said could be corroborated. We also had a problem with motive. The jury probably couldn't believe that Walker and Ramsey would murder Derwin just because Dorsey—who had lost the election—promised them jobs in the sheriff's department. Most people would think that doesn't make sense. Only those of us who deal with murders every day know that most murders usually don't make any sense.

"Even though Cuffy and Skyers are witnesses who carry a lot of baggage," I said, "I'm absolutely convinced they're telling the truth."

"The paper did a number on you this morning. How are you holding up?" Tom asked.

Cynthia Tucker, an award-winning columnist for the *Atlanta Journal-Constitution* (the *Atlanta Journal* and *Atlanta Constitution* merged in November 2001), wrote in her column that morning: "Morgan made a deal with the devil, and the devil is winning. If he doesn't convict Dorsey, he should immediately resign from being district attorney of DeKalb County." When I read her column, the first thing that popped into my head was the song "The Devil Went Down to Georgia" by the Charlie Daniels Band.

"I'm okay. I understand the perception that I made a deal with the devil. We have to figure out how to get the next jury to move beyond Cuffy and look at the evidence. We need to see the evidence through the lens of a jury," I said.

"How are we going to do that?" Tom asked.

"I need to return a phone call when we get back to the office, and I will fill you in," I said.

We finished around noon, with a score not worth remembering, and I drove to the courthouse. It would be a long time before I saw the green of a golf course again. After the gut-wrenching loss of the Walker and Ramsey trial, we were galvanized to learn from our mistakes and not leave any stone unturned in our preparation for the Dorsey trial.

***

Before the Walker and Ramsey trial, I had received a solicitation from a jury consulting firm out of Texas. I always threw solicitations like that in the trash because no prosecutor I knew had ever used a jury consulting firm. Their services were routinely used by big civil law firms involving cases where millions of dollars were at stake. What caught my attention was this firm, based on the letter, had already done a great deal of research and knew a lot about our case. It also offered a service I was unfamiliar with, a presentation of evidence before a mock jury. When I got to the courthouse, I called them up.

After I heard what they had to offer, I felt so strongly about the value this firm could provide that I hired them without consulting Tom and Petrey—contrary to my normal leadership style. I told them afterward, of course, and asked them to keep the decision completely confidential. Petrey, true to form, asked where the money—$5,000 plus expenses—

was coming from to pay for this endeavor. I told him we would take it out of money confiscated from drug dealers; not a dime would be from taxpayers.

In late April, Tom, Shawn LaGrua, and I drove to Augusta, Georgia, a town that resembled DeKalb County demographically. Though Augusta had been in the running as a location for the Dorsey trial in June, we had recently learned that it would not take place there.

We told the Texas firm that, based on the Walker and Ramsey trial, we anticipated the Dorsey jury would be composed primarily of Black jurors, with a majority being Black women. The firm had assembled twenty-four mock jurors—two panels of twelve—from the voting list to fit that demographic. After signing nondisclosure agreements, mock jurors would be paid $100 each to hear evidence in a case and reach a verdict.

We walked into the large meeting room where the trial would take place. Almost all the mock jurors were Black women, with a few Black men and two white women, waiting to hear the "evidence." We were told to stay in the background. The consultants did not want the jurors to know which side was paying for this exercise.

Our job beforehand had been to write a succinct account of what we believed the evidence would show from both sides, without any commentary. Tom volunteered, before I could ask him, to write the prosecution and defense presentations. Since we had just been through a trial, he knew the vulnerabilities with the murder charge against Dorsey, and Tom could surmise what the defenses to the RICO count might be.

The mock jurors were seated in folding chairs and given legal pads if they wanted to take notes. One member of the consulting firm read the prosecution's summary of the evidence, and another then read the defense summary. Both spoke in monotone voices, and there was no closing argument from either side. The presentation of both sides took almost two hours.

Next, the group of twenty-four heard a scaled-down version of the jury charges, the instructions a judge would give a jury before their deliberations. They split up into two groups of twelve and went to separate rooms to deliberate both charges in the case. Cameras were installed in both rooms so we could watch the deliberations, which were also being recorded. After the "verdicts," the consultants interviewed each juror individually regarding their backgrounds and thoughts on the evidence, to be included in their report to us.

I was intrigued to witness how twenty-four strangers would view and analyze an impartial showing of the evidence in our case. Their deliberations could give us insights on the strengths, weaknesses, and potential outcome of the real case.

As we watched via closed-circuit televisions, both juries immediately skipped over the first count, the murder count, and started deliberating on the RICO charge. Petrey and I had been debating how much emphasis to put on what we deemed the "lesser fraud allegations." These charges included Dorsey ordering employees to pick up his kids from school, take a Happy Meal to school each day for one of his children, and drive his daughters to and from college. Should our time and energy be dedicated to the charges of making employees work at banks for his security firm and the bribes paid by Shirley McMichael, we wondered?

The women mock jurors quickly answered that question for us.

"I can't imagine ordering someone to take my boy a Happy Meal at his school because he doesn't like the school lunch!" one female juror exclaimed. "If my boy doesn't like what the lunch lady serves, he goes hungry."

Another said, "I pay hard-earned money to have someone look after my kids after school every day. My tax dollar has no business taking care of someone else's kids."

"And what about ordering his employees to take his daughter to and from college?" another juror mused. "Doesn't Greyhound go to Atlanta?"

I made a note to tell Petrey not to forget the small stuff. These jurors were more upset over these charges than the bribery payments made by McMichael to Dorsey.

Both juries took approximately twenty minutes to go through the allegations on the RICO count and vote "guilty." They now turned their attention to the murder count. Neither jury liked that Cuffy and Skyers were not going to jail. That was no surprise. One juror lamented, "I find it hard to convict a man for murder when two other men are allowed to just walk away free."

I also wanted to know how the jurors would react to the fact that another jury had acquitted Walker and Ramsey. A male juror summed it up nicely: "That verdict was about two men who aren't on trial here today. We don't know what those jurors heard. Besides, that trial was in Atlanta, and this ain't Atlanta."

I knew we'd have a problem convincing a jury that Dorsey was guilty of murder given that he was at a party with his wife when the assassins were doing the killing. Georgia law on parties to a crime is a difficult concept for many jurors to understand. Again, a different male juror nailed it better than any law school professor.

"Osama bin Laden may not have been flying those planes that crashed in New York City, but he is just as guilty as those sons of bitches who killed all those people!"

I got a line for my closing argument from his response. It was worth the cost of this entire exercise.

Another issue I wanted to hear the jurors comment on was a fact only Phyllis Brown knew. After the murder, Dorsey never went to see her, never called her, and never wrote his condolences to say how sorry he was over Derwin's death.

A woman mock juror commented, "The only reason that man did not go see the widow is because he was responsible for her husband's death."

I would make sure I asked Phyllis about this when she took the stand in our next trial.

One mock jury found Dorsey "not guilty" on count one, murder. The other group voted "guilty." Two sets of twelve adults, who heard and processed the exact same words, arrived at diametrically opposed verdicts.

Which way would the jurors vote in the real trial?

Several lawyers had previously said in the media that, since we lost the Walker and Ramsey trial, Dorsey would be much harder to convict of murder. I told Tom and Shawn as we were leaving, "Well, at least we know we have a fifty/fifty shot of a guilty verdict on the murder count. That's better odds than what Vegas and the media pundits are giving us."

Then I asked them, "If Dorsey's lawyers come to us and tell us he will plead to the RICO count if we drop the murder count, what do we do?"

"Let's cross that bridge if it ever happens," Tom said.

It never did.

Phyllis Brown called me and said, "J.Tom, I'm concerned you might dismiss the murder count after the Walker/Ramsey verdict. I hope that won't happen. I want you to know I still have faith justice will prevail."

I assured her, "Phyllis, I have no intention of dropping the murder charge. We are going to trial on all counts."

***

On a beautiful spring day, Cuffy led Petrey, Chris, and me on a walk-through of the murder scene. We met at a cul-de-sac near the church where Skyers parked the night of the shooting. Sheriff's deputies transported Cuffy to the scene and removed his handcuffs for the walkthrough. Once again he was wearing his orange jumpsuit.

We took a short stroll through the wooded lot from the dead end where the car was parked to the end of the cul-de-sac where Derwin lived, fifty yards at most. We were on the path where Ramsey dropped his weapon as he was running from the scene. I was puzzled why no one had ever found the gun. Ramsey searched for it during the early morning hours after the shooting. The police did a thorough search of the property after Cuffy's confession. Where was the gun? We would never know.

Derwin's home was the second house from the end of the road. I noticed there was no streetlight to illuminate the property. Cuffy pointed out where he hid behind a car across the street from the Browns' house and waited for Derwin to arrive. As before, he spoke in that matter-of-fact voice without emotion or regret. Cuffy also showed us where Ramsey was hiding in the woods and where Walker was waiting next to a car in the driveway. I understood now why Cuffy was out of the line of sight for the actual shooting.

I was glad I went to the crime scene on the night of the murder. I realized now that on a clear, sunny day, Derwin would have seen the shooter. However, on a cold, dark, rainy night, he walked right into a death trap. Derwin could not have seen the assassins lying in wait for his execution. Although the day was warm, I shivered when I remembered that night in December.

Following up on the information that Cuffy provided about Mary Fischer, the writer for *GQ* magazine, we needed to subpoena her to appear at trial. The journalist privilege, rooted in the First Amendment, allows journalists to keep the sources of their published material confidential. I wasn't sure if that privilege applied to the testimony I wanted to elicit from Fischer regarding Cuffy's meeting with Dorsey in her hotel room at a Ritz-Carlton in Atlanta. I assigned the problem to Jeanne Canavan, a bright lawyer working in the appellate division, whose research showed that we did indeed have the right to subpoena Fischer.

Because Fischer lived out of state in Los Angeles, we had to get a superior court judge in California to issue the subpoena. I wasn't surprised when the attorneys for *GQ* filed a motion to quash the subpoena on the grounds of journalist privilege.

Jeanne and I flew to California so she could make the argument why the privilege did not apply in this case. Jeanne had me testify that I only wanted Fischer to corroborate what we already knew—that she gave Cuffy a key to her hotel room at the Ritz-Carlton and that Dorsey was waiting for Cuffy in her room. The judge agreed with Jeanne's argument, and he ordered Fischer to testify to those limited facts. Ultimately, the defense agreed to stipulate in writing to Fischer's testimony, and we did not have to bring Fischer to Georgia for the trial.

With Dorsey in custody—he was being housed in a jail outside Atlanta—we were able to get a DNA sample from his saliva and confirm that his DNA was on the washcloth and panties that Shirley McMichael had preserved in a stapled paper bag after she first had sex with Dorsey. We also located the house where that happened. We could use this evidence to corroborate her testimony about providing sexual favors in exchange for conducting a bonding business in DeKalb County.

During trial preparation, we talked to McMichael again, and she told me a story I had not heard before. She said that after the election, but before she first talked to Fred Mays, she had lunch with Dorsey in downtown Atlanta. "Sheriff Dorsey looked exhausted and had lost weight," she said. "He told me his losing the election was wrong, and that people had made up lies about him." Dorsey told her there was going to be a special election for sheriff, and his name would be on the ballot.

"Where's Derwin Brown going to be during this special election?" McMichael asked, puzzled. He told her that Derwin Brown was "not going to be around." She showed me how Dorsey put his hand and index finger to his temple as if it were a gun and then pushed his thumb down on his finger—firing a shot.

Because I was somewhat skeptical of this story and wondered why I was hearing it for the first time, I asked McMichael if she had told anyone this before. She said, "I told Agent Mays when I first spoke with him, after the runoff but before Derwin was killed." Fred confirmed this conversation with McMichael, but said he had brushed it off as Dorsey being nonsensical.

As we were preparing for trial, Clarence Mosley, Dorsey's trusted chief of staff, independently relayed to me a similar story. Before Derwin's murder, Mosley said, Dorsey told him that Derwin would not be around to take office in January. Dorsey said he would be selected by the judges to be the interim sheriff and would then win the office in a special election. We added Mosley to our list of key witnesses.

Because Cuffy had lost control during cross-examination in the Walker and Ramsey trial, which destroyed his credibility, we impressed upon him the importance of maintaining his composure during cross-examination. He seemed to recognize that the way he handled the prior cross-examination by Richardson was a disaster. Tom spent hours preparing him for another grueling cross-examination in the Dorsey trial.

Another weak link in the Walker and Ramsey trial was our inability to convince the jury that the mere promise of jobs if Dorsey regained power was sufficient motive for them to commit murder. To prove Dorsey's motive to commit murder, however, we had ample evidence of corruption during his administration to show that he was consumed with power and was willing to take desperate measures—including murder—to regain it. We weren't able to present this evidence in the Walker and Ramsey trial since Dorsey was not on trial. Because the evidence of corruption was critical to proving Dorsey's guilt in the murder trial, we focused during our preparations on making sure our corruption case was airtight. This was where the special grand jury investigating corruption was extremely helpful. We were able to hear live testimony and gather evidence before the grand jury that we could later use in trial. With this information, Petrey and John Floyd had prepared an indictment that read like a novel, detailing corruption in a sheriff's department. Using RICO to show a criminal enterprise allowed us to present the corruption evidence in an organized and persuasive way. The RICO charges not only proved that Dorsey was a corrupt sheriff but also provided convincing evidence of Dorsey's motive to murder Derwin Brown. However, relying on RICO in this case—which would be a first against a public official in Georgia—was not a slam dunk. A judge would make the ultimate decision whether a jury could even consider the RICO charges in rendering a verdict.

CHAPTER 17

On April 5, 2002, Judge Becker sent both sides an order regarding the change of venue of the Dorsey trial to a location outside the Atlanta media market. Much to my surprise, it would not take place in any of the three Georgia cities we and the defense team had suggested. When I got the order, the first person I called was Ken Hodges, the district attorney in Dougherty County.

"Ken, you will never believe where the Dorsey case has been shipped to for trial," I told him.

"Savannah?" he said.

"Nope. Try again."

"Augusta?"

"Try again."

"Columbus?"

"Close," I said, "but no cigar."

"I give."

"Albany."

"Albany! What the hell! Don't they know you were born and raised here?"

"Apparently, nowhere else in the state with similar demographics to DeKalb could accommodate a five-week trial. I wonder if Judge Becker and the defense lawyers know where I grew up. But it doesn't matter. I no longer have any close ties to Albany."

"Well, you just tell me what I can do, and I will get it done."

I'm sure Ken did not know what was in store for him when he made that generous offer. I didn't.

I spent the first twenty years of my life in Albany. Three generations of my family were buried in the sandy soil, though none of my close family still lived in Albany, and I had not lived there in over twenty-five years. However, I did know how to find the Dougherty County courthouse—I had taken the oath to practice law there twenty-two years before.

Ken Hodges grew up there, too, but he lived on a one-thousand-acre plantation with a swimming pool and a tennis court outside Albany. Ken could walk out his back door and go quail hunting. I grew up in a middle-class neighborhood and had never fired a gun before becoming a district attorney. Ken attended private schools through high school; I went to Albany's public schools. During my senior year at Albany High School, I sorted mail at the post office from 11:00 p.m. to 7:00 a.m. to save money for college. I slept in the late afternoons and early evenings and tried to store sleep like water in a camel on the weekends.

Ken got his undergraduate degree from Emory University in Atlanta. I completed my freshman and sophomore years at the local junior college and graduated from the University of Georgia in Athens. Ken and I did share one educational experience: We are both proud graduates of the University of Georgia School of Law. A couple of years later, Ken returned to Albany to be with his father, who was critically ill. After his father's death, Ken defeated the incumbent district attorney in 1996 and became one of the youngest DAs in the state. That's when I met Ken, and despite our different paths, I instantly liked him. He's smart and funny, and he became an integral part of the prosecution team in *State v. Dorsey*.

At the outset I told Ken, "I need you to help us find a place to live for five weeks."

"Whatever you need, J.Tom."

"Would you mind helping us during jury selection?" I asked a couple of weeks later. "You may have some insight as to some of the potential jurors."

"Whatever you need, J.Tom."

"What about you actually participating in the trial and questioning a few of the witnesses?" A local prosecutor would help with the optics, I thought. I knew the defense team had added a local defense attorney to their table.

"Whatever you need, J.Tom."

Finally, after much consideration, and discussing it with Petrey and Tom, I called Ken and said, "I think it would be beneficial if you made the opening statement to the jury. Petrey and I have decided to split closing arguments. He is going to argue the corruption and RICO charges. I am going to argue the murder charge. We want you to set the stage with your opening."

"Whatever you need, J.Tom."

Although Dougherty County and DeKalb County were demographically and racially similar on paper, I knew that culturally they were worlds apart. DeKalb County is part of the metropolitan Atlanta area, home to prestigious educational institutions, such as Emory University, Agnes Scott College, and Oglethorpe University, and to the national public health agency of the United States, the Centers for Disease Control and Prevention (CDC). Dougherty County, with approximately one-seventh the population of DeKalb County in 2002, relies on agriculture, including pecan groves, some manufacturing facilities, and a major Marine Corps supply center. I heard it often said that there are two Georgias: Atlanta and the rest of the state. As the mock juror said back in Augusta, "This ain't Atlanta." I'd spent the first twenty years of my life in one culture and my adult career in another. I would now be returning to my childhood culture to try the biggest case of my career.

***

Petrey, Carol Ellis, and I made a road trip to Albany to look for accommodations. Judge Becker had sent both sides a letter saying she and her court staff would be staying at the Merry Acres Inn, and we would have to look elsewhere. That was the first place I was hoping to stay. We also struck out at several chain hotels, so, as I'd warned Ken, I called and asked him for suggestions. I was worried that we might have to split up the team in different lodgings.

Ken called me back promptly and said he found a place where we could all stay for five weeks, a hunting lodge called Winfield that was closed for the summer, located in a remote area about fifteen miles outside the city limits. I was skeptical, but also desperate.

We followed Ken's county-issued car on a state highway that led us west out of Albany. We passed the campus where I attended junior college thirty years earlier. Not much had changed. When we got to the outskirts of town, I noticed entrances to a few gated communities with nice-looking homes. They weren't there when I was growing up in Albany.

The land immediately changed to farmland just a mile past the city limits sign. South Georgia is flat as a pancake. Most of the land is at sea level, and below that is swamp land. Crops of corn, soybeans, wheat, and cotton were newly planted in the fields. We also passed acres upon acres of pecan groves.

We eventually arrived at a nondescript dirt road. Unless you knew where you were going, you'd miss the turnoff to Winfield. On the right side of the entrance road was a barbed-wire fence and a cow pasture. On our left was a field of pine trees, another important South Georgia crop. After about a mile we came to the lodge.

South Georgia is famous for quail hunting. People from all over the world fly into Albany's small airport on private planes and are shuttled in late-model blacked-out SUVs to prime hunting locations outside of town. When I was a kid, my grandmother and I would sometimes eat at a Mexican restaurant inside the airport to watch the planes take off and land. I was mesmerized. We wondered who these people were who were flying to our town in their own airplanes, when neither one of us had even been on a commercial airplane.

Ken introduced us to Bill, the Winfield property manager, who explained that the big building we'd seen first contained the dining hall and kitchen. Two residential buildings each had two bedrooms and one bath, and a cabin sat in the back of the property. Since the property was not used during the offseason, we could have it for the cost of utilities and evening meals if wanted. Bill led us to the cabin on the back of the property, which was a short walking distance from a small pond. Having grown up in South Georgia, I wondered how many alligators lived in that pond. When I learned to water-ski as a teenager, I was motivated to stand up quickly and avoid the 'gators.

The cabin looked very old, and the posts for the walls were rough-hewn local cypress trees. Petrey, who grew up in rural Alabama only one hundred miles away, appreciated the cabin's country feel, as I did. Inside the front room was a long, wood-planked dining room table that would be perfect for stacking our papers and files. There were two small bedrooms, one bathroom, and a small kitchen. I doubted we would be cooking any meals. An assortment of taxidermied animals adorned the room, including a deer head, a rattlesnake, and a raccoon that Petrey aptly named "Sidrac," in honor of Dorsey's first name, Sidney. And he quickly dubbed our quarters the "Snuffy Smith Cabin," after the long-running comic strip featuring an Appalachian hillbilly by that name who lived in "Hootin Holler."

In the main room, toward the back wall, there was a steep ladder, which appeared to go up through a hole in the ceiling.

"Where does that lead?" I asked.

"There's a bed and a chest of drawers up there, nothing else," Bill said. "No one ever stays up there. Not sure why it's even there, but you can have a look. It's actually kind of a neat place."

I climbed up the ladder, and I knew where I would be sleeping that summer. The room was small, just large enough for a double bed and a chest of drawers. But what drew me to stay there were the four walls. Each wall was glass halfway up to the ceiling. I could turn in any direction and see out over the fields and the pond. I could also see anyone coming to the cabin from any direction for more than a mile, sort of like a widow's walk.

We decided that Petrey and Chris would stay with me in the cabin and that all the trial materials would be stored in the cabin under Chris's supervision. Roz, Carol, and Shawn would stay in one of the two residential buildings, and Tom and John Floyd would stay in the other. Fred wanted to stay in town closer to the courthouse.

The cabin had electricity but no phone, television, or internet. However, it did have an effective alarm system. On a stretch along the dirt road between the dining hall and our place were several kennels that housed dogs used for hunting and retrieving quail. On our first night at Winfield, we learned that the dogs—all of them—would let us know if a rabbit or a deer was within one hundred yards of the kennels.

The Snuffy Smith Cabin would be my home away from home for the duration of the five-week trial. The rest of the team and I lived together, worked together, planned together, ate together, and stressed together for five weeks. This kind of intense bonding during a trial was unique and, I'm convinced, valuable. We developed a camaraderie and cohesion that helped us put on the best case we possibly could in front of the South Georgia jury.

As we prepared for the trial back in Decatur, I told Petrey, Tom, and Chris that I would head down to Albany a week early so that I could get settled in the Snuffy Smith Cabin, outline the direct examination of my witnesses, start drafting my closing argument, and make sure Ken was covering everything in his opening statement. What I didn't mention was that I wanted to reacclimate myself to my South Georgia roots—I wanted the jury to relate to me as someone from Albany, not Atlanta.

None of us believe we have an accent. People from somewhere else are the ones who talk funny. In Albany, the proper noun "Jordan" is pronounced "Jurden." When Jimmy Carter was elected president, only those of us from South Georgia knew how to pronounce the last name of his chief of staff, Hamilton Jordan, who grew up in Albany. Cairo, a small town south of Albany, is pronounced "Kāro." And, of course, Albany itself is pronounced "All-benny."

Somewhere during my five years of school in Athens, and my move to and career in Atlanta, I lost my South Georgia accent. My wife Carol was the first to point this fact out to me. "You don't sound like you did when I first met you in Athens," she said after we were married. However, whenever I visited my mom in Albany, I'd return home and my kids would say, "Dad, we can tell when you have been visiting Gran. You don't sound the same when you get back home." I wasn't sure how long it would take for me to regain my accent, but I knew if I listened and talked to enough people, I would get it back.

Before the trial, one of my grandmother's dear friends sent me a handwritten note. She said she had seen me being interviewed on television and suggested that I put my suspenders, bowtie, and French cuff shirts in the closet when I came to Albany so I wouldn't look like an Atlanta lawyer. I took her sage advice and found some long ties, belts, and regular dress shirts to wear in court.

After I drove the three hours or so from DeKalb County to Albany, my first stop the next morning was to visit the cemetery where my grandparents were buried. My mother would later be buried there as well. This cemetery was the oldest in town and bordered the Flint River.

Albany, which at the time of the trial had a population of roughly seventy-five thousand, was named after Albany, New York, a transportation city located on a river. Albany's founding fathers believed that barges would float down the Flint River from Albany to the Gulf of Mexico carrying bales of cotton, which would then be loaded on waiting steamships. Unfortunately, the shallow shoals on the Flint River prevented any significant barge traffic from flowing south.

I found my grandparents' graves with the help of the caretaker and a map. My grandfather died before I was born. After paying my respects to my grandparents, I drove through what was still the Black section of Albany. It was here that one of the most influential people in my life had lived. I realized that she, along with the other women who raised me, shaped my views of race and Black Americans more than the fact that I grew up in South Georgia.

I was born two months early on Thanksgiving Day, when my mom, who lived in New Orleans, was in Albany visiting her mother. Wanting to raise her son in Albany, she and my father moved in with my grandmother (her husband, my grandfather, had recently died). Mom scrambled to find a job as a teacher and a childcare provider for me.

Sarah Hightower was the daughter of a sharecropper in Arlington, a small hamlet about thirty miles west of Albany. She married an abusive man who suffered from alcoholism. One day, after picking cotton, she walked to the highway and hitchhiked to Albany with her son, where some of her family had moved years earlier. I'm not sure how she learned my mother was looking for childcare, but Mom said that the moment Sarah held her infant child, she knew she wanted her to take care of her son.

Five days a week and half a day on Saturday, Sarah would take the bus and come watch over me. She did housework, too, but Mom made it clear that taking care of me was Sarah's first priority. My mother also made certain that I and, later, my little sister Claire knew we were always to obey and mind Sarah.

Sarah loved me unconditionally, and I loved her that way in return. When I was very young, I pulled a percolator of scalding hot coffee on my body while sitting in a highchair. I still have the scars on my arms. During my two-week hospital stay, the only person who I would allow to hold me was Sarah—not even my own mother could comfort me.

Around the time I was eleven years old and Claire was six, we were hanging out with a bunch of neighborhood kids across the street. Sarah called us in for lunch. As we started to go home, one of my playmates, "Larry," as I'll call him, asked why we had to leave.

"Because Sarah called us to come in for lunch," I told him.

"You don't have to do what she tells you to do," Larry said. "She's just a nigger!"

I am not, by nature, a violent person. It takes a great deal to push me over the edge. I don't know whether what happened next amazed Larry or me the most. I jumped on him with both fists flying. He fell backward onto the ground, and I landed on top and began pummeling his face with my fists. It took three of our friends to pull me off Larry. We were both crying, and the blood from his nose got all over my T-shirt.

When I was held a safe distance away, Larry shouted through the blood coming down his face, "You are a nigger!"

Somehow, that did not bother me in the least.

Luckily, Sarah had gone into the house before the fight started. I told her I was "tussling" with another boy, and that he got a nosebleed but was okay. I knew that story would not satisfy Mom when she got home from work and saw the bloody T-shirt.

After dinner, Mom made me stay in the kitchen and told Claire to go to her room. My grandmother, who was usually my ally when I was in trouble, was nowhere to be found. Mom poured herself a bourbon and Coke, lit a Salem cigarette, and told me to sit down.

"Son, I heard you were in a fight today," she began.

"Yes, ma'am," was all I could say—no denying the truth and the bloody T-shirt.

"I thought I taught you to fight with words, not your fists," she scolded me.

"Yes, ma'am."

"Who did you get in a fight with?"

"Larry, Momma."

"Larry!" she exclaimed. "Why on earth were you and Larry fighting?"

"Because he called Sarah that n-word, Momma."

Mom had told me never to use that word, or I would get the whipping of my life, and I didn't want to risk getting a whipping. "That's a hateful and mean word," my mother had told me earlier, "and we are not hateful and mean people."

She didn't say anything at first. Mom took a gulp of her bourbon and a deep draw on her cigarette and looked away for a minute. She then turned back, looked me in the eyes, and said, "You should have hit him harder. Go do your homework."

Long after Claire and I no longer required childcare, Mom continued paying Sarah, and Sarah kept coming to visit; she was there for every Thanksgiving, Christmas, Fourth of July, and birthday. After Sarah died, Claire and I were shocked to learn that she had saved money throughout her life to leave to the two of us.

One of my most vivid childhood memories was when Sarah and I stood in our long fenced-in backyard watching a parade going down Slappey Drive, the main highway running north and south through Albany. I was six or seven years old. Sarah and I stood silently, and I remember holding her hand with my left hand and my dogs, Victor and Missy, on my right side barking at the parade marchers.

I didn't realize then that I was watching a man with a dream—Martin Luther King Jr.—walk by my house. Some forty years later, I was prosecuting a murder trial in the same courthouse where Dr. King had been prosecuted for disorderly conduct and leading a march without a permit.

Next, I drove to Albany High School. I pulled into the parking lot between the stadium where I played football and the main school building. It had seen better days. I walked into the empty stadium, sat down on a bench, and mused about the circumstances that brought me to this moment.

Despite all their cultural differences, Dougherty County and DeKalb County did share some history, a commonality that made Albany a suitable location for the Dorsey trial. The counties' similar racial demographics in 2002 had their roots in the late 1960s. The Supreme Court ruled more than a decade earlier in *Brown v. Board of Education* that state-sanctioned school segregation—under the "separate but equal" doctrine—was unconstitutional. But many communities simply didn't comply. So forced busing was enacted to achieve desegregation of public school systems.

"Separate but equal" certainly did not exist in Dougherty County, where the Black school buildings were in disrepair, the teaching materials were inadequate, and many of the teachers were denied access to higher-quality training. I was aware of these problems because my mother, who had become a public school administrator in Dougherty County, would discuss the situation with me at the dinner table.

I know of what I write. I rode those buses. I attended an all-white elementary school in my neighborhood, then I was bused to recently integrated Albany Junior High School, although another junior high school was closer to my home. I never gave it much thought that I was going to school for the first time with Black kids. We were all middle schoolers, which, by definition, meant that we were all foolish and immature.

Then I began attending Westover High School, the one closest to my home. I formed many friendships there, and in the spring of my sophomore year I went out for football; I was also elected a student council officer for my upcoming junior year. Before school started in the fall of 1971, we'd already had two weeks of football practice when, around 3:00 p.m. on the day of our first game, Coach Clark called us into the locker room. He was visibly upset; we could tell by the look on his face this was not going to be a pep talk for that night's game. Something was terribly wrong.

"Boys," he began, "I have some bad news that I just learned this afternoon. For reasons I can't explain because I am not sure I understand, some of you, along with some other students from Westover, are no longer going to be students here after tonight. You'll be attending another high school Tuesday morning, after Labor Day. For those of you remaining at Westover, our team will look very different on the practice field Tuesday." Coach Clark tried to explain to us that a federal judge in Macon, Judge

Wilbur Owens, had issued a desegregation order that afternoon, which included forced busing.

Because Westover was already bursting at the seams with mostly white students, a significant number of students—including twenty-two of us football players, sixteen of those starters—would need to be bused to Albany High to make room for more Black students. Albany High's student body was 60 percent white and 40 percent Black. Students from Monroe High, which was 100 percent Black, would be bused to Westover.

I was upset, as were my teammates and classmates, at being forced out of the school we loved so other students could take our place. We didn't care if the other students were Black or white, Martians or Earthlings. Who and what the hell was a federal judge, and how could he disrupt our lives like this just two days before classes were to begin?

Mom—the first in her family to graduate from college and the first administrator in the Dougherty County School System to obtain her PhD—told me that the purpose of high school was to prepare me for college, that Albany High had good teachers, and that my job was to learn and do well on the SAT. She said Judge Owens had been her classmate at Albany High School, that he was a smart and good man. Without saying these specific words, she told me to "get over it."

In a balm to our earlier frustration, we won more football games that season at Albany High than the Westover team did. I also managed to salvage my nascent political career: Later that year, I was elected student council president.

Forced busing had the same unintended consequence in both Dougherty County and DeKalb County: mass exodus of white people leaving the public schools, with many moving to neighboring counties not specifically covered by the court order.

The census data is astounding. In 1970 the racial composition of DeKalb County was 86.07 percent white, 13.69 percent Black. In 2000, the census data showed that DeKalb County was 54.23 percent Black, 35.83 percent white. Dougherty County was no different. In 1970,

Dougherty was 66 percent white, 34 percent Black. Thirty years later, the percentages were 71 percent Black, 25 percent white.

So here I was, full circle, back in my hometown, due to a twist of fate and the racial history that entwined Dougherty County and DeKalb County.

CHAPTER 18

On the eve of trial, I decided, on a whim, to visit the church I attended from childhood through my teenage years, the First United Methodist Church of Albany. As in many towns in South Georgia, the churches, post office, and courthouse were in proximity to each other. On Sunday mornings, the only traffic heading into town was bound for the churches.

At one time, I could name every member of the congregation. This morning, I did not recognize a soul. Everyone I had known had either died or moved away. I sat near the back of the sanctuary and gazed at the large, beautiful stained-glass window behind the pulpit. It was a picture of Jesus praying in the Garden of Gethsemane before his crucifixion.

The artist depicted Jesus with tan, almost white skin, and long, flowing, light-brown hair over his shoulders. I wasn't savvy enough when I was a kid to realize that Jesus probably didn't look anything like this depiction.

During the summer before my senior year of high school, I let my hair grow slightly over my ears. Football players were required to have short hair above their ears. When I reported to summer camp, Coach Henry, our head coach, walked over to me and said, "J.Tom, when you go home this weekend, you'd better find time to get your damn hair cut if you want to play on this team!"

In a half-rebellious, half-pleading reply, I said, "Coach, Jesus had long hair. Why can't we have long hair?"

Coach Henry gruffly retorted, "Morgan, when you can walk on water, you can grow your hair long." I cut my hair.

As I was leaving the church after the service, I stopped to introduce myself to the pastor standing by the door. I told him I had attended this church before I left for college. He said, "We heard you were back in town," which I thought was odd since we had never met. The encounter immediately made me think of the Jimmy Buffett song, "I Heard I Was in Town."

The prosecution team—Petrey, Clegg, Chris, Fred, John Floyd, Shawn, Carol Ellis, and Roz—arrived at Winfield that afternoon. Although they knew we'd be living in the country for the duration of the trial, they were shocked and very pleased to see how remote we were from civilization. Shawn asked, "This place is amazing! Is there a place we can shoot skeet?"

"Actually, there is," I replied. "The manager of the property told me he would provide the shotguns, but you will have to furnish the shells. There is a sporting goods store in town where you can get all the shells you want to shoot. Shooting skeet may be a good way to release our trial frustrations."

After everyone had settled into their living quarters, we drove into town to meet Ken at the courthouse. The church traffic had long gone home, and the streets were empty. Ken had a key to the courthouse as well as to the courtroom where the trial would begin the next day.

Ken wanted to review his trial opening statement for accuracy and suggestions. We sat in the jury box, where the real jury would eventually sit, while Ken began to read from his prepared remarks. He revealed a theme he believed would be ideal for the trial, and one he wanted to introduce in his opening statements. It helps a jury to focus on the evidence when lawyers can sum up a complicated trial in a simple statement, such as "If it doesn't fit, you must acquit," the defense mantra in the O. J. Simpson murder trial.

"This case is about a culture of corruption and lust for power in the DeKalb County Sheriff's Department," Ken began. "A culture of corruption so pervasive, it ultimately led to the assassination of the sheriff-elect, a man who had just won election to eradicate the corruption."

Petrey interrupted, saying, "Culture of corruption and lust for power is a theme we can build on, and J.Tom and I can hit home in our closing arguments. Keep going."

After we finished offering our suggestions, Ken said he would memorize his opening statement in time for trial. Since it was seventy typed pages and took him fifty minutes to deliver, he had a monumental task before him.

That evening, at the Snuffy Smith Cabin, I shared an idea with Petrey and Chris for a visual presentation to accompany my closing argument to the jury. I was fairly confident this jury would find Dorsey guilty of RICO; both juries in the mock trial we'd conducted had returned that verdict. But the other results were troubling: Just one of those twelve-person groups had "convicted" him of murder. And back in March, a real-life jury had acquitted Walker and Ramsey on their murder charges. I needed to devise a new and innovative tactic for my summation, to present the evidence in a more convincing and visually compelling way.

When I told them what I wanted to do, Petrey spewed, "That's the dumbest idea I have ever heard! If it falls apart, there goes the murder conviction, and you will be the poster child in this country on how not to present a closing argument. However, it could make a pretty good *Saturday Night Live* skit."

I never took what Petrey said personally because he was usually correct, and I needed his input. Still, I replied, "Okay, if you are so damn smart, do you have a better idea?"

Before Petrey could respond, Chris offered, "J.Tom, write down your thoughts, and I will take them to a graphic artist in Atlanta and see what he can do."

***

The next morning, June 3, 2002, we drove from Winfield to the courthouse to begin jury selection. It took us less than twenty minutes to drive the fifteen miles, which would be impossible in Atlanta. When we arrived at the courthouse, it looked far different from the way it did the night before. Well over one hundred prospective jurors, without a clue as to what kind of trial they might serve on, were waiting in line to pass through security. Ken was waiting for us at a side entrance, where he would meet us every day so we could avoid the security detectors.

We took our seats at the table closest to the jury box. In criminal cases, because the prosecution has the burden of proof, the prosecutors sit closest to the jury. Petrey, Clegg, Ken, and I sat at the table while the rest of the team sat on the bench behind us. Steel and Samuel were already seated at the defense table along with Carl Bryant, a well-known and respected civil rights attorney in South Georgia. He would be a good addition to their defense team. Since today's focus was on jury selection, the courtroom was sparsely attended. Although jury selection is an extremely important segment of a jury trial, little is seen or heard that would entertain an audience. Roz told Phyllis and Brandy they did not need to be present until jury selection was over, and she would keep them posted. A pool camera sat on a tripod in the corner of the courtroom. Attached to the camera was a cable that led to a monitor in another room. In that room the press could sit, take notes, talk, drink coffee, and call their pressrooms without disturbing the trial. I was wondering if Dale Cardwell, or any of the other reporters I knew, were even present for jury selection. With few spectators and without a television audience, the lawyers for both sides were more at ease.

Dorsey was brought in by two deputies, wearing a coat and tie, with his hands handcuffed behind his back. When the deputy removed the handcuffs, Steel hugged his client, and Dorsey sat down between Steel and Samuel.

Judge Becker entered the courtroom from a door on the wall behind the judge's bench as the bailiff barked, "Everyone rise! The Superior Court of the Stone Mountain Judicial Circuit is now in session. The Honorable Cynthia J. Becker presiding." Although we were physically in Dougherty County, the trial was under the jurisdiction of DeKalb

County Superior Court. Judge Becker took her seat, and then she told everyone to be seated.

She began, "Have the parties joined issue?" Joining issue is the formal beginning of a criminal trial where the defendant signs the indictment and either pleads "guilty" or "not guilty" to the charges. His attorney and the prosecutor must also sign the indictment. In this case, Dorsey pled "not guilty."

"We have, Your Honor, "I replied.

"Then let us begin," she said in a tone that conveyed who was in charge. "I have a couple of preliminary matters to go over while the jurors complete their juror questionnaires." As in the previous trial, both sides had submitted numerous questions for the jurors to answer before the judge and the lawyers individually questioned the jurors. "First, we will begin each day promptly at nine o'clock and try to end by six. Be on time and prepared, without wasting the time of the jurors and myself. Also, we will recess for the weekend at the end of the day on Thursdays."

This scheduling was a brilliant decision on her part, and both sides were in complete agreement. Jurors would be more amenable to participating in a multi-week trial if they had four days on and three days off. Additionally, it would give the lawyers an extra day to prepare for the upcoming trial week. And I would have three uninterrupted days in the Snuffy Smith Cabin each weekend to write, fine-tune, and memorize my closing argument.

The bailiff ushered in the first panel of twelve prospective jurors into the jury box, where they were first questioned by Judge Becker, followed by questions from lawyers representing each side. I thought I recognized the first juror, a male, but for the life of me, I could not remember how or where I had seen him.

Judge Becker questioned the jury pool, "Is there anyone seated in the jury box who is related to, or who knows, personally or professionally, any of the lawyers involved in this case?" and she then called out our names.

The first juror raised his hand and responded, "I don't know if this counts, but I am a pastor at a local church, and Mr. Morgan introduced himself to me yesterday as he was leaving our morning service."

Petrey gave me an incredulous look and whispered, "You went to church yesterday?"

I whispered back, "We need all the help we can get."

Another juror raised her hand. "I don't know Mr. Petrey, but if he is related to any of the Petreys in Alexander City, Alabama [Petrey's hometown], I know his great-aunt. She is a fabulous teacher."

A juror in the back row raised her hand and offered, "I don't know Mr. Hodges personally, but I do know some of the abused children he has helped as our district attorney."

Judge Becker excused these jurors for cause at the request of the defense team. This meant that the defense did not waste any strikes removing them from the panel.

None of the first twelve prospective jurors knew any of the defense lawyers.

The jury questionnaires, along with direct questions from the judge and the lawyers, would hopefully yield a fair and open-minded jury. Of course, both sides wanted to know what, if anything, a juror had heard about this case. As prosecutors, we wanted to know if a juror was familiar with the earlier acquittal of Walker and Ramsey. We decided not to bring it up during questioning, but rather to give jurors the chance to volunteer that information. Because the defense was allowed to strike twice as many jurors as the prosecution, we had to be particularly judicious when deciding which jurors to strike.

Some of the questions we asked them were:

1) Do you believe that you, or any member of your family, has been falsely accused of a crime by law enforcement? (These people have an automatic bias against the state, and we would need to strike them.)

2) Have you ever had an unpleasant experience with law enforcement? (Usually, only prosecutors want to know the answer to this question, but since Dorsey served a career in law enforcement, the defense also wanted to know the answer to this question.)
3) What are your job responsibilities? (People who supervise others and have a high degree of responsibility are usually good at sifting through evidence and making difficult decisions.)
4) What is your educational background? (This was going to be a technical, document-loaded case, because of the RICO charges. We needed jurors with analytical skills.)
5) Are you or have you ever been a teacher? (Teachers, having dealt with many types of different and difficult personalities, are good at judging character and truthfulness.)
6) Do you enjoy watching true crime television or reading true crime stories? (Those who follow true crime have an increased understanding of the criminal justice system, and they are especially cognizant that powerful and influential people can commit horrible deeds.)

The defense lawyers were looking for that juror, or jurors, who would not bend or compromise their positions. The prosecution must prove guilt beyond a reasonable doubt to all twelve jurors. It only takes one juror to hang up a jury and cause a mistrial, which prosecutors would like to avoid. Sometimes prosecutors will dismiss a case to avoid a retrial. This is particularly true if a jury reaches a guilty verdict on some of the lesser charges, but they are unable to reach a unanimous verdict on the most serious charge. In this case, that would be murder. Some of the questions the defense attorneys asked were:

1) If you have a firm belief or opinion, would you change your opinion to please others and to make it easier on yourself? (Entrepre-

neurs, people who work alone and not in groups, and people who appear to have antisocial tendencies make good defense jurors.)

2) Are you aware that in our great country, it is the prosecution's burden to prove guilt beyond a reasonable doubt, and the defendant is never obligated to prove anything? (This is one of Steel's favorite questions to prospective jurors.)
3) Have you, or any member of your family, ever served in the military? (Because veterans and families of veterans are typically pro-prosecution jurors, the defense wants to strike them off the jury.)

It became clear on the first day of questioning prospective jurors that none of them had ever heard of Sheriff Sidney Dorsey, or indicated that they were aware of an earlier acquittal. Only a few people were even aware of the assassination of a sheriff-elect in the Atlanta area. Atlanta might as well have been a million miles away with problems that were not their own.

This case would ultimately be decided in a vacuum by people who had not been influenced one way or the other by the media or other external factors. After two weeks of intense questioning by both sides, twelve jurors—eleven women (nine Black and two white) and one Black male—were seated to hear the evidence and reach a verdict in the case of the *State of Georgia v. Sidney Dorsey*.

CHAPTER 19

"You never get a second chance to make a good first impression" is a truism that applies to the first day of a jury trial. All the lawyers were trying to look their best in pressed suits. The men wore starched white shirts and freshly polished shoes. Everyone had their hair cut or styled over the weekend, including Judge Becker.

It was Monday, June 17, 2002. The courtroom had an electric, tense feeling. Unlike during jury selection, all the benches were filled with spectators. It was the largest courtroom in the courthouse and could comfortably seat over two hundred adults on the wooden benches. Phyllis and Brandy sat a few rows back in the center of the courtroom. Roz's job was to sit with the family members during the trial and answer any questions they had about procedure. The media room overflowed with television, radio, and print reporters covering the first day of the trial. Outside, media trucks with satellite dishes on top were lined up in front of the courthouse.

The defense lawyers and their client were sitting patiently at their counsel table. Looking at the judge's bench from the back of the courtroom, the defense table was located to the right, and the prosecution table was positioned to the left, closest to the jury box. As he would every day, Dorsey wore a trim, fine-tailored suit, crisp shirt, and tie. Although he was in custody, the law requires that a defendant be allowed to wear street clothes in the presence of the jury during a criminal trial. The rationale is that jurors will have an inherent bias against a defendant wearing inmate clothing. If this is true, the law makes sense. A defendant's guilt or innocence should not be determined by the clothes he wears. And Dorsey was the finest-dressed defendant I had ever seen in a courtroom.

I was anxious and ready to get started, even though it was unlikely that any of my assigned witnesses would testify on the first day. I noticed the only item Ken had placed on the table before him was a blank legal pad and a pen. Chris was sitting behind us with a typed, numbered list of all the documentary and physical evidence we intended to introduce during the trial. With more than three hundred items on his list, he would be responsible for providing us with the evidence we needed to present to a witness during examination. Petrey laid down the law early on in our preparation, which suited us well. The lawyers would work with duplicates when preparing a witness, but Chris always kept control of the originals. Physical evidence, such as guns, bullets, recordings, and photographs, was always in his possession. In this case, Chris was serving a dual role as case investigator and paralegal.

After Judge Becker and everyone else in the courtroom were seated, she instructed the bailiff to open the door and guide the jury into the jury box. The jurors had a bewildered look on their faces when they surveyed the courtroom and saw it was full of people. If they did not know already, they certainly knew now the gravity of the decision in their hands. Judge Becker explained to the jurors that the trial would begin with opening statements and that the prosecution would go first, as it bears the burden of proof. "Mr. Morgan," she said, "you may now proceed with opening statements."

I stood up and spoke loudly, "Your Honor, Mr. Hodges will be giving the opening statements for the prosecution." I knew this would come as a shock to the defense team and the reporters following the case. They believed I added Ken to the team for the optics of having a local prosecutor sit at the counsel table, but not really to participate in a meaningful way. Why wasn't the district attorney in charge of the case making the opening statements? How could someone who did not even work for the district attorney, and who lived in South Georgia, be competent and prepared to handle a key component of the state's case?

I sat down, and before Ken could stand up, I put my arm around his shoulder and whispered into his ear, "Brother, a million people are watching you on television. Don't fuck it up."

He whispered back in my ear, "I won't." And he didn't.

Shakespeare said, "All the world's a stage." This was Act One, Scene One, and Ken was ready to deliver his lines. He walked to face the jury without a note or piece of paper in his hand. Wearing a dark navy suit, a white shirt, and a red tie with an American flag lapel pin, he looked the epitome of the Hollywood prosecutor. Instead of contacts, he was wearing silver wire-rimmed glasses, which I had never seen before. I suspected he wanted to look more serious and professorial. He began in a voice that sounded authoritative and yet conversational:

"Power. Ladies and gentlemen, this case is about power, the power of a man so consumed by power that he could not and would not let it go; a man so corrupted by power that he used the office to which he was elected, the sheriff of DeKalb County, for his own personal use; a man so consumed by power that when a man announced he was going to run against him and reform the sheriff's office, and when that man won, he devised a plan to assassinate him so he could take the office back. The man that was full of corruption, that was so consumed by power that he had a reform candidate for sheriff assassinated at his direction, is the defendant, Sidney Dorsey.

"On December 15, 2000, a decorated, respected, and dedicated police officer with the DeKalb County Police Department was returning home from the Georgia Public Safety Training Center where he graduated from the Sheriff's Academy, but he never made it. At the defendant Sidney Dorsey's direction, four men—Patrick Cuffy, Paul Skyers, David Ramsey, and Melvin Walker—assassinated Derwin Brown. They carried out the defendant's order in carrying out that assassination. And on that day the defendant took away the life of a twenty-year veteran of the

DeKalb County Police Department, husband of twenty-three years, a father of five, a grandfather of six, a career public servant, and the reform candidate for sheriff. He was gunned down in front of his house with his wife and children at home.

"Now, December 15 was a culmination of all the defendant's corruption, and for you to get a clear picture of what happened, I'm going to have to take you back in time and run you through everything."

Ken patiently and meticulously walked the jury through all the witness testimony we would present regarding the corruption allegations, everything that happened the day and night of the murder, and Cuffy's admission and plea deal. Ken addressed the snake in the woodpile: the plea deal with Cuffy:

"Now, you won't like Patrick Cuffy, and you won't like the deal that was made for his testimony, but his statement and his cooperation led to the discovery of testimonial evidence, physical evidence, documentary evidence, ballistic evidence, and witnesses, all of which you will hear and see, which will corroborate Cuffy's testimony."

Ken also needed to address the prior acquittal before the defense could bring it up:

"Ladies and gentlemen, the evidence will also be that there was a trial in DeKalb County, and that David Ramsey and Melvin Walker were acquitted of charges relating to the assassination of Derwin Brown in that trial. The evidence, however, will be that the DeKalb County trial against Ramsey and Walker was for different charges. There was different evidence. There were different defendants and there was a different motive. . . . Ladies and gentlemen, those charges did not include the underlying reason for Sidney Dorsey ordering the assassination of Derwin Brown, and that was his inability to lose the power that he gained through his office. . . . Sidney Dorsey did this because he could not stand to lose his power."

Ken spoke for fifty-seven minutes without a note and without ever losing his train of thought. Petrey and I looked at each other like two football coaches who made the right call for the starting quarterback.

It was now Steel's turn. I had gone up against Steel in other jury trials, and I knew he would be just as prepared and effective as Ken to deliver a powerful opening statement for his client.

I instructed everyone to take meticulous notes during Steel's argument. We had no clue what the defense was going to be in this case until Steel opened his mouth and spoke to the jury. Unlike civil cases, where depositions and discovery are used, in most criminal cases, the prosecution has no knowledge of the defense's theory until the day of the trial. It is trial by ambush, and prosecutors have to be able to form quick rebuttals to defense arguments. Steel watched Cuffy's and Skyers's testimony in the prior trial. He knew their vulnerabilities, and I was sure he would exploit them. But what was their motive to kill Derwin if Dorsey was not somehow involved?

Another reason to keep good notes is to track any promises that an attorney makes during opening statements about what the evidence will prove during the trial. The opposing lawyer will then remind the jury during closing arguments if a promise was made to introduce evidence that never made it into court, probably because the evidence never existed.

Steel began by introducing his client and discussing his background and wonderful accomplishments:

"Five-year-old Sidney Dorsey was put on a train by his parents in Brooklyn, New York, bound for Decatur, Georgia, DeKalb County. Sidney was raised by his aunt, and in Georgia in the 1940s a child who did not live with his parents could not attend public schools, so Sidney was forced to attend private school. Finances were an issue, and since the age of seven Sidney had to work to earn money for himself and his family. In school he cleaned the toilets at the school he attended in exchange for his tuition.

"In 1959, after graduating from high school, Sidney did a very honorable thing. He joined our armed forces, the army. He was stationed mostly in Germany, and after being honorably discharged, Sidney continued to civic service in 1964, joining the City of Atlanta Police Department. For the next twenty-eight years, Sidney served as a dedicated officer. He completed college and law school while an employee of the City of Atlanta Police Department, with commendations up and down his chest. He solved the horrible murder of the wife of the Honorable Horace Ward, the federal judge who desegregated the University of Georgia."

Judge Ward, the first Black judge in the Northern District of Georgia, was appointed by Jimmy Carter to the federal bench. His wife was tragically murdered, and Dorsey was one of the several homicide detectives working on the case. I had never heard until this morning that Dorsey was responsible for solving the murder, but defense attorneys were prone to exaggerate their clients' accomplishments.

"He was a case agent," Steel continued, "the lead case agent on the infamous Atlanta missing-children murder cases in the early 1980s. He solved five cases in five weeks and was nominated employee and officer of the year. There is a Sidney Dorsey Day celebrated by the City of Atlanta Council."

The only way personal information about Dorsey's background could come into evidence was for Dorsey himself to testify. Was Steel's opening statement a signal that Dorsey would take the stand and be subject to cross-examination by Clegg? I saw Clegg furiously taking notes.

Steel told the jury that Dorsey tried to help Patrick Cuffy because Cuffy was "down on his luck." Cuffy was hired after Dorsey's first election after volunteering in Dorsey's campaign. When Dorsey was up for reelection, Cuffy volunteered again after being promised a promotion to internal affairs. Cuffy recruited his friend, Paul Skyers, to help on the campaign. Skyers was promised a job in the sheriff's department for his services.

Then Steel's statements to the jury turned bizarre. "Patrick Cuffy and Paul Skyers in May 2000 concocted a plot to rig the election for sheriff. They took out an insurance plan to ensure that they could not be taken away from their lifelong dreams and a lot of money. Cuffy and Skyers decided that whoever dared to defeat Sidney Dorsey in the August election would be slain." Steel did not make it clear how killing whoever might defeat Dorsey would give them "insurance" or help them procure well-paying jobs in the sheriff's department.

Steel, having heard Cuffy's prior testimony, knew the planning for Derwin's assassination. He outlined the plot much as Ken had a few moments earlier, but he left out Walker's and Ramsey's participation. He also told the jury that Dorsey had no knowledge of this scheme and would have absolutely put a stop to it.

Surprisingly, he accused Skyers of having the murder weapon. With the flair of a good storyteller, Steel said, "Suddenly Paul Skyers came running from the darkness, his right hand outstretched, and fired sixteen times at the Honorable Derwin Brown. As Derwin Brown tried to run away to get to safety, Skyers continued pursuit, striking Derwin Brown twelve times from his toes to his knees to his private parts to his chest to his throat. As a dying Brown lay in a puddle of blood screaming his last screams, Paul Skyers ran down the driveway and got in the car with Patrick Cuffy driving, and the two of them fled into the darkness."

"*Really*?" I thought. The absurdity of this would be laughable if only the jury knew what we knew. Of the four assassins, Skyers seemed the meekest and weakest—the least capable of pulling the trigger. I spent hours with Skyers when I interviewed him and later prepared him for each trial. He struck me as someone who was too timid to kill anyone, but would blindly follow his friend Cuffy by taking a more passive role in a crime. When it came time to draw straws as to who would be the triggerman, his partners did not even include him in the drawing. Surprisingly, given his nervous nature, they trusted him to be a reliable getaway driver.

Steel also told the jury, "In March 2001, Cuffy and Skyers were told by the authorities—that's the police—that if they had any information on the murder of Derwin Brown, they would be granted immunity."

I had no idea how Steel was going to extract this information from any witness because it was not true and never happened. Law enforcement has no authority to offer immunity. The district attorney is the only person who can offer immunity from prosecution, and I did not offer that to Cuffy and Skyers until their interviews in November 2001. Petrey would need to refute this assertion when our law enforcement witnesses testified.

"On November 29, 2001," Steel continued, "Patrick Cuffy met the Honorable DeKalb County District Attorney J.Tom Morgan and manipulated him. Patrick Cuffy is as sly as a fox." Steel described the immunity agreement and said that I was tricked into believing Cuffy, and he told the jury not to let Cuffy trick them in the same way.

Steel explained to the jury that Cuffy had to point the finger at two innocent men, Melvin Walker and David Ramsey, because I would not enter into an immunity agreement with the triggerman, who, in Steel's version of events, was Skyers. Therefore, Cuffy and Skyers had to concoct a conspiracy in which they were not the triggermen. This was also the reason Cuffy had to point the finger at Dorsey, according to Steel. Since the DA would not make a deal with the real instigator, Cuffy had to make Dorsey the mastermind and sole instigator of this murderous plot. Most of Steel's argument addressed Count One, the murder.

Steel's arguments refuting the RICO counts and corruption counts were wide ranging, like a pig's breakfast of different theories in hopes that the jury would latch onto the one they liked best.

Steel made Shirley McMichael out to be a seductress who trapped Dorsey into giving her a bonding company. "You will learn that when Shirley McMichael came to interview with Sidney to be a bondsperson, she wore a very short skirt. She sat down. She opened her legs and exposed her private parts. For the next four years, Sidney and Shirley McMichael had a consensual sexual relationship.

"You will learn that though Sidney was married to Sherry Dorsey, they slept in different rooms. They stayed together for their young son." Steel said the evidence would show that Dorsey accepted only legitimate campaign contributions from McMichael.

Again, how was Steel going to prove McMichael's seduction of Dorsey without Dorsey testifying? Was this another signal that he would?

We knew Dorsey had listed at least one campaign contribution from McMichael. Unfortunately, due to the cash-only payment method, we had no paper trail to indicate how much money McMichael gave to Dorsey. It would be her word and her credibility on the stand.

Steel told the jury that Dorsey received legal advice telling him that he could use sheriff's employees to transport his wife and children for their personal safety. I wondered whether a lawyer would actually take the stand and testify that he gave Dorsey that advice.

Steel told the jury that Dorsey had no personal involvement in the management of his family security company and no knowledge of on-the-clock deputies providing private security. In any event, the hours worked by deputies on the DeKalb County clock were minimal.

Steel told the jury that the prosecution started the corruption investigation and added the corruption counts to "prop up a failing murder investigation."

I would need to make sure, with Fred's testimony, that the jury knew and understood we started the corruption investigation months before the assassination of Derwin.

Finally, Steel told the jurors that another jury saw that Cuffy and Skyers were liars, and acquitted two innocent men, Walker and Ramsey, of a horrible crime.

"Melvin Walker went to trial," he said, concluding his opening. "The state put up the same evidence. Melvin Walker was found not guilty of conspiring with Sidney Dorsey to murder Derwin Brown. David Ramsey went to trial: He was found not guilty of conspiring with Sidney Dorsey to assassinate Derwin Brown.

"Sidney Dorsey stands before you charged with serious crimes in the state of Georgia: the murder of Sheriff Brown, racketeering, bribery, violation of office. Sidney is not guilty. Thank you."

I was starting to see Steel's defense strategy, and it was a smart one. He and Samuel were never going to concede that Dorsey was guilty of RICO and corruption. They were going to fight those charges like hell. But, since lawyers know juries like to compromise if they are having a hard time reaching a unanimous verdict, Steel wanted his energy focused on the murder charge. If the jury couldn't reach a verdict on murder, the jury could compromise and find his client only guilty of corruption.

If Dorsey were acquitted of the murder but found guilty of corruption, it would be a win for the defense. The RICO and corruption charges did not include any acts of violence. They were only money crimes, and a conviction would result in only a few years of actual prison time. If the jury found Dorsey guilty of murder, he would die behind the bars of a Georgia state prison.

CHAPTER 20

Beginning on June 17, 2002, and continuing over the next two and a half weeks, the prosecution presented its evidence supporting both corruption and murder charges against Sidney Dorsey. Dr. Gowitt led the state's witnesses. The defense offered to stipulate that Derwin's cause of death was from gunshot wounds. Stipulation is a common ploy by defense lawyers to prevent the jury from hearing the gruesome nature of the injuries and from viewing pictures of the victim's body riddled with gunshot wounds. We did not agree to stipulate; we were not going to let the defense sanitize this murder. We wanted the jury to know from the start: This is a murder trial, and Derwin's murder was horrific and brutally painful. The jurors needed to see, not just hear, the consequences of the assassins' actions.

Clegg started by asking Dr. Gowitt to explain to the jury the requirements to be qualified as an expert witness regarding the cause of death from gunshots. Again, the defense offered to stipulate that he was an expert witness, but we wanted the jury to hear Dr. Gowitt's impressive background. His academic career included four years of medical school, another year of specialty training in forensic medicine and death investigations, followed by an internship with a medical examiner. He said, "In my career now, it spans almost twenty years, I have conducted or supervised approximately seven thousand autopsies, I have been involved in approximately twelve thousand death investigations and I have qualified as an expert witness in the field of forensic medicine and pathology approximately five hundred times here in Georgia as well as fifteen or twenty other states." Many Americans have seen actors portray medical examiners on television, but few have ever seen one testify in the real world. I knew Dr. Gowitt would keep the jurors riveted during his testimony.

My professional relationship with Dr. Gowitt spanned many years. I had talked with him one-on-one and heard him testify on numerous occasions, but I only realized that afternoon who he reminded me of—in appearance, voice, and demeanor—Burl Ives, the short, stocky, bespectacled narrator of the animated children's Christmas special, *Rudolph the Red-Nosed Reindeer*.

Clegg offered the first piece of evidence in the trial, exhibit number one. Standing before the jury, next to Dr. Gowitt, was a life-size foam manikin, made the same height and depth as Derwin's body. There were twelve rods, each representing a gunshot entering the body. Seven rods passed through the manikin. Five of the rods entered the manikin but did not exit.

Dr. Gowitt stepped down from the stand and explained, "This was purchased by my office as part of what we would call the workup for Mr. Brown's case. There were so many gunshots—it is difficult to follow twelve gunshots. No matter how clear I am in explaining it, the manikin says more than I do, believe me. What we did was take a rod and put it in the entry area of the wound and then out the exit area of the wound. The rods generally follow the trajectory of the bullets as I saw them at the time of the autopsy."

That manikin with the twelve metal rods inserted, and Dr. Gowitt standing next to it just a few feet from the jury, will be an image forever etched in my memory.

Clegg asked whether any shots fired were in close range to Derwin. Dr. Gowitt answered, "Of the twelve gunshot wounds that Mr. Brown sustained, only one had what I will call stippling or gunshot particles around it, and that was a wound located on the back of his middle finger of the left hand." I remembered that Derwin's wedding band was deformed when I saw his body at the morgue. Dr. Gowitt testified that this was probably a defensive wound Derwin suffered when he first saw the shooter and the gun pointed at him, instinctively raising his hand.

Dr. Gowitt testified Derwin then turned to run, and one bullet struck him, traveling through his left arm and lodging in some papers in the front pocket of his suit jacket. Dr. Gowitt then pointed to three rods entering the back of the manikin. "The next three shots entered his back as he was trying to run away," he explained. "One bullet went through the spleen, lung, and heart." Pointing to another rod, Dr. Gowitt said, "This one went through the liver, diaphragm, and lung. And the third bullet entered the back and lodged near the heart. These three shots were fatal wounds, but death would only come after a few minutes from the bleeding."

The medical examiner went on to show the rod in the face from the gunshot that shattered Derwin's jaw. After passing through the face, the bullets severed the jugular vein in the neck. "This was the knockdown shot. Mr. Brown was still alive, but in excruciating pain." Dr. Gowitt sounded more like a teacher than a doctor while speaking to the jury.

"The final shots to Mr. Brown occurred when he was balled up on the ground in a fetal position. The shooter was standing over him from two to three feet away and fired the remaining shots into Mr. Brown's legs and scrotum. He probably became unconscious within thirty seconds to a minute after hitting the ground, and he died a few minutes later.

"I cannot tell you how many shots were fired at Mr. Brown that night," he continued. "But I can tell you he was struck sixteen times, with twelve of the bullets entering his body. Four bullets passed through his clothing, but did not touch flesh."

As Dr. Gowitt was testifying, Clegg introduced photographs taken of Derwin's body before the autopsy. The photographs were displayed solely to the jurors and the defense lawyers. They were not seen by the spectators in the courtroom.

Dr. Gowitt's testimony was painful to listen to, and I could only imagine what Phyllis and Brandy were feeling. They knew what was coming, as they had heard it before in the first trial, but I was sure hearing it again was not any easier. I was glad Roz was sitting with them in the courtroom.

When it came time for Steel to cross-examine, he got right to the issue at hand. Steel began, "Dr. Gowitt, the Honorable Derwin Brown suffered a horrific death, correct?"

Dr. Gowitt replied, "Based upon my examination during the autopsy, I would agree that Mr. Brown suffered excruciating pain before he lost consciousness."

Steel continued, "However, Dr. Gowitt, you have no way of knowing who pulled the trigger that caused this horrible death, correct?"

"That's correct," replied Dr. Gowitt.

"And you have no way of knowing who was or was not involved in Sheriff Brown's murder, correct?" asked Steel.

"That's right," answered Dr. Gowitt.

"And did you not testify in another trial where Melvin Walker and David Ramsey were accused of Sheriff Brown's murder?" asked Steel.

"I do not remember the defendants' names, but I did testify as to Mr. Brown's cause of death in another trial," answered Dr. Gowitt.

"And you are aware that the jury in that case found Mr. Walker and Mr. Ramsey not guilty of Mr. Brown's murder?"

"Someone told me they were acquitted of the charges," replied Dr. Gowitt.

"Thank you, Dr. Gowitt, for your testimony. That's all I have," and Steel sat down.

***

After Dr. Gowitt's testimony, we turned to building the corruption case and showing the motive for Derwin's murder—greed and power. We would revisit the murder evidence with our final witnesses. Petrey was responsible for organizing the presentation of the corruption case and RICO charges. The next fifty witnesses each had a piece to place in the puzzle that would show Dorsey was guilty of the corruption and racketeering charges.

Ken called Sheriff Tom Brown to explain the legal duties and responsibilities of the elected Georgia sheriff. Sheriff Brown said the sheriff was not accountable to any other officeholder. "I report to the people of DeKalb County. I am voted in and out of office every four years." Sheriff Brown told the jurors there were 425 employees in the DeKalb County Sheriff's Department, and that he could hire and fire any of them at will.

Sheriffs run county jails, Brown explained to the Dougherty County jurors, noting that "the DeKalb County jail is not just the biggest jail in Georgia, it is also the biggest jail east of the Mississippi River. It holds 3,600 inmates, and it costs the DeKalb County taxpayers $53 million a year to operate." He also told them that it was solely within the discretion of the Georgia sheriff as to who would be allowed to operate bonding companies serving the jail in their county.

Because we were planning to call Lieutenant Baker, the sheriff's aide-de-camp, in a few days, we wanted Sheriff Brown to explain his position. Brown told the jury that an order from Baker had the authority of a direct order from the sheriff. He said Dorsey kept Baker, who'd served in the previous administration, and Brown kept Baker in that position because of his institutional knowledge of the sheriff's department.

Sheriff Brown further testified that the Georgia sheriff is not authorized by law to accept fees from bonding companies; cannot order employees to transport private persons, including family members, to and from personal appointments; cannot order a lawyer working for the sheriff's department to perform personal legal services for the sheriff or his friends and family; and cannot send sheriff's deputies to provide private security while on the county clock.

"After I was sworn in as sheriff following Derwin's assassination," Sheriff Brown continued, "I found thirty-five copies of dismissal letters written by Derwin in personnel files directed to employees he was going to fire the day he took office. These letters were mailed to the recipients in

November. One of those dismissal letters was directed to Deputy Sheriff Patrick Cuffy."

Samuel, during cross-examination, elicited from Sheriff Brown that the Georgia sheriff is sheriff twenty-four hours a day, seven days a week while he is in office. The defense was trying to lay the foundation for the argument that Dorsey was entitled to a driver and security, even if his family members were also present.

Fred Mays was the first witness I called. We needed to solicit Fred's testimony on the record so that he could sit with us in the courtroom. A witness is not allowed to hear other witnesses testify before taking the stand.

Fred looked sharp in a new suit, but it could not hide Fred's muscular build. Although not intentional, our first two law enforcement witnesses—a sheriff and a GBI special agent—were Black. In retrospect, having these two witnesses lead off the corruption portion of the trial may have reassured the jurors that this case was not a white persecution of Dorsey.

After being sworn to testify and stating his occupation, I asked, "Agent Mays, were you involved in the investigation of the defendant, Sidney Dorsey?"

Fred answered, "Yes, my boss, Director Buddy Nix, told me there had been a request for my services to conduct a criminal investigation of a Georgia sheriff."

"Who made that request, Agent Mays?"

"You did, Mr. Morgan."

"And when was that request made, Agent Mays?"

"Monday, July 10, 2000."

"And do you know the date that the victim in this case was gunned down in his front yard?"

"I know the date well. It was December 15, 2000."

"Therefore, the corruption investigation involving Sheriff Dorsey began six months before Sheriff Brown's assassination, correct?"

"That's right," said Fred.

I wanted the jury to fully understand that there was an ongoing corruption investigation of Dorsey long before the homicide. I needed to refute Steel's opening statement that the corruption allegations were only brought against Dorsey to "prop up a failing murder investigation."

"Agent Mays, what was the initial allegation that you were requested to investigate?"

"An Atlanta television station reported that some DeKalb County sheriff's deputies were providing private security at local banks while on the clock, and that Sheriff Dorsey owned the security firm. At your request, Mr. Morgan, I scheduled a meeting with Sheriff Dorsey in his office. I knew Sheriff Dorsey personally and professionally."

"When did that meeting take place, and was anyone else present for the meeting?"

"The meeting took place at 10 a.m., July 27, 2000, in the sheriff's private office at the jail. Chief Investigator Carol Ellis from your office and Lt. Roy Baker from the sheriff's department were also present at the meeting."

"Were you wearing a recording device during the course of that interview?"

"Yes sir, I was."

"Did you tell Mr. Dorsey that you were recording the conversation?"

"No sir. He asked me was I recording it."

"What did you tell him?"

"I told him I had a recorder on me, and he asked me was it on, was it recording, and I told him no."

"Did you record the conversation, Agent Mays?"

"Yes sir, I recorded the conversation."

In preparation for this trial, I listened for the first time to the recording that Fred had put in the evidence locker almost two years earlier. I introduced the cassette into evidence. I am sure the jury thought they were about to hear the recording, but they would have to wait. I had other plans for Dorsey's voice.

Fred told the jury that Dorsey and Baker explained that Sgt. Joe Murray was not on the clock when reporter Dale Cardwell saw Murray providing security at the bank. They told Fred it was a clerical error, which they corrected, and that Murray should have been placed on unpaid leave that afternoon. Fred told the jury that his investigation, prior to the interview, revealed that Murray had never asked for leave to work at a bank. Murray was never told by anyone he had to take leave when he was directed by Lieutenant Baker to provide security at a bank.

Fred told the jury that he interviewed about twenty employees from the sheriff's department. They were also directed to provide private security at banks while they were on the clock.

I asked Fred, "Agent Mays, do you know an owner of a bonding company, Shirley McMichael? If so, when did you first meet her, and where did y'all meet?"

"Ms. McMichael contacted me and said she needed to see me. We met on September 27, 2000, at Rehoboth Baptist Church. That was our first meeting."

"What did y'all discuss at this meeting?" I asked.

"She told me Sheriff Dorsey forced her to have sex, and that she had given him money so that she could keep her bonding company business."

"Did she say anything about a meeting with Sheriff Dorsey not long after his election defeat?"

Fred responded, "Yes, she told me something about meeting with Dorsey after he lost, and [Dorsey] telling her he was going to be elected sheriff in a special election because Derwin Brown would not be around to take office."

"What were your thoughts when she told you that Dorsey told her he was going to win in a special election?"

"I wrote it off as Sheriff Dorsey being nonsensical. It didn't make any sense to me. Derwin Brown was going to be the sheriff."

Samuel cross-examined Fred. "You lied to Sheriff Dorsey when he asked you if you were recording the conversation?"

"That's correct," said Fred matter-of-factly. It did not legally matter if Fred lied to Dorsey about the recording; it was still admissible under Georgia law.

"Did Shirley McMichael tell you that she feared for her life while Sheriff Dorsey was in office?" asked Samuel.

"Yes. She said she feared for her life, and that she feared for Derwin Brown's life after he won the election."

I wondered why Samuel asked Fred whether McMichael told him she was scared of Dorsey. His response seemed more helpful to the prosecution than the defense. I realized later that Samuel had a reason for eliciting this testimony.

Petrey was responsible for presenting Sgt. Joe Murray's testimony to the jury. Murray told the jury that he was a detention officer in the jail. After Dorsey was first elected in 1996, he was promoted to community relations, assigned a marked sheriff's car, and issued a uniform and a gun. To his knowledge, he was the only person with a detention officer rank who had a car and a gun.

Murray told the jury that when school was in session, it was part of his regular job to pick up Dorsey's children from school in the county patrol car. Sometimes he would take the boys to buy toys or to get a haircut, but usually he took them back to the sheriff's department, where he helped watch over the kids.

Petrey asked him, "How long did this continue, sir, that your duty was to pick the sheriff's children up from school. Are we talking a few weeks, a few months, a few years?"

"Years," said Murray.

Petrey asked, "Sergeant Murray, did you ever have occasion to transport Sheriff Dorsey's daughter?"

"Yes, sir," he replied. "Sheriff Dorsey ordered me on two occasions to pick up his daughter from college in Statesboro, Georgia."

"Were you in uniform, Sergeant Murray?"

"Yes, sir.

"What vehicle did you drive?"

"The patrol car assigned to me."

"Where did you get the gas for these trips to Statesboro?"

"The county pumps."

I glanced at the female jurors and noticed several of them taking copious notes during this testimony. Perhaps the female mock juror in Augusta was not alone in her views regarding government employees transporting and babysitting a politician's children.

Petrey began the questioning about the incident that set the corruption investigation in motion. "Sergeant Murray, were you ever ordered to provide security at banks while you were on duty?"

"Yes, sir."

"Who gave you those orders?"

"Lieutenant Baker. Sometimes Sheriff Dorsey."

Murray told the jury that, to the best of his recollection, he provided security at least fifteen times at five different banks. Sometimes he was at the bank a couple of hours; a few times he was at the bank from 10:00 a.m. to closing.

Petrey asked him, "What exactly did you do when you got to the banks, Mr. Murray?"

Murray replied, "Just security. I just stood there and watched the bank like security."

Petrey asked, "At any time that you were driving Sheriff Dorsey's children or providing security at banks, did you take annual leave, or sick leave, or leave without pay?"

"No sir, I was always on duty. The only time I took leave without pay was when Lieutenant Baker docked my paycheck after the reporter saw me working at the bank."

Murray told the jury he had no idea why a reporter was filming him at a bank, and he reported the incident to Lieutenant Baker that day.

In a subsequent meeting with Baker and Dorsey, Baker told him that he was going to deduct four hours' pay from his paycheck that week, but he would get it back in the next paycheck. Murray didn't understand why he was docked four hours.

"Did you see the television story about you working at the bank?" asked Petrey.

"Yes, sir."

"What, if anything, did you do after you saw the story?"

"I talked to my wife and my son and decided I needed to tell someone the truth. I thought I was just doing my job when I was at the bank," answered Sergeant Murray. He ultimately spoke with Fred Mays.

Samuel cross-examined Murray for the defense. He began, "Sergeant Murray, after you were moved to community relations, you worked more than forty hours a week, correct? You worked maybe fifty and sixty hours and sometimes weekends, correct?" Lawyers can ask a witness leading questions during cross-examination.

"Yes, sir."

"And every week you worked all those hours, the county only paid you for a forty-hour workweek, including the weeks you worked at a bank, correct?"

"Yes, sir."

It took me a few minutes to figure out where Samuel was heading with this line of questioning, but then it hit me. Murray always reported forty hours of work each week, never requested overtime even when he worked more than forty hours, and was only paid for forty hours each week. The defense could argue that all the extra time he spent transporting Dorsey's kids and working at the banks was at no cost to the county—no harm, no foul. Petrey would need to argue in his closing that if Murray had not been at the banks or transporting Dorsey's kids, he would have been performing work for the county. Murray never "volunteered" his time to work at the banks or transport Dorsey's children.

During one of the jury's breaks, when they could not hear what was being said in the courtroom, Judge Becker told the lawyers from the bench that she had been informed that Dorsey had stopped eating and refused anything served to him. I wondered, *Was this a scheme by Dorsey to disrupt the flow of the trial*? Judge Becker, in a firm and commanding voice, looked straight at Dorsey and said, "Mr. Dorsey, you must eat. If it comes to it, I will have you physically examined and pump you full of whatever a doctor tells me to if I have to." Dorsey said he understood and that he would start eating again.

Petrey called Lieutenant Baker to testify. Baker testified that he was an aide-de-camp for Sheriff Morris. When Dorsey defeated Morris, Dorsey kept him on. Then, when Dorsey was defeated and Sheriff Brown was appointed after Derwin Brown's death, Sheriff Brown kept him on as well.

Baker confirmed what Sheriff Brown had said: that any order he passed on to an employee, even those above him in rank, had "the same authority as the sheriff himself, because I am passing on the sheriff's order through me."

Baker told the jurors that Dorsey ordered him to direct Sergeant Murray and others to transport Dorsey's children to and from school. The orders also came from Dorsey for Baker to direct Murray and others to provide security for the banks when needed. Baker said that when Murray called him about the filming at the bank, he met with Dorsey, and they agreed it would be a "political embarrassment." He said they decided the best way to handle the matter would be to change Murray's timesheet to show that he was actually on leave while at the bank.

Petrey asked Baker, "Do you have any doubt, sir, what would have happened to your job and your career if you had ever refused to carry out an order from Sidney Dorsey?"

"No, sir, I have no doubt."

"What would have happened?"

"I probably would have been replaced."

Turning to the subject of Shirley McMichael, Petrey asked, "Lieutenant Baker, do you know Shirley McMichael, the owner of Speedy Bonding Company?"

"Yes, Ms. McMichael had a personal relationship with Dorsey."

"What do you mean when you say personal relationship?"

"Ms. McMichael often showed up in the sheriff's office to see the sheriff without an appointment. She had greater access to Dorsey than employees of the sheriff's department or other bonding companies."

Baker also testified that when he went to Dorsey's residence on business after the murder of Brown, he saw Melvin Walker leaving Dorsey's residence.

When Samuel cross-examined Baker, he asked, "Lieutenant Baker, you told Mr. Petrey that Shirley McMichael often came to the sheriff's office without an appointment, correct?"

"Yes, sir. Most of the time she came to the sheriff's office uninvited."

Samuel continued, "How was she dressed when she came to the sheriff's office uninvited?"

"She sometimes dressed provocatively in short skirts and revealing tops. She was usually barefoot."

McMichael's attire was news to Fred and me. She had not shared this surprising information with us.

***

Early in the trial, I noticed three elderly gentlemen sitting on the back bench in the courtroom. Courtroom watchers, sometimes called trial junkies, are people with time on their hands who would rather watch real, live drama in a courtroom than fake drama on daytime television. I asked Ken, "The old dudes in the back, fans of yours? They walk in together at three o'clock and leave exactly at five o'clock each day."

Ken looked at the three men and said, "Nope, never saw them before the trial. I'll go check them out. They could be voters."

After talking with the three men, Ken returned. "Well, they are not here to watch the lawyers. They are here to watch Judge Becker. It is the first time they have seen a female judge, and they think she is hot. They leave at five to go to happy hour."

"I suggest we wait until after the trial to tell Judge Becker," I said with a smile.

***

As the trial progressed, we adopted a routine that suited us well throughout the trial. On Monday evenings, the Winfield kitchen staff prepared a delicious Southern meal for us to consume while we reviewed the day's testimony. Quail, fried chicken, catfish, pork chops, fresh corn, okra, green beans, pickled cucumbers, cornbread, and banana pudding were served. On Tuesday and Wednesday evenings, we ate at local restaurants. After dinner, we drove back to Winfield to discuss the day's events and prepare for the next day's testimony.

On Thursday evenings, after Judge Becker recessed the trial, everyone would return home, but I would stay in Albany to work on my closing argument. Ken often came to the Snuffy Smith Cabin to assist with my closing and discuss trial strategy. On Sunday afternoons, we all gathered again at Winfield to plan the next week's trial testimony and to let Carol Ellis know the order of witnesses we would need for court. Her responsibility was to ensure that all witnesses were present and ready to appear in court.

The night before I called Shirley McMichael to testify, Fred and I met her at a table by the hotel pool where she was staying. It was a hot, humid Georgia summer night, and the mosquitoes were the size of small birds. I reviewed the questions I would ask her the next day. Her answers were the same I had heard before. She returned to her room, and Fred said, "There's more to her story. She ain't telling you everything." I respected Fred's intuition about human nature, but I didn't have any evidence to refute McMichael's version of events.

CHAPTER 21

The next morning, McMichael, dressed professionally and with a short hairstyle, told the jury that Dorsey personally interviewed her when she applied to operate a bonding company in the county. "During the second interview, Sheriff Dorsey told me I had been approved. He told me I was the first woman, and the first Black person, to operate a bonding company in DeKalb County." She said she grossed $600,000 her first year, and that her personal income that year was $150,000. I am sure the jury was surprised to hear that a bonding company could be so lucrative in a short time.

Then McMichael said that after she'd operated the bonding company for six months, Dorsey asked to see her, and he told her to meet him at a Church's Fried Chicken. She met Dorsey in the parking lot and got in his car—an unmarked Crown Victoria—and he drove her to a deserted house. "And then we got into the house, and then he just kind of like, you know, started getting all over me. He told me there was a price I had to pay for giving me the bonding company. Then he started, you know, having sexual intercourse with me." She told the jury that she locked the panties she wore and a washcloth she used that day in a safe, and years later, she handed them over to Agent Fred Mays. McMichael started crying as she told the story, and Judge Becker ordered a fifteen-minute recess so McMichael could regain her composure.

When the court resumed, McMichael told the jury that Dorsey would call her and tell her to reserve a hotel room. She couldn't remember how often this occurred; she believed it was several times, and she always paid for the room with her credit card. "Dorsey liked to call himself 'Big Daddy' or 'Big Man' when they were alone in the hotel room," she told the jury.

McMichael also told the jury that Dorsey demanded cash payments. She paid him $2,500 to $10,000, depending on how many bonds she wrote that day for inmates who were granted bonds. "One time, I wrote a check for $2,500. He told me, 'You know better than to give me a check!' and he tore up the check." McMichael told the jury she gave in to Dorsey's demands because he controlled her livelihood.

I asked McMichael if she had a meeting with Sheriff Dorsey shortly after his election defeat in August 2000. She told the jury, "I met with Sheriff Dorsey not long after he lost the runoff. I asked him about his plans for the future when he would no longer be sheriff. He said, 'I am going to run for sheriff in a special election and I will win.' I asked him, 'What about Derwin? He told me, 'Well, Derwin won't be, Derwin won't be there.' Then he put his finger to his temple." McMichael demonstrated the gesture to the jury, pointing at her head with her fingers looking like a gun. "He told me Derwin wouldn't make it to take office."

"Did you ever tell anyone about this conversation with Sheriff Dorsey? If so, when?" I asked.

"I told Agent Mays when he first interviewed me. I don't remember the date, but it was before Derwin Brown was murdered." I wanted to be sure the jury understood that McMichael had this conversation with Dorsey after he was defeated in the runoff election but before Derwin Brown was murdered.

McMichael also recounted her visit to O'Charley's restaurant in fall 2000 when she wore a wire at my request. She said Dorsey could tell she was nervous, and he wrote a note on a paper napkin and handed it to her. It read, "Are you wired?"

McMichael said, "After I read the note, I was shaking. Sheriff Dorsey grabbed the napkin and tore it up. He stood up and said, 'Don't ever talk to me no more!' and he left the table."

I thought McMichael did fairly well on the stand. Still, I was glad we had corroboration: my investigator watching Dorsey and McMichael passing the note at the restaurant, hotel receipts with McMichael's name and credit card numbers, and Dorsey's DNA on her panties. However, she was about to undergo a grueling cross-examination from Samuel.

He began, "Let me ask you about how many times you had sexual relations with Sheriff Dorsey."

"I can't give you the number of times, but I know it was several times, and every time it was against my will."

"Several times?" Samuel asked.

"Uh-huh. Many, many times."

"Would you say that he came to your house for sex as many as sixty times?" asked Samuel.

"Like I said, I don't know," replied McMichael.

"A hundred times?" the defense attorney asked.

"I don't know."

"Possibly 150 times?" asked Samuel in an incredulous tone.

"No. I wouldn't say that," replied McMichael.

Samuel hammered on, "Can you tell me why it is that when Fred Mays interviewed you on February 14, 2001, you told Agent Mays you had only had sexual relations with Dorsey a total of eight times?"

"Because I was ashamed," McMichael told the jury.

Samuel had just proved that McMichael lied to a GBI agent during an interview, even though Fred told her to be truthful about everything, even if it was embarrassing.

Samuel also questioned McMichael about another event she failed to relay to Fred and me. Apparently, McMichael hosted a fundraiser for Dorsey's reelection campaign at a local comedy club. She gave a speech at that event in which she sang Dorsey's praises. The event was a success, and she raised a lot of money for Dorsey.

Samuel wasn't finished. "Over the course of time you bought presents for Sidney Dorsey, did you not?" he asked. "And you didn't tell the GBI or J.Tom Morgan about these presents, did you?"

McMichael responded, "I believe I did. I'm not really sure." Fred and I knew the truthful answer to that question was "no."

McMichael admitted on the stand that she bought Dorsey a $1,500 watch as a gift. "You also bought him a smoking jacket, did you not? Do you remember buying him this smoking jacket?" asked Samuel. At that moment, Samuel removed his suit jacket and donned a very nice burgundy velvet smoking jacket from Neiman Marcus, prompting Judge Becker to quip, "Are you sure that's going to fit?" Her remark brought laughs from the jurors and me.

In addition, Samuel made McMichael admit that she lied on a résumé for a job when she claimed she had completed two years of a four-year degree at Emory Law School. Fred and I had not seen or heard about the résumé. Samuel's cross-examination of McMichael was classic. If you can show the jury that a witness will lie about some things, you can argue to the jury that the witness will lie about everything.

We would now need to explain to the jury that, even if McMichael willingly participated in the bribery in order to operate her business, Dorsey would still be guilty of bribery. A simple quid pro quo is still bribery. Both the person making the bribe, and the person accepting the bribe, are guilty of bribery. Had McMichael been more forthcoming with us regarding her relationship with Dorsey, we may have changed our strategy and treated her as an unindicted coconspirator for bribing the DeKalb County sheriff instead of presenting her as a victim. We also would have been better able to prepare her for Samuel's cross-examination questions.

After McMichael's testimony, Fred asked me, "J.Tom, what kind of watch costs $1,500?"

I replied, "Fred, not any kind of watch that you and I will ever wear."

Fortunately, many other witnesses testified about corruption in the sheriff's department under Dorsey's supervision. Noah Heimlich, as well as other employees, testified about the many excursions they made to transport Dorsey's family members. Because deputies were now free to speak without fear of retribution from Dorsey, several of them testified that they were ordered to provide private security while on the DeKalb County clock. Unlike Sergeant Murray, these deputies were paid overtime if their work at the banks exceeded their regular working hours. Donna Stone, the computer programmer in the payroll department, testified about the thousands of dollars the county paid in overtime to these employees who were performing personal services for the sheriff. She also testified that Sheriff Dorsey authorized Patrick Cuffy to be paid almost $50,000 in overtime in 2000.

Our final witness regarding the corruption charges was Ronald Ramsey, a licensed Georgia lawyer. He told the jury Dorsey hired him with the understanding that his job was to handle employee-related matters and contracts involving the sheriff's department. However, Dorsey ordered him to provide private legal services, including court appearances, for Dorsey's family and friends.

Petrey asked him, "Mr. Ramsey, were you ever compensated for the work you did for private individuals while working for the sheriff?"

"No, I just received my county salary," Ramsey replied.

Ramsey knew he could not ethically represent private citizens while working for the county, and he eventually resigned.

Supported by the incriminating testimony of fifty witnesses, Petrey, with John Floyd's input, presented the foundation for the first RICO conviction of a public official in Georgia. Now, in the trial's second week, it was time to turn to the prosecution's proof of Count One, murder.

***

We decided the best witness to lead off the murder allegation was Clarence Mosley, Dorsey's chief of staff and a close personal friend. Mosley, seventy-three years old, had an impressive work history before joining the sheriff's department. He spent twenty-two years in the military and received several medals for his service. He had been the director of compliance for the Franklin Mint and the assistant city manager for Philadelphia. He retired and moved to DeKalb County, where he met Sidney Dorsey and volunteered in Dorsey's first campaign for sheriff. Dorsey put Mosley in charge of a program intended to reduce the victimization of senior citizens in the county. Mosley greatly admired Dorsey and considered him a close friend. Dorsey sometimes stayed overnight at Mosley's home.

I asked, "Mr. Mosley, did you have a meeting with Sherriff Dorsey shortly after he lost the runoff election?"

The distinguished-looking, gray-haired gentleman softly replied, "After Sidney lost the runoff election, I went into his office to see how he was holding up and what his plans were for the future. Sidney was not happy. He told me he had been skewered by the media. He made the statement that Derwin Brown would never assume the office of sheriff. There would be a special election. First, there would be an interim sheriff appointed, and then there would be a special election. Sidney said he would enter that race and that he would win."

Mosley told the jury that Dorsey's statements and manner so troubled him that the next day, he called his pastor for advice. After talking with this pastor, he called Tom Brown—then the DeKalb County director of public safety, who later became sheriff—and told him about the conversation. Brown told him to put his statement in writing and put it in safekeeping. However, Mosley said he didn't do what Tom Brown suggested.

In April 2001, four months after Derwin's murder, Mosley had lunch with Dorsey. During that meeting, Dorsey tried to get Mosley to remember a different version of their earlier conversation after his defeat. It was after this lunch, and much prayer, that Mosley knew he needed to report the earlier conversation with Dorsey to the district attorney. Mosley called Tom Brown to arrange a meeting with me; that's when I learned of Mosley's conversations with Dorsey for the first time.

Steel only questioned Mosley about his hearing deficiencies, but Mosley said he was in the sheriff's office and only a few feet away when he had the first conversation with Dorsey.

Clegg was responsible for questioning Patrick Cuffy. He'd questioned Cuffy during the first trial and had developed a rapport with him. In the time between the two trials, I saw sheriff's deputies escort Cuffy to Clegg's office and wait for him. Clegg wanted to make sure Cuffy understood why he was such a disaster in the first trial.

Cuffy took the stand wearing a suit and tie since he was no longer in custody. Clegg questioned Cuffy in a methodical way, and Cuffy's testimony was entirely consistent with what he said when we interviewed him in November 2001 and at the trial of David Ramsey and Melvin Walker in March 2002.

Cuffy spoke in the same monotone, slightly accented voice I heard the day I interviewed him in secret. He seemed to be incapable of empathy. I wondered what the jury was thinking. They looked intense, but who wouldn't after hearing him describe the methodical planning and consummation of this brutal murder?

Clegg asked Cuffy to explain his understanding of the immunity agreement with the district attorney. "My attorney, Keith Adams, and I met with Mr. Morgan, Mr. Petrey, and Mr. Harvey. Mr. Morgan told me that if I cooperated with the state and told the truth about what happened regarding the circumstances of Derwin Brown's killing, I would not be charged with murder, and my statements could not be used against me. Mr. Morgan told me that if he caught me lying, I would be charged with murder, and I could face the death penalty. Mr. Morgan also agreed to let me plead to the original charge of tampering with evidence at my house and dismiss the murder charge [related to the shoot-out at Cuffy's house]. I pled guilty and got a year to serve."

Clegg asked his last question, "And Mr. Cuffy, is your testimony before this jury the truth today?"

"Yes sir. It is," responded Cuffy.

Steel stood up and walked close to Cuffy and asked his first question, "You are an admitted liar, are you not, Mr. Cuffy?" Steel had seen how Cuffy exploded and deteriorated under cross-examination when he was called a liar in the first trial.

Cuffy calmly responded, "I have been untruthful in the past regarding my involvement in the killing of Derwin Brown." Under Clegg's tutelage, Cuffy was better prepared to avoid outbursts of anger when answering cross-examination questions.

"In fact, you lied to Sergeant Stewart on December 22, 2000, when you said you had nothing to do with the assassination of the Honorable Derwin Brown, correct?" asked Steel.

"I did not tell the police the truth when they interviewed me shortly after the Brown killing," Cuffy said in the same monotone voice he used with Clegg.

"And you kept lying until Mr. Morgan offered you a sweetheart get-out-of-jail-free card, correct?"

"I told my attorney the truth. He arranged a meeting with Mr. Morgan where if I told the truth, it would not be used against me. That's when I told the authorities the truth," said Cuffy.

"But you only made up this story involving Sidney Dorsey when you were facing life in prison for a murder that occurred at your house. Now that's the truth, isn't it?" asked Steel.

"I had nothing to do with that killing. I didn't even have a gun. But somehow, I was charged with felony murder. And I don't think that the DA could prove I was guilty of murder. My testimony regarding Sidney Dorsey's involvement with Mr. Brown's murder is the truth," said Cuffy.

After witnessing Cuffy's meltdown in the prior trial, I was shocked and pleasantly surprised at his demeanor in this trial. I wrote Clegg a note, "How much Xanax did you put in Cuffy's water glass?"

"Mr. Cuffy," Steel continued, "you testified against Walker and Ramsey, and that jury knew you were lying and found Walker and Ramsey not guilty of the murder of Mr. Brown. You are telling the same lies to this jury, correct?"

"I was truthful to that jury, and I'm telling the truth today," Cuffy said without emotion.

Steel asked Cuffy about his long friendship over the years with Paul Skyers. Cuffy acknowledged they had been friends for a long time. Steel, preparing for Skyers's testimony, said, "Mr. Cuffy, when you found yourself in a jam charged with murder, you concocted these lies with your best friend, Paul Skyers, against Mr. Walker, Mr. Ramsey, and Sidney Dorsey. If y'all could trick Mr. Morgan into believing your lies, you'd walk away from two murders, right?"

"I was never charged with Mr. Brown's murder. Mr. Morgan did not know about my involvement until after I told him," Cuffy replied.

"You knew Mr. Morgan would never agree to immunity if you pulled the trigger or were the instigator of the murder of Mr. Brown. That is why you had to fabricate a story involving Mr. Walker, Mr. Ramsey, and Mr. Dorsey. Isn't that true, Mr. Cuffy?" asked Steel.

"I wasn't the instigator or the triggerman, which is why I talked to Mr. Morgan," said Cuffy.

Steel hammered Cuffy for over three hours, yet Cuffy retained his composure and irritatingly monotone voice.

Subsequent third-party witnesses corroborated aspects of Cuffy's testimony:

- Officer Harris, a DeKalb County school resource officer, told the jury that he saw Cuffy and others parked at Glen Haven Elementary School on a Saturday night before the murder. Cuffy called Dorsey, who assured Officer Harris that Cuffy was on special assignment for him.

- DeKalb County police officer Logan testified that prior to Derwin's murder she spoke with Cuffy and Walker in a DeKalb County park at night when they were talking next to Cuffy's car.
- Faith Harley told the jury that Cuffy was at her home at 4:00 a.m. on the morning after the murder when Cuffy got a phone call and said he needed to leave to go get Ramsey.
- A former Fulton County deputy sheriff testified that Cuffy asked to purchase a TEC-9, but he did not sell it to him.

We also introduced into evidence a receipt showing Ramsey's return of the metal detector that Cuffy said had been purchased from Radio Shack after the murder to try to locate the gun that Ramsey lost in the woods as he was fleeing the scene of the crime.

I called Paul Skyers to testify. Skyers was wearing street clothes. After asking his name, I asked Skyers to tell the jury his age, height, and weight. "I'm twenty-seven years old, and I am five feet, four inches tall and weigh 140 pounds." Skyers certainly did not fit the image of an assassin. He appeared extremely nervous on the stand.

Skyers testified he met Cuffy when they both worked at SID, Inc. He also said he volunteered in the 1996 and 2000 election campaigns for Sheriff Dorsey. He said he interviewed for a job with the sheriff's department, but he never made it past the first interview.

I asked him if he had a meeting with Cuffy after Dorsey lost in the runoff. Skyers replied, "Cuffy asked me to come to his house. David Ramsey was there when I arrived. We went for a walk to a pond, and Cuffy pulled out a note that said, 'Kill Derwin Brown.' I asked Cuffy, 'Where is this coming from? The Man?' The Man meant Sheriff Dorsey. Cuffy said, 'Yes.' Then Cuffy ripped up the note and gave each of us a piece and told us to chew it up. About three weeks later, Melvin Walker became involved in the plot."

"How was the shooter determined?" I asked.

"I told him I couldn't do it, but I could be the getaway driver. Walker drew the short straw."

"Where were you on the night of the shooting?" I asked Skyers.

"Cuffy told me we had to kill Brown that night because he was under a lot of pressure from Dorsey. I was at work, and left around nine to go to Cuffy's house."

I interrupted him, "Were you and Mr. Cuffy at any time that evening present at a restaurant called MVP?" I asked this question because in Steel's opening statement, he said the defense would prove that Cuffy and Skyers were stalking Brown at the restaurant the night Brown was murdered.

"No. And I had no idea Mr. Brown was there that night until I heard about it later."

"Please continue," I directed.

"I drove the four of us in my Honda Civic to the back of a church parking lot. This parking lot was next to some woods that bordered Mr. Brown's neighborhood. I parked the car, and the other three got out. I had one walkie-talkie, and Ramsey had the other walkie-talkie. I sat there until I heard what sounded like firecrackers and Ramsey's voice on the radio yelling, 'Let's go, let's go, let's go!' A few seconds later, Cuffy jumped in the front seat, and Walker and Ramsey got in the back seat. We drove off, and the windshield kept fogging up because of the adrenaline and the heat from the weapon used by Walker. Cuffy had to keep wiping the windshield so I could see.

"When we got back to Cuffy's house, I said I would dispose of the TEC-9. I dislodged the firing pin and the bolt and threw everything in a drain on the way home. We all discussed our alibis, and if anyone asked us, we were at Cuffy's house most of the night of the murder."

"Were you facing any criminal charges related to the murder of Derwin Brown when you came to see me in Rockdale County in November 2001?" I asked.

"No," he responded.

"Then why did you talk with me, Mr. Petrey, and Mr. Harvey?"

"Cuffy called me and told me to come see you, and I did. When I got there, Cuffy told me to tell you the truth about what happened and that everything would be okay. You promised me that if I told the truth, my statements would not be used against me. That's why I talked to you."

"After you talked with me, did you take a GBI agent to the drain cover where you disposed of the weapon and its parts?" I asked.

"Yes, and he was able to pull the gun out of the drain," said Skyers.

During cross-examination, Steel questioned Skyers about his lengthy friendship with Cuffy. "Isn't it true that you visited your best friend, Patrick Cuffy, every day at the jail after he was arrested for the murder at his home?" asked Steel.

"I did go see him often after he was arrested," said Skyers.

"And it was during these conversations when your friend was in jail that the two of you came up with the idea to fabricate a story that would get him out of jail!" Steel shouted.

"We never talked about the case because we thought someone might be listening," said Skyers.

Steel asked, "At any time did you have a conversation, either in person or on the phone, with my client, Sidney Dorsey, having to do with the murder of Derwin Brown?"

"No. I never met Sidney Dorsey personally, or talked with Sidney Dorsey. Cuffy always relayed the messages from Dorsey to us," Skyers replied.

After Skyers was cross-examined, two witnesses from the DeKalb County Sheriff's Department testified that Dorsey requested preferential treatment for Ramsey, Skyers, and Walker prior to the murder. Jerry Keefer in the human resources department said that in fall 2000, Dorsey ordered him to hire Ramsey and Skyers as deputies even though Keefer did not believe they were qualified. Keefer intentionally delayed hiring them since Dorsey was only going to be in office a few more months.

Officer Skandrett, who was director of training for the sheriff's department, told the jury that in October 2000, Dorsey ordered him to fast-track Walker into "mandate school," even though Walker was not qualified and other qualified deputy sheriffs were ahead of him. This training is required in order for deputy sheriffs to be certified as law enforcement officers with powers to arrest, search, and seize evidence. However, Walker was not admitted into mandate school.

Shawn called Bernadette Davy, the GBI firearms examiner to the stand. Of all the lawyers on our team, Shawn knew the most about guns. Her husband, an FBI agent, made sure of that.

Ms. Davy explained to the jury that the hammer of a gun—the part of a gun that strikes the cartridge that houses the bullet—leaves a unique "fingerprint" on the cartridge. Davy had a semiautomatic weapon to demonstrate to the jury the various parts of the gun and how they work together. Davy explained that she was given sixteen cartridges (which she used interchangeably with the term shell casings) that came from the crime scene where Derwin Brown was killed.

Shawn asked, "Ms. Davy, did you examine the sixteen cartridges, and if so, what were your findings?"

"Using a comparison microscope, I examined the sixteen cartridges and determined they were all fired from the same weapon," testified Davy. "Furthermore, based on my knowledge and expertise of firearms, I was able to conclude that the weapon used was either an Intratec, AA Arms, or Feather Industries 9mm pistol."

"Did you examine any bullets related to the murder of Derwin Brown?" asked Shawn.

"Yes. I received eight bullets from the medical examiner's office for examination. When a bullet is fired from a weapon, it spins as it moves through the barrel. These turns leave microscopic markings on the bullet, visible under a microscope. Every bullet fired from that weapon will have identical markings. I determined that the eight bullets were fired from the same gun."

Shawn handed Ms. Davy the gun from the storm drain. She asked Ms. Davy, "Were you able to match the cartridges or the bullets with a particular gun?"

"No," she said. "The only weapon given to me for comparison purposes is the weapon you just handed me, and it was too damaged to conduct a test firing."

"Can you determine the type and manufacturer of the weapon I just handed you?" asked Shawn.

"This gun is a semiautomatic Intratec 9mm pistol," said Ms. Davy.

There were no questions from the defense.

That evening the prosecution team was having dinner at a local restaurant when Shawn quipped, "Anyone else notice anything strange about Dorsey's hair?"

"Huh, what do you mean by strange?" I asked.

"It looks like it slides down and to the left as the day moves on," she said.

"I don't get it. How could it do that?"

"J.Tom, you are so clueless at times. I bet he is wearing a hairpiece," Carol said. I admitted I had known Dorsey for years and never imagined that it was not his real hair.

"Ask the deputy who escorts Dorsey into court if he knows what is happening with Dorsey's hair," I directed Shawn.

The next morning, I saw Shawn talking to the deputy before court resumed. After speaking with the deputy, Shawn came over and said, "The deputy told me that Dorsey wears a wig, but the glue that holds the wig to the scalp is contraband in the jail. He is trying to keep the wig attached to his head with toothpaste. The deputy said Dorsey is as bald as a bowling ball."

Our last two witnesses were family members. We knew their testimony would be emotional and impactful. I called Robert Brown, Derwin's son who had been eighteen at the time of the murder, to testify. I met Robert for the first time as we were preparing for trial. All my communications with the family had been with Phyllis, and sometimes Brandy when she accompanied her mother. I remembered how heart-broken Robert had been when he spoke at his dad's funeral. When I finally met him during trial preparation, I told him his eulogy was remarkable.

Robert told the jury he had just graduated from high school the spring before the murder and was still living at home. He said, "My father came home around ten. I could see him through the family room door. He got out of the car and was walking up the driveway, smiling, with shopping bags in his hands. Then he left my field of vision. I heard like 'pow, pow.' It sounded like firecrackers. I was wondering who was popping firecrackers so close to the house. Then I heard rapid fire and my mother yelling for all of us to get down. I ran to get my dad's handgun, but I could not find it. I grabbed a machete.

"Uncle Crowder told me not to go out there, but I did. I started calling my daddy's name, but I didn't get a reply. Then I saw him lying on the ground. My mother had already been outside, and she was calling 911. I checked my daddy for a pulse, but I could not find one. I slapped him, slapped him, slapped him across the face, thinking I could get him to move, but he just lay there."

"Your witness," I said to the defense.

Steel was very cordial and sympathetic to the son and asked him only a few questions about the distance from his home to the MVP restaurant. Robert said it was about five minutes by car.

I called the last witness for the prosecution: Derwin's widow, Phyllis Brown. She seemed very frail as she climbed the steps to the witness chair. I walked her through her life with her husband and how she supported his campaigns for sheriff. Then I turned her attention to the night of the murder. "Please tell the jury what happened after you got home on the night of December 15, 2000," I said.

She summoned strength from somewhere deep inside her and said, "I left the celebration early at MVP. I wanted to surprise Derwin with the new uniform he would wear for his swearing in. I hung the uniform on the door so that it would be the first thing he saw when he walked into the house.

"It was dark, and it was raining. I heard what sounded first like firecrackers. I realized after two pops it was gunfire, and I thought it was coming from the neighbor's house. I told everyone to get down. I peeked through the blinds and I could see Derwin's car. I ran to the family room expecting him to walk through the door. I opened the door and called his name, but there was no answer. Crowder told me not to go outside, but I walked out and looked to my left and Derwin was lying there. His head was at the top of the steps. He almost made it inside.

"I knelt and looked into his eyes, and I knew he was gone. There was a trickle of blood coming out of his mouth. I still had the cordless phone in my hand. I told the operator, 'Captain Brown has been shot.' The ambulance came and took him to the hospital. My daughter and son-in-law drove me to the hospital."

"Ms. Brown, prior to your husband's murder, had you ever met Sidney Dorsey?" I asked.

"Yes. We spoke on several occasions," she said.

"After your husband's murder, did Sidney Dorsey ever call you or write to you to express his condolences for the loss of your husband?" I spoke slowly so the jury could digest every word.

"No. He never expressed any condolences whatsoever," replied the widow.

"Thank you very much, Ms. Brown," I concluded.

There were no questions from the defense.

I let Judge Becker know the state rested our case.

Though we had presented all our evidence on the RICO and murder counts, we had one more thing to do before the defense presented its case: to address the defendant's motion to dismiss the RICO counts. John Floyd, who sat patiently and watched almost three weeks of trial from the bench behind the counsel table, was now front and center. Judge Becker excused the jury so she could hear arguments from both sides regarding the defendant's motion.

Samuel argued that the facts did not support a RICO indictment, and the Georgia legislature never intended for it to be used against a politician for acts done while in office. Floyd, the nation's expert on RICO, walked Judge Becker through the history of RICO charges from the Nixon administration to the present. He said that nothing in the federal or state laws prohibited a prosecutor from charging a corrupt politician with RICO, although this case was a first in Georgia.

Judge Becker faced a tough decision. If she threw out the charges, no prosecutor would try to charge a politician again under RICO. If she allowed the charges to go forward and there was a RICO conviction, it could open the doors for similar prosecutions by other district attorneys. After hearing arguments from both sides, Judge Becker decided from the bench not to dismiss the RICO charges and ruled that the jury would decide whether Sidney Dorsey was guilty of RICO violations.

***

Now it was the defense's turn to present evidence. Everyone was wondering the same thing: Would Dorsey testify in his own defense? If he did, we were ready. I told Clegg months earlier that I needed him to prepare to cross-examine Dorsey. Of all the lawyers I had seen cross-examine defendants in my career, Clegg was the best. He had an unassuming, nonconfrontational manner when he questioned a defendant. He never raised his voice, and several times during questioning, he would tell the defendant, "I am sorry. I have a hard time hearing [which was true]. Could you please repeat your answer?" Conveniently, every time Clegg asked a defendant to repeat an answer, it was a response that Clegg wanted the jury to hear twice. I have seen Clegg lead many defendants to their convictions with their own words.

Clegg told me he'd prepared two hundred questions to ask Dorsey if he chose to take the stand, and those were just for starters. But Dorsey decided to keep his mouth shut. The law makes it clear that the decision to testify is solely the defendant's. Outside the jury's presence, Judge Becker told Dorsey to stand.

"Mr. Dorsey," Judge Becker addressed the defendant. "Your attorneys have told me that you have decided to exercise your Fifth Amendment right and not testify on your own behalf. Is that correct?"

"Yes, Your Honor," Dorsey replied.

"Do you understand that if you choose not to testify, that fact cannot be used against you, and that I will instruct the jury that they cannot consider your failure to testify as evidence against you?" asked Judge Becker.

"Yes, Your Honor," Dorsey again replied.

"Very well. You may be seated," she told him. "Let the record reflect that the defendant has been advised of his Fifth Amendment right not to testify and that he has chosen to exercise that right."

I knew this decision had to be difficult for Dorsey and the defense team. Dorsey was charismatic and persuasive and would have made a good witness. However, Clegg had a reputation as an excellent cross-examiner, and I made sure early in the trial that the defense attorneys knew Clegg would assume that role in this trial. Also, Walker and Ramsey did not testify in the previous trial, and their silence certainly did not hurt them.

Once Dorsey sat down and the jury had returned to the courtroom, Steel stood up and in his loud voice said, "If that's the State's case, Your Honor, we rest," and he sat down. After almost three weeks of trial testimony, the defense presented no evidence to the jury. Defendants in criminal cases often do not present evidence at trial. The burden is on the prosecution to prove guilt beyond a reasonable doubt. Now both the prosecution and the defense had rested their cases.

Because of the July 4 holiday, Judge Becker recessed the jury on Wednesday, July 3, 2002, and instructed that closing arguments would begin on Monday morning, July 8, 2002.

CHAPTER 22

"Ladies and gentlemen of the jury, on behalf of the citizens of DeKalb County, I want to thank you for your service. You were called upon to render a verdict for a crime that did not even occur in your county. However, you have been constantly attentive and patient with us during this trial, and there is nothing more that our criminal justice system can ask you other than your verdict speak the truth. In fact, the word 'verdict' is derived from the Latin term for truth."

I was alone; my "courtroom" was the Snuffy Smith Cabin. No jury was present, unless you count the assortment of taxidermied creatures surrounding me. Instead of a suit and tie, I wore a polo shirt with the district attorney badge embroidered on the front, khaki shorts, and tennis shoes with no socks.

Petrey and I spent the time the jury was recessed between July 3 and July 8 practicing our closing arguments. On Sunday, our final day to prepare, Petrey volunteered to practice on the dock at the pond behind the cabin. I ran through several practice sessions inside.

The closing argument I'd built focused on the direct evidence of Cuffy's testimony, since he'd received orders personally from Dorsey. The circumstantial evidence I'd draw on included testimony from the medical examiner; from Paul Skyers, the other coconspirator who'd been granted immunity, but had not spoken to Dorsey; as well as from Clarence Mosley and Shirley McMichael, both of whom said that Dorsey told them Derwin would not be around to take office.

I had already practiced my closing out loud many times, memorizing every word. I recorded and listened to these practice sessions and made adjustments: slowing down and pacing myself, emphasizing certain words, clarifying some of the substantive points, and being mindful of my gestures. On this Sunday, I did three more run-throughs and timed myself at fifty-seven minutes for each one. The extra three minutes gave me time to address any defense arguments.

After hours of listening to myself talk, I decided I'd had enough. I grabbed a Budweiser from the refrigerator and walked out onto the front porch. The evening was warm but not uncomfortable, surprising since the heat and humidity can be downright miserable in a South Georgia summer. As I looked out on the field of grain where dove hunters would be walking in the fall, I had a sudden realization; I'd go so far as to call it an epiphany. The next day I'd be giving the most consequential and scrutinized speech of my life, and I would be doing so because of a teacher.

In seventh grade, I knew I wanted to be a lawyer after reading Harper Lee's *To Kill a Mockingbird* and watching Gregory Peck play Atticus Finch in the movie. However, I had what seemed like an impossible obstacle to overcome: stage fright. When I ran for president of the seventh grade and gave a speech to the entire class, I fainted. Not surprisingly, I was not elected.

During an eighth-grade English class, the teacher assigned me to stand before the class and read the poem "If—," by Rudyard Kipling, which is about becoming a man. I tried to read, but no words could escape my mouth—not one. I was petrified. If this was what becoming a man required, I was doomed to an eternal childhood. So much for a career in a courtroom.

The next year, I was fortunate to have Joanne Stripling for homeroom and English. She told the class we would be studying Shakespeare, and one of our assignments would be to memorize various passages and recite them before the entire class. After class that day, I told Mrs. Stripling, "I don't think my memory can hold all of those words, and I'm sure I can never repeat them in front of my classmates." She told me, "Come back after school, and I will teach you how to memorize passages."

Mrs. Stripling was young, probably not long out of college, tall, with long brown hair falling over her shoulders. She was a dynamic teacher who enunciated her words clearly and loudly, and commanded respect from her students. In our afternoon sessions, Mrs. Stripling taught me to "memorize the first line of a passage, recite that line from memory; memorize the second line, recite both lines together; and continue until you've memorized and can recite the entire passage without looking at a note."

Passages from *Hamlet*, *As You Like It*, and *Romeo and Juliet* ("Ah, what light through yonder window breaks. It is the east, Juliet is the sun!") will forever be etched in the recesses of my brain. I might forget the name of someone I met yesterday, but I will never forget the lines Mrs. Stripling had me memorize and recite before the classroom. I discovered, thanks to Mrs. Stripling, I no longer had stage fright when I recited lines from memory.

By the time of the Dorsey trial, I'd given countless speeches from memory, including all of my closing arguments to juries. Tomorrow would be the culmination of my work and her guidance. *Mrs. Stripling*, I thought, *this Bud's for you*.

I could still hear Petrey's voice behind the cabin. I walked to the pond slowly and quietly so as not to disturb him. As I drew near, I caught sight of him standing on the dock, facing the water in his T-shirt, shorts, and Birkenstocks. Tall and slim with his glasses perched on the end of his nose and his hair a little disheveled, Petrey was delivering a persuasive argument to what appeared to be an empty pond. Across from the dock, though, I spotted the gray snout and black eyes of an alligator intently watching Petrey's argument, the rest of the animal still and immersed in the water. The sun was shining from that direction; due to the light and his terrible eyesight, Petrey couldn't see the alligator. That old gator was the most attentive juror he had ever addressed.

***

The next morning, Monday, July 8, 2002, closing arguments began. I dressed as my grandmother's friend suggested, in a dark suit with an American flag on the lapel, a white starched shirt, and a red tie decorated with small blue triangles. The courtroom was packed, with people standing in the back. Phyllis and Brandy sat a few rows behind the prosecution table, as they had every day of the trial.

Under Georgia law, the prosecution has the right to open and conclude the closing arguments. Petrey would open to address the RICO charges, and before I concluded with the Count One murder charge, the defense attorneys would make their equivalent arguments sandwiched between the two of us.

Petrey was classic Petrey, methodically making a complicated subject—in this case RICO—simple to understand. He took all the various components of the evidence, testimonial and documentary, and showed the jury why the crime of RICO was proven beyond a reasonable doubt. Petrey's demeanor was not theatrical; he didn't slam a podium or throw things on the floor. Yet his words and body language conveyed his outrage at Dorsey's actions, telling the jury in clear and colorful terms:

"[Dorsey] turned the sheriff's department into a personal chauffeuring, babysitting, Lexus/Mercedes/limousine-repairing, go-kart-toting, door-unlocking, Happy Meal–fetching, bribery-infested, scandal-ridden organization that crushed the pride and the morale of the good men and women who worked there.

"The defense told you in his opening statement that the corruption case against Sidney Dorsey was the last-ditch effort to bolster the murder case. That is absolutely, incontrovertibly ridiculous. The reason for that is the corruption case had begun almost six months before Derwin Brown was assassinated. District attorney J.Tom Morgan notified the defendant's attorneys a month before Derwin Brown was assassinated that he was considering a special grand jury to investigate the bribery and theft charges.

"Sidney Dorsey stole that election from a man who had the courage to stand up and say I'm going to clean up the cesspool that Sidney Dorsey created. By 2000, the gravy train was derailed. Sidney Dorsey, you heard, was losing the Citizens Trust Bank contract, he was losing the power to have sex with women who dared not refuse him, he was losing the power to line his pocket with bribes, he was losing the power to use the people and the property of DeKalb County as his own, as though he were some medieval warlord. The assassination of Derwin Brown was a desperate move by a panicking man whose fool's paradise was being snatched out beneath him."

Don Samuel led off the defense team's closing arguments, addressing the RICO charges. With a scruffy beard and a mischievous smile, Samuel has a disarming and nonthreatening style. Using a calm and conversational approach, he gave a thorough, detailed, thoughtful, and unemotional analysis of why Dorsey was not guilty of corruption.

"The decision that you will make here, whether it's today, tomorrow, or however long it takes, the decision you will make will be one of the most important decisions that you will ever make in your life.

"You know you can always sell a house. If you have to, you can divorce your spouse. Those decisions can be changed. But the decision in a murder case, the decision about what to do with the terminally ill member of your family, those decisions are irreparable. And that is why the decision you will make in the jury deliberations room will be one of the most important decisions of your life. And that's why the judge will tell you, when we finish with arguments, that before you make this decision, before you can find any human being in this country guilty of a crime, any crime, you must be convinced of the person's guilt, beyond reasonable doubt.

"Beyond reasonable doubt needs proof of such a convincing character, the formation is so strong and compelling that you don't hesitate in making your decision, that your mind is not wavering at all about the correctness of the decision you are about to make. Proof of such a convincing character that you would be willing to rely on it, at the time, for your most important affairs without wavering, without question, the decision is that clear. I suggest to you that the information you've heard in this courtroom from the witnesses presented by the state is not sufficient. You would not buy a house based upon this information; you would not make a decision about a terminally ill member of your family; you wouldn't even choose a flavor of ice cream based on the quality of the information that the state has presented to you."

Like Petrey, Samuel presented his case with cerebral aplomb, arguing that his client was only guilty of bad judgment, not criminal behavior. He blamed other people in the sheriff's office and hammered the point that the sexual relationship between Dorsey and Shirley McMichael was consensual and had nothing to do with bribery. He emphasized that McMichael had not been truthful with Fred and me about the true nature of her relationship with Dorsey, and therefore none of her testimony was trustworthy. Samuel took his full hour and not once raised his voice.

***

Then it was showtime: Murder, Count One. Brian Steel, who had a runner's physique and close-cropped hair, went next. I was sure Steel and I would give the jury the forceful and emotional closing arguments they expected from watching TV. We had plenty of material—this was about the assassination of an elected official.

What Samuel lacked in stridency, Steel made up for; he was loud and argumentative. Although the podium in front of the jury was a few feet from where I was sitting, I felt like he was screaming in my ear. He repeatedly told the jury not to be duped by the likes of Patrick Cuffy and Paul Skyers.

"How dare they! How dare they!" Steel yelled, working himself up with righteous indignation. "There is no evidence that Sidney Dorsey is involved. And they are telling a murderer, 'We know you are involved, but you can walk out of here if you just say the name Sidney Dorsey.'

Read this immunity agreement. It states that if Cuffy and Skyers are not truthful, if they don't fully cooperate, their immunity can be ripped away from them and they can be prosecuted for the murder of Derwin Brown.

"Twelve people in DeKalb County unanimously said, 'Rip the immunity agreement away from the State of Georgia.' Make it twenty-four to nothing. Make it twenty-four to nothing! This is wrong! This is wrong! Make North Georgia and South Georgia come together in unison and find Sidney Dorsey not guilty."

"They" clearly referred to us, the prosecution team. While Steel did not actually point his finger at me for making a deal with the devil, he was implying exactly that. When he finished, Judge Becker gave the jury a fifteen-minute recess before I gave the final murder argument. I needed the time, too, to take a deep breath and clear the air of Steel's heated words before I began.

I'd delivered over one hundred closing arguments, but I had never experienced a sensation like I did that afternoon. When I stood up to face the jury, I felt a magic bubble envelop me and those twelve people, sealing us from the outside world. Gone were the cameras, reporters, spectators, lawyers, deputies, judge, and defendant. Gone was the weight of the moment, what it meant to stand in a courthouse in Albany, minutes from my childhood home, arguing the case of my lifetime. I began talking to them as if they were sitting in my living room, and I needed to tell them something important.

"Ladies and gentlemen of the jury," I began, just as I'd rehearsed and memorized it, leading into, "there is nothing more that our criminal justice system can ask you other than your verdict speak the truth. In fact, the word 'verdict' is derived from the Latin term for truth.

"Mr. Hodges told you in his opening statement that this case was about the culture of corruption in the DeKalb County Sheriff's Department, which culminated in the assassination of Derwin Brown, the sheriff-elect. Mr. Petrey just explained to you why Sidney Dorsey was criminally responsible for that culture of corruption. And now it is my job to show you that Sidney Dorsey is guilty beyond a reasonable doubt of the assassination of Derwin Brown."

I didn't read from notes during my closing; none of the other lawyers did either. But from this point forward I relied on the new tactic I'd come up with weeks earlier for presenting the evidence. This idea was the one Petrey jumped all over, saying its demise could serve as a *Saturday Night Live* skit. But Chris and the graphic artist he'd worked with in Atlanta had realized my presentational idea, just as I'd hoped—even better than I'd expected. I turned to an easel holding a very large board, about five feet high and four feet wide. It sat just a few feet from the jury, but at this point they could see nothing except some seams crisscrossing the board's surface. The seams corresponded to magnetized pieces of black vinyl. In the middle of the board was a piece of vinyl much bigger than the other pieces. Fourteen smaller pieces of vinyl surrounded it, with seven pieces running up the left side and seven pieces running down the right side. I'd distilled my argument to fourteen evidentiary points.

As I discussed each of the following evidentiary points, I removed the vinyl piece that corresponded to the evidentiary point with words in black print on a yellow background.

• *Clarence Mosley, Chief of Staff*

"'Derwin Brown will not take office, and I will win in the special election'—said to whom? Clarence Mosley. Clarence Mosley is the confidant of Sidney Dorsey. He is then Sidney Dorsey's chief deputy." I noted that this conversation between Dorsey and Mosley took place after Dorsey's election defeat but before Derwin's murder. I also pointed out that Mosley had a subsequent conversation with Dorsey in March 2001 after the murder. When Dorsey tried to get Mosley to remember a different version of their prior conversation, Mosley was concerned enough to meet with me.

• *Shirley McMichael*

"After the election defeat, before the murder, Ms. McMichael was having lunch in Atlanta with the defendant Dorsey. She asked him what is going to happen now. And he said, 'Derwin Brown will not be around to take office, and I will win the special election.' Isn't it amazing that Mosley and McMichael say almost identically the same things? And she says, 'Well, why won't Derwin be around to take office?' And he puts his finger to his head and pulls the trigger. Now, you say, well, why didn't Ms. McMichael tell someone? She did, remember, she told Special Agent Fred Mays before the murder took place. And what did Agent Mays tell you? 'I just brushed it off; I didn't think Dorsey was serious.' We can't fault Fred Mays; just like the FBI agents who maybe should have paid closer attention to the September 11 warnings, no one, including Agent Mays, could ever have imagined that something as horrific as the murder of a sheriff-elect would ever take place."

I peeled the third piece of vinyl on the left side, revealing the name of a key witness.

• *Patrick Cuffy*

"Who was called on to do the deed? None other than Patrick Cuffy. If Patrick Cuffy is a monster, he is a monster of Sidney Dorsey's own creation. He mentored him, he hired him, and he gave him the tools to do the dirty work. Cuffy was transferred to community relations for one reason, to help plan the murder. My goodness. Who would have put Patrick Cuffy with children, who would have put Patrick Cuffy as an ambassador for the DeKalb County Sheriff's Department? That was absolutely a ridiculous idea unless you had another motive in mind. And that motive was to plan the murder of the sheriff-elect."

• *Three More Conspirators*

"Three more conspirators are added. Melvin Walker, David Ramsey, Paul Skyers, all of whom had worked for Sidney Dorsey before. Why call upon these people? He knew them, he could trust them, he had something on them, he could offer them something in return." I reminded the jury of another famous elected official who, when he wanted to commit a felony against a political opponent, called in the people closest to him, his political insiders, to do his bidding: Richard Nixon.

I told the jury that any person who aids, abets, encourages, or solicits another to commit a crime is guilty of the entire crime, regardless of the person's role. I said, "Osama bin Laden may not have been flying those planes into the World Trade Center or the Pentagon or in that Pennsylvania cornfield, but he is just as guilty as the pilots who did. If you find that Sidney Dorsey encouraged, aided, or abetted the murder of Derwin Brown, then he is guilty of the murder." I saw a juror nod in understanding.

I discussed the testimony of third parties that corroborated how Cuffy, Walker, Ramsey, and Skyers worked together: Cuffy and Walker speaking to school resource officers at a DeKalb County park when Ramsey and Skyers were hiding in the bushes, Ramsey's attempted purchase of a TEC-9 from a friend, police surveillance of Cuffy's and Ramsey's 2:30 a.m. drive after the murder, Cuffy telling a girlfriend at 4:00 a.m. after the murder that he needed to go get Ramsey, and Ramsey's return of the metal detector to Radio Shack after the murder.

I reviewed the law on conspiracy. "If you are involved in a conspiracy, the planning stage of it, the actual crime itself, the concealment stage, all of that, even if you don't know what the other conspirators are doing, as long as they are about the purpose of the conspiracy—here, the purpose is to kill Derwin Brown—then all are guilty of a conspiracy."

- *Paul Skyers*

I told the jury that we needed corroboration of Patrick Cuffy's statement after we spoke with him. The logical person was another conspirator who wasn't the triggerman or the instigator—Paul Skyers—who gave a statement that corroborated Cuffy without speaking to Cuffy beforehand. "Once these two men started talking, the dominos started falling, pieces of the puzzle started fitting together.

"There's been a lot of talk about the immunity agreement for Cuffy and Skyers. It is a reality of our criminal justice system—no one likes to deal with criminals, certainly when they are murderers. But if you are prosecuting the Mafia, if you are prosecuting the Klan, it doesn't matter; if it's a corrupt criminal organization, you've got to have someone on the inside willing to talk. And people don't talk about murder unless you have something to give them in return." I pointed out that in this case, Cuffy and Skyers only received immunity if they were truthful; if they were caught in a lie, we could use statements made against them and seek the death penalty for the murder.

- *Glen Haven Elementary School*

I reminded the jury about the school resource officer who testified he saw a car late one evening at Glen Haven Elementary School near Derwin's residence. "He goes to check on the car, Cuffy gets out of the car some distance away, there are two or three people in the car, one with maybe braids or dreads, Cuffy dressed all in black, without any identification, and he gets Sidney Dorsey on the phone, someone who the school resource officer knows. And Dorsey, at 9:46 on a Saturday night, at a closed elementary school, says, 'Patrick Cuffy is on special detail for me.'"

- *Fast-Track Hirings of Ramsey and Skyers*

I reviewed the testimony of the head of human resources, Jerry Keefer. "Before the murder, Keefer gets a phone call from his boss: 'Come up to my office.' He goes up there. And who does Dorsey say hire? Skyers and Ramsey. Only those two people. Keefer says they are totally unqualified, they do not meet the minimum requirements, they have no business in the sheriff's department, but the sheriff orders him to fast-track these people and get them on board now."

- *Fast-Track Training for Walker*

I noted that Walker, who had been promoted to deputy sheriff, had not received mandate, or certification, training, which would allow him to have full law enforcement powers. Dorsey ordered Walker to receive this training in October 2000. "Officer Skandrett says, 'Wait a second, this guy is not qualified, there are people ahead of him who meet the qualifications who are waiting in line, and it's five days before mandate school starts. Sheriff, this is not the right thing to do.' And Dorsey tells him, 'What part of my request do you not understand? I'll handle it myself.'"

- *Walker at Dorsey's House*

"After the murder, Walker is seen at Dorsey's residence by Roy Baker."

- *Meeting at Apartment Complex*

In addition, I pointed out that after the murder, an off-duty DeKalb County deputy sheriff who was providing security at an apartment complex testified that he recognized Dorsey, Cuffy, and Walker having a private conversation late at night in the parking lot of the complex.

- *Meeting at Lawyer's Office after Shoot-out at Cuffy's House*

I recounted the evidence that just a few days after the shoot-out at Cuffy's house, a meeting occurred at Dorsey's lawyer's office. "Dorsey is worried about Cuffy, who's just been arrested on a misdemeanor. And who is invited to the lawyer's office representing Sidney Dorsey at that time? Not just any Joe Blow, not just any member of the sheriff's department—amazingly enough, it's the four people who at Dorsey's orders directed the murder: Walker, Skyers, Ramsey, and Cuffy."

- *Meeting at the Ritz-Carlton*

"Who arranges the dinner party at the Ritz-Carlton? Sidney Dorsey. Using the reporter Mary Fischer from *GQ* magazine as sort of a pawn that gets these people together. Why? Dorsey wants to meet with Cuffy, but he wants to meet privately. He doesn't want to be seen with these people. Remember he is a homicide detective; he doesn't want to be seen with the people that he ordered to direct this murder. Dorsey is worried about how Cuffy is holding up. And Cuffy tells him, 'I am going to take it to my grave. You don't have to worry about it.'"

• *Mary Fischer's Room*

I reminded the jury: No one disputes that the dinner meeting at the Ritz-Carlton or the private meeting between Dorsey and Cuffy in Mary Fischer's room took place.

The last piece of vinyl that I removed revealed a gripping piece of evidence.

• *Dorsey's Own Words*

"The most telling words of this case, the most telling words of this trial, come from the defendant himself." I then played the tape of the conversation Fred Mays had secretly recorded during his interview with Dorsey regarding the corruption probe before Derwin was assassinated. For the first time the jury, and the courtroom, heard Dorsey's venomous voice:

"I don't know what they promised Brown, or what Brown promised them, but that is the lowest son of a bitch, and I have never cursed in my life in this building, but he is the lowest scumbag I have seen in my life! He is awful! He is awful! You don't know. He'll stop at nothing."

You could hear and feel the hatred Dorsey had for Derwin in that recording. When I switched off the tape, the courtroom was eerily silent.

There was only one magnet left, in the center of the board. I pulled off the final large magnet, revealing Dorsey's book-in picture—his mugshot—when he was arrested on the murder charge.

I looked directly at the jury and said, "The only person who had the motive to kill Derwin Brown is none other than Sidney Dorsey himself. Why? You can imagine the agony of defeat on August 8, 2000. Sidney Dorsey was about to lose power. Power to order people to do his personal tasks at his bidding. Power to order sheriff's employees to perform at his private security firm. Power to control the bonding business of DeKalb County and to take bribes. Power to control the $51 million budget."

It was now time for me, standing close to the front of the jury box, but not so close as to invade their space, to give the final minutes of argument that I had so carefully rehearsed.

"Mr. Hodges said in his opening, this case is about power and one man's total obsession with power and what he will do to keep power at all costs. Ladies and gentlemen, this story is as old as the Bible, as old as Cain and Abel. Abraham Lincoln had these words to say about power: 'Nearly all men can stand adversity, but if you really want to test a man's character, give him power.'

"There was a coercive culture of corruption in the DeKalb County Sheriff's Department from 1997 to the year 2000. We, the citizens of DeKalb County, are here to ask you, the citizens of Dougherty County, for justice. For those of us who were growing up here in Albany in 1961, we remember a significant event that summer. As a small child, standing on Slappey Drive, I thought I was watching a parade walk by. I did not realize I was watching history go down the street. At the end of that march in Kiokee Baptist Church, Dr. Martin Luther King Jr. said, 'If justice is not for everyone, then there can be no justice for anyone.' I repeated for emphasis, 'If justice is not for everyone, there can be no justice for anyone.'

"Ladies and gentlemen, there must be justice for the good men and women of the DeKalb County Sheriff's Department who were demeaned when they had to perform personal tasks for their boss, the sheriff.

"There must be justice for the taxpayers of DeKalb County who were robbed of the good work of their government employees when a corrupt sheriff had the government employees working in his private business.

"There must be justice for the citizens of DeKalb County who were denied their right to vote, their right to be represented by the sheriff of their choosing when a man was so consumed with power that he had the rightful sheriff assassinated.

"There must be justice for the family of Derwin Brown: for Phyllis Brown, who lost a loving and caring husband of twenty-three years; for the Brown children, who lost a caring father; for the Brown grandchildren, who lost a devoted grandfather; for Derwin's mama, who lost a son.

"And finally, ladies and gentlemen, there must be justice for Derwin Brown, a man who saw wrong and tried to right it; a man who was not scared to take on the unbeatable foe, but paid the ultimate price for having done so; a man who challenged corruption with honesty and integrity and, three days before he was to take office as sheriff, was viciously gunned down in his front yard while his family waited for him inside their home.

"He was gunned down because one man who had taken an oath to uphold the law broke that law. Because one man was so consumed with power that he could not give it up.

"Ladies and gentlemen, justice demands a verdict of guilty on each and every count in this case. Thank you very much."

CHAPTER 23

On Monday afternoon, July 8, 2002, the jurors listened attentively as Judge Becker took over an hour to give them instructions about the law and their responsibility to apply the evidence presented during the trial to the law. She also read the fifteen counts in the indictment, told the jurors to consider each count separately, and emphasized that the defendant could only be found guilty on any count if all twelve jurors determined guilt beyond a reasonable doubt.

"A defendant is presumed innocent and is not required to produce evidence of the defendant's innocence," Judge Becker noted. "The state is required to prove beyond a reasonable doubt each and every element of the charges against the defendant. If the state fails to meet its burden of proof, it is the duty of the jury to acquit the defendant of the charges. This principle is the bedrock of our system of criminal justice in the United States."

The jury deliberated a few hours without reaching a verdict, which was not unexpected. The jury had heard almost three weeks of testimony from over sixty witnesses. This case was complicated—actually, two cases wrapped into one trial—a murder case and a corruption case involving a public official. A quick verdict does not usually bode well for the prosecution, at least in my experience. Judge Becker released the jury at 7:00 p.m. so they could go to dinner and their respective hotel rooms before resuming deliberations the next morning.

Judge Becker decided to sequester the jury during deliberations until they reached a verdict. This precaution was extraordinary in a non–death penalty case; the law only mandates jury sequestration in death penalty cases. Judge Becker wanted to ensure that no outside influences could impact the verdict. Jurors were prohibited from all news sources or contact with family members until a verdict was reached. They were under the close watchful eyes of sheriffs' deputies.

That evening, the prosecution team and I ate dinner together at a crowded steakhouse in Albany. We were still on pins and needles, but at this point we had done all we could do. As we were finishing, our server handed me a note that read, "J.Tom, thank you for picking up the tab. Patrick Cuffy." I thought, *What the hell!* I stood up to look around the restaurant. In the corner, Brian Steel and Don Samuel were laughing uncontrollably. At Roz's prodding, I put the note in my mouth and ate it.

The jury continued to deliberate all day Tuesday, again without reaching a verdict. Ken allowed the prosecution team to wait in his conference room while the jury deliberated. The tension in the room was palpable, so we took turns leaving the room to take walks around the town. Three blocks from the courthouse, I walked past the Albany Theater, where community plays and musical events are performed. My grandfather, who died before I was born, was a stonemason and helped lay the foundation for the building in 1927. I thought how rewarding it must be to help build something that will serve future generations.

I found a chance to slip away Tuesday evening and visit Sybil Thomas, my music teacher when I was in high school. Sybil had the distinction of being the first Black person from Albany to graduate from The Juilliard School in New York. She was also an activist; she helped organize the sit-ins at a Woolworth's lunch counter in Greensboro, North Carolina, in 1960.

Sybil said that she had not been able to see the trial for herself, but she was reading about it each day in the local paper. She said the "street committee" informed her that our team had done a good job putting up a case against Dorsey.

Before the Black community had universal access to telephones, newspapers, or radio stations in Albany, the news traveled within the

Black community via the "street committee." The name was derived from the ways that important information was passed: before and after church services, over fence posts, at the Laundromat, and riding the bus to and from work. Most of the shared information during the Civil Rights Movement was via street committees. Although times had changed, I was not surprised news still traveled that way in Albany's Black community.

On Wednesday morning, July 10, 2002, the jurors sent Judge Becker a note that read, "We have reached a verdict on all counts, but for one count. We are hopelessly deadlocked ten-two on that count." Judge Becker called the prosecution and defense teams to the courtroom to review the note. Even though the jurors did not identify which count, everyone suspected it had to be the murder count. But which way? Was it ten to convict for murder? Or was it ten to acquit Dorsey of murder? My experience with the mock jury in Augusta told me it could go either way. Judge Becker ordered the jury to continue their deliberations and to make every effort and try their best to reach a unanimous verdict on all counts.

Three hours later, the jury sent Judge Becker a note stating they had reached a verdict on all counts. What I now know is that, as we suspected, the jurors had been deadlocked on the murder count. After the jurors received Judge Becker's note asking them to try their best to reach a unanimous verdict, the jury foreman, the only man on the jury, told all the jurors to hold hands in prayer. The foreman prayed out loud and asked God to give all the jurors direction to reach a just and true verdict. The jurors once again, without signing their names, wrote their verdict on a piece of paper and handed the paper to the foreman. This time they were unanimous on the murder count.

For the last time, the jurors filed back into the jury box in the Dougherty County Courthouse. Judge Becker directed her gaze and voice to the jury. "Mr. Foreman, please rise. Has the jury reached a verdict?"

"Yes, Your Honor," said the sole male on the jury.

"Please hand your verdict to the deputy," she said. The deputy took the verdict form to Judge Becker, and she looked at the verdict.

"Mr. Morgan, Mr. Steel, please approach the bench to review the verdict," she ordered. Steel and I reviewed the verdict together. After we reviewed the verdict, she told Steel to sit down at counsel table and instructed me to read the verdict from the podium.

I stood at the podium and looked out at the courtroom, packed with stoic and silent people.

I then looked down at the verdict and began to read.

"We, the jury, find the defendant, Sidney Dorsey, on Count One, Murder, Guilty. Count Two, RICO, Guilty."

I continued to read the verdicts on the remaining thirteen counts in the indictment. Out of the total fifteen counts, Dorsey was found guilty on twelve counts. He was found not guilty on the two counts involving bribery and Shirley McMichael and on one count involving theft by taking for using employees in his campaign.

While reading the verdict, I could hear a faint sob in the courtroom. I looked up to see Phyllis gently crying with her hands covering her face. Before the verdict was read, Judge Becker had ordered everyone to refrain from outbursts in her courtroom, but I was sure she would not say anything to Phyllis.

After I finished reading the verdict, the defense asked that the jury be polled, a procedure in which each juror stands and is asked two questions by the judge: "Is this your verdict? Is it still your verdict?" Both answers must be in the affirmative. Each juror confirmed the verdict.

After the polling of the jury, Judge Becker announced that court was adjourned. Sentencing would take place in DeKalb County in two weeks. I confirmed with her before she left the bench that the gag order was no longer in effect. Before I entered the public seating area, I stopped to shake hands with Brian and Don. I told them their closing arguments were the best I had ever heard.

Phyllis was waiting for me on the wooden bench where she had sat the entire trial with her daughter Brandy. Derwin's mother was also there for the reading of the verdict. When I got to Phyllis, she fell into my arms sobbing out loud. My first thought was how frail and weak she had become since I first met her in the hospital on the night of Derwin's death. The next morning, the Albany paper ran a picture on the front page of Phyllis crying in my arms.

The world is one big circle. The courtroom where I took the oath to be a lawyer twenty-two years earlier was now the background for a picture that would be seen by thousands of people.

I walked through the front doors of the courthouse to a large crowd of reporters, with their cameras, notepads, and microphones, assembled in a large semicircle at the bottom of the courthouse steps. Other than when my impulsive mouth caused me to be fined by Judge Becker, I had not publicly spoken to a reporter since Dorsey was indicted.

I was prepared for the first question, which I knew would be on everyone's mind. "Why was this verdict different from the Walker and Ramsey verdict?"

"This was a very different case," I responded. "This case was about a corrupt sheriff who would stop at nothing, even murder, to remain in power. We could tie a corruption case with a motive for murder. We could not do that in the first trial."

I spoke with the reporters for over an hour, until they all finally left to report their stories, except for Dale Cardwell. We shook each other's hand. I knew there would be a later time when we could unpack the past eighteen months together. He said their companion radio station was still reporting live and asked if I would answer one last question for the evening. I agreed.

"J.Tom, the trial is over, what are you going to do now?" Dale asked.

"Dale, I am going to gather my Jimmy Buffett CDs, a six-pack of beer, and head to blue water," I said. That statement was replayed many times over the next twenty-four hours.

Meanwhile, my wife Carol was boarding a plane to Atlanta in Washington, DC, after a business trip when she heard other passengers excitedly exclaiming, "He's guilty!" She knew they had to be talking about the Dorsey trial, and she immediately called her mother in Decatur to confirm that Dorsey had indeed been convicted. John was standing at home in the living room with his fingers crossed watching me on live television, and when I read the verdicts, he was overcome with happiness. He then assumed the role of my personal answering service as hundreds of congratulatory calls poured in to our home phone. Caroline, who was attending an academic summer camp at Davidson College in North Carolina, was glued to the television and sobbed when she heard the verdict. My family finally felt a sense of relief. We could get on with our lives.

Ken had patiently been watching the news conference from behind the crowd so he could talk to me. With much relief, we gave each other a hug. Ken said, "J.Tom, I can't thank you enough for inviting me to join your party. What a ride!"

"We could not have done it without you," I responded. "Your opening statement was brilliant, and your mere presence gave credibility to our case."

"You are damn lucky," Ken said. "You were able to assemble a helluva team of great prosecutors and investigators to back us up."

"You are only as good as the people you hire," I said.

Fred Mays and I rode together one last time to the Snuffy Smith Cabin. I thanked him for everything he had done to help bring this case to a just conclusion. I told Fred his recording of Dorsey's voice before the murder was probably the deciding piece of evidence in the jury's verdict.

I have never met a prosecutor who celebrated wildly after a guilty verdict. The feeling is one of solemn gratitude—gratitude that justice prevailed. The same was true that evening. We did open a couple of bottles of champagne at the Snuffy Smith Cabin, and then we gathered as a group one last time at a local restaurant for dinner. We focused on the future and talked about what we were going to do when we got home, and where we were going on vacation, instead of the events of the past six weeks. We had lived it together. We knew we had experienced something extraordinary over the past eighteen months, and we needed time to process our thoughts and emotions.

Back at the cabin after dinner, Petrey and Chris said good night, and I made my last climb up the ladder into the widow's walk. I remembered that I had turned off my phone so we could eat in peace and enjoy the last evening together. I turned the phone back on to check messages.

The office was answering hundreds of calls, not just from Atlanta, but from people across the country who heard the verdict read on the major network channels. The staff at the district attorney's office in Decatur was trying to distinguish those calls that were personal—family, friends, and colleagues—from the general public's. They forwarded the personal messages to me so that I could respond in kind. I called the office answering machine on my flip phone to retrieve the messages; there were over one hundred calls. Both my phone and I were going to run out of energy before I could listen to them all.

The last call I listened to that evening was not from someone I knew. My assistant, however, believed I should hear it. I'm glad she did. The voice was that of a woman, a stranger to me, with the thickest of Southern accents:

> *Mr. J.Tom Morgan, you don't know me from a hill of beans. My name is Sonya and I am just a typical girl. I live in Gwinnett County. I am forty years old, and I drive a dump truck. But I want you to know that for the last year, I have learned more from watching you on this case. You very much impacted my life. I thought that the people would get away with killing Mr. Brown, and I hate to see his wife look so sad. So today, I sat in my dump truck and I listened to you read the verdict, and I was overwhelmed for you because I knew it was very important for*

> *you to win and I am very proud of you, and DeKalb citizens should be very proud also.*
>
> *I left a note with Diane Hill* [our receptionist], *and I want you to know that I mean it when I say I would rather meet you than meet Tom Cruise because you are a real man, and you are a good man. I want you to know that. I don't want you to call me back, but I want you to know that you are a smart man. Take care.*

The Georgia rain began pelting the tin roof above my head. A smile came to my lips, tears slid down my cheek, and I went soundly to sleep.

EPILOGUE

After a murder conviction, the defendant, the victim's family members, and the prosecution have the right to make statements before the judge pronounces the sentence. At the sentencing hearing for Dorsey on August 15, 2002, the prosecution declined to make a statement. Dorsey did so from the witness stand. However, he was now dressed in jail-issued inmate clothing. Maintaining his innocence, he said while raising his hands, "I do not have the blood of Derwin Brown on my hands." He also said he would "always be free" while in prison because he was innocent.

Phyllis Brown also made a statement. Seated in the witness box, she looked directly at the man who'd ordered her husband of almost twenty-four years killed. Even though the death penalty was off the table, she told him, "I will not ask anyone to take your life. What I wish for you is that every night when you go to sleep you have a picture of Derwin when you close your eyes—because that's all I have."

Judge Becker told Dorsey to stand. She then sentenced him to life in prison plus twenty-three years consecutive to the life sentence.

Dorsey's attorneys later appealed his convictions to the Georgia Supreme Court. John Floyd and Barbara Conroy from my office wrote the appellate brief for the state, and John gave the oral argument to the Georgia Supreme Court. The court upheld Dorsey's conviction on all counts without any dissents.

In 2007, five years after the trial, Sidney Dorsey admitted to a DeKalb County assistant district attorney that he was involved in the planning and murder of Derwin Brown, but claimed that he had attempted to call it off. He died in a Georgia prison in March 2026.

Melvin Walker and David Ramsey did not remain free for long. They were indicted by a federal grand jury in Atlanta in 2004 for depriving Derwin Brown of his civil rights by killing him, a federal crime. The protection against double jeopardy under the Fifth Amendment does not apply if a person is charged in both state and federal courts. Walker and Ramsey, who were tried and acquitted in state court, were both found guilty by a federal jury in 2005. They are serving life sentences without parole in federal prison.

Phyllis Brown died on Christmas Eve 2006, at age fifty-two, from complications of a stroke. She is buried next to her husband, Sheriff-elect Derwin Brown.

ACKNOWLEDGMENTS

The successful investigation and prosecution of those responsible for the assassination of Derwin Brown was a team effort—and so was the writing of *A Rainy Night in Georgia*. Many friends, family, colleagues, and even a few strangers read the original manuscript I wrote and offered words of encouragement and much-needed critique. I am especially grateful to my children, Caroline Morgan Berchuck and John Morgan, for providing valuable details and insights as only those who were intimately connected to this experience could do.

My niece Laurel Simmons offered constructive advice on both content and writing style, which helped improve the book. John Petrey, who had a significant role in this story, gave his typical honest and beneficial criticism and helped shape the true crime focus of this book. Chris Harvey, who's also important in this story and has a penchant for details, helped with recollection of facts. My administrative assistant, Carol Sowell, provided first-rate support with administrative details, including preparing drafts of the manuscript and obtaining permission for photographs.

I am deeply appreciative of several professionals and friends who took the time to read my manuscript and provide both constructive comments and a written review: Dale Cardwell, Richard Deane, Melita Easters, Norm Eisen, Diane McPhail, and Bill Torpy. I owe a special thank-you to Deborah Norville. We met when we were both students at the University of Georgia—I was in law school, and she was studying to be a broadcast journalist. I have followed her distinguished career for many years and am honored by her endorsement of the book.

Ken Poston, a Georgia lawyer who has written his own successful true crime novel, advised me, "Lawyers compartmentalize and hide their feelings. You need someone to dig into your soul. I know I did." I am indebted to Ken for introducing me to his literary agent in New York, Linda Konner.

Linda appreciates a good story and graciously took me under her wing. She introduced me to John Capouya, a professional writer and editor, who helped me "dig into my soul" and humanize this story, reorganize the original manuscript, and bring the story to life. His help has been nothing short of invaluable.

Linda also introduced me to the publisher of this book, Globe Pequot, and to Jake Bonar, an acquisitions editor at Globe Pequot. Jake's positive support and astute comments have been immensely appreciated. Ann Seifert, copy editor of this book, has impressed me with her remarkable attention to detail and insightful comments. I am grateful to Anthony Pomes, publicist with Globe Pequot, who has embraced this book with enthusiasm.

Sherry Boston, the current district attorney for DeKalb County, and her paralegal, Jolene DeVries, went above and beyond to find and retrieve the original file and trial manuscripts and provide me access and a place to work while I was in her office.

"A Rainy Night in Georgia," the song made famous by Brook Benton's hit version, was written by Tony Joe White. I thank his widow, Leeann White, for permission to use the song title for the title of this book.

Russell Carter, a law school classmate and agent for the Indigo Girls, helped me secure permission to quote lyrics from two of the Indigo Girls' songs that are among our family's favorites.

Finally, there would be no *A Rainy Night in Georgia* without Carol Ellis Morgan. Carol, a former corporate lawyer and retired law school professor, has an uncanny eye for detail that can be both exhausting and essential. There is not a word, sentence, paragraph, or chapter in this book that she did not scrutinize for accuracy and clarity. Most importantly, she knows this story well because she lived it with me. She is aware of the impact of this story on our children and me, and she helped me put it into writing. Thank you, Carol.

This book reflects both personal memory and careful research, and any mistakes are mine alone.

ABOUT THE AUTHORS

J.Tom Morgan

J.Tom Morgan served as the elected district attorney of DeKalb County, Georgia, from 1992 to 2004. In recognition of his successful prosecution of Sheriff Dorsey, he was the first recipient from the United States to be awarded the Special Achievement Award from the International Association of Prosecutors in 2003.

Prior to becoming DA, he served as an assistant district attorney in DeKalb County for nine years and was the first prosecutor in Georgia—and one of the first in the nation—to specialize in the prosecution of crimes against children. He has appeared in numerous documentaries on child abuse issues, the prosecution of Sheriff Dorsey, and other criminal cases, and he is a frequent commentator on criminal justice matters for regional and national print and broadcast media.

He is the author of *Ignorance Is No Defense: A Teenager's Guide to Georgia Law* and coauthor of *Ignorance Is No Defense: A College Student's Guide to North Carolina Law*. He currently teaches criminal law at Western Carolina University and lives in Cullowhee, North Carolina. An experienced and popular speaker, he is available for speaking engagements on a limited basis.

John Capouya

In his journalism career John Capouya wrote and edited for magazines including *Newsweek*, *SmartMoney*, and *Sport*, and for the newspapers *New York Newsday* and *The New York Times*.

From 2008 to 2020 he taught journalism at the University of Tampa as well as nonfiction narrative, memoir writing, and creative nonfiction in UT's Master of Fine Arts (MFA) program.

He is the author of three nonfiction books. His most recent book, *Florida Soul*, which *The Wall Street Journal* called "compelling," is a history of R&B in that state. The biography *Gorgeous George: The Outrageous Bad-Boy Wrestler Who Created American Pop Culture*, is currently under option for a feature film. And *Real Men Do Yoga*, which *Publishers Weekly* called "an excellent introduction," has sold more than 50,000 copies.

In addition to collaborating on *A Rainy Night in Georgia*, Capouya coauthored *Bikram Yoga* for yoga teacher Bikram Choudhury.

He currently does developmental editing, proposal writing, and "book doctoring" for a variety of clients.

www.ingramcontent.com/pod-product-compliance
Ingram Content Group UK Ltd.
Pitfield, Milton Keynes, MK11 3LW, UK
UKHW031931250826
8166IPUK00002B/27

9 781493 094837